QUANTITATIVE METHODS FOR MANAGERS

Arthur Godfrey

Senior Lecturer, Department of Computing and Quantitative Studies, Western Australian Institute of Technology

Edward Arnold

© Arthur Godfrey 1977
First published 1977 by
Edward Arnold (Publishers) Ltd
25 Hill Street, London W1X 8LL

ISBN 0 7131 3348 1 Cased Edition
     0 7131 3349 X Paper Edition

Printed in Great Britain by **Unwin Brothers Ltd, The Gresham Press,**
Old Woking, Surrey.

PREFACE

Quantitative methods are concerned with measuring and provide the tools used in many aspects of management. The methods are mathematical and statistical in nature, characteristics which might give a daunting first impression. This typical response is an unfortunate one and usually stems from a poor introductions to maths at school level and possibly no introduction to statistics at all. My solution is to relate each theory to a practical purpose and, since this book sets out to produce better managers, not mathematicians or statisticians, the purposes are specifically management ones. Thus each chapter includes applications of the techniques developed in it, giving concrete bases to the abstract concepts.

Most managers cannot attend Diploma in Management Studies courses, but this book, like the others in the series, is intended to be of value to all managers, at all levels. I hope that its practical approach to a theoretical and often awesome subject will appeal both in and away from the classroom. The approach was developed over some years of teaching on DMS courses at the School of Management Studies, Polytechnic of Central London.

A.I.G.

To my wife Hazel and to Elizabeth Scott, with affection and grateful thanks

CONTENTS

APPENDICES (*continued*)

PART I

I

A REVIEW OF THE
MATHEMATICS ASSUMED
TO BE KNOWN

In September 1972 I bought some shares in the Hongkong and Shanghai Banking Corporation at 12¾. I subsequently received as scrip issues 1 for 1, 1 for 10, and again 1 for 10. In July 1975, the share price was 27½. Was I right to be satisfied?

Should a firm provide cars for its employees for business use or should it pay them to use their own cars?

It is known that a certain production process yields about 2% of defective products overall. The works manager picks up a handful and finds that 2 of the 47 products he holds are faulty. Is he right to make a fuss?

The answers to these three problems are judgements, with some room for disagreement. Managers with relevant experience might give snap answers and could even be correct in given circumstances, though argument might continue. However, by using mathematics, i.e. by putting figures for the circumstances and then performing calculations, we can reach an objective view so that the judgements are not only right, but are also seen to be right.

It is well known that mathematics provides a kit of tools for solving numerical problems. Unfortunately, the rules for choosing and using the tools are often put to the young in such a way that as adults they either solve problems without understanding them, or (more usually) feel that the difficulties are beyond them and do not try. This is a pity, for not only is the use of maths essential in management—it is also quite easy. Three simple problems will illustrate what happens in maths:

A farmer delivers 8 sheep to a slaughter-house on each of 3 days. For how many sheep must he be paid?

A stair carpet costs £3 per metre run and a woman buys 8 metres. How much must she pay?

How many wheels are there on 8 tricycles?

The answers all come from multiplying 3 by 8, or alternatively 8 by 3, to get 24 sheep, £24 and 24 wheels respectively. The 3 and the 8 and the calculation were identical for all the problems. Why? Because the sheep, carpet and tricycles were all 'translated' into the language of numbers which thereafter *represented* the real-life situation while being operated on with the language's own rules of grammar and syntax. After these operations, the result (24 in all cases here) is translated back into the original situation to become so many sheep, pounds or wheels.

We have in fact constructed a *model* of the real-life situation, manipulated this model and then interpreted the result. All mathematical work is just modelling, and without realizing it we all model in many aspects of life. For instance, the lens-made image of a television newsreader at work (a translation) is further translated into electrical voltages, radio signals, voltages again, then into lines of light of varying brightness and/or colour. This pattern we interpret as 'seeing the newsreader'. If we choose we can see the lines of light, but we usually prefer to interpret the TV model.

This volume deals with the use of mathematical modelling in the management sphere. As we review the grammar of the mathematical language in this chapter we shall also see how to decide which way to model when faced with a problem.

The language of mathematics

Mathematics uses *numbers* to represent quantities. Where the quantities are known precisely they may be represented by such symbols as 4, $168\frac{3}{4}$ or 19.672. Where they are not known it is convenient to use letters of the alphabet for them; thus C and X are numbers, but we do not know just what quantities they stand for. One of the objects of our work will be to find the unknown quantities, by comparing them in stated circumstances with other, known quantities. In fact maths is concerned with *relationships* between quantities.

Equality and inequality. These are the most fundamental relationships; two (or more) quantities are either equal or they are not. The number (quantity) of wheels on a tricycle *equals* the number of feet in a yard. Both are *less than* the number of legs on a dog, but *greater than* the number of my legs. Mathematical *notation* enables these rather wordy relationships to be written much more briefly:

$$3 = 3$$
$$3 < 4 \ (3 \text{ is less than } 4)$$
$$3 > 2 \ (3 \text{ is greater than } 2)$$

All the notation we shall use is just a very short way of writing long ideas and relationships. Once learned, it should lose its terrors, e.g. $x > y$ merely states that x is a larger number than y.

Operations to change quantities. These are addition, subtraction, multiplication and division, or extensions of them. Naturally they involve at least two quantities, which modify each other according to the operator used. Examples are $5 + 7$, $A \times 4$, $B - C$, $X \div 2.2$. Such operations are valid as ideas but are not very useful until combined with a relationship such as $=$. This brings out solutions, $5 + 7 = 12$, enabling us to use 12 instead of $5 + 7$ at all later stages in the calculation. This relationship is reversible in several ways, e.g.

1. $5 + 7$ or $7 + 5$ may be replaced by 12
2. 12 may be replaced by $5 + 7$ or by $7 + 5$
3. $12 - 5 = 7$ or $12 - 7 = 5$ (subtraction as the opposite of addition).

We must further note that 5, 7 and 12 are just numbers, representing quantities of anything, but it is implicit that before the operators $+$, $-$, $\times$ or $\div$ can act between them, the quantities must be compatible. 5 pence plus 7 bicycles do not normally equal 12 of anything. Hence when dealing with unknown quantities we must express them separately until we know otherwise. Known numbers may, however, be mixed with unknowns where appropriate; two As and three Bs are $2A + 3B$, but this is as far as we can go.

Positive and negative numbers. Since one cannot remove 10 tons of goods from a warehouse that contains only 8 tons, it might seem that a larger number may not be subtracted from a smaller one. However, there are many real-life cases where quantities can fall below zero. For example, if my bank balance is £8, i.e. the bank owes me £8, and the manager allows me to withdraw £10, then I owe the bank £2. It is often convenient to consider all transactions from the same point of view, e.g. how much of my money is in the bank. Credit or zero balances raise no problem, but overdrafts need an extra symbol to indicate the opposite direction of the owing/owed relationship. The minus sign meets this need and is used in any situation to indicate a quantity of less than zero in this sort of sense; my balance becomes $-£2$.

We calculate with negative numbers just like positive numbers, but logic calls for a few special rules:

1. If no sign is used, positive is understood.
2. Multiplying by a negative number changes the sign, e.g.
   $$(-3) \times 5 = -15; (-3) \times (-5) = 15; (-A) \times B = -AB.$$
3. It follows that the negative of a negative number is (the same) positive number, e.g. $-(-6) = 6$; $-(-P) = P$.
4. With negative quantities, the smaller the size of the number itself (apart from the sign), the larger the negative number, e.g. $-4 > -27$ (-4 is greater than -27).

Order of attack. There is a need for priority rules to govern the order of using intermixed operators. For example, consider the following sequence:

$$4 \times 8 + 2 \times 10 - 6 \times 3$$

Tackling this from left to right gives

$$32 + 2 \times 10 - 6 \times 3$$
or
$$34 \times 10 - 6 \times 3$$
or
$$340 - 6 \times 3$$
or
$$334 \times 3 = 1002$$

If we use parentheses to isolate pairs or triplets and then replace the amounts inside brackets with their calculated values we might have, among many possibilities,

$$(4 \times 8) + (2 \times 10) - (6 \times 3) = 32 + 20 - 18 \qquad = \qquad 34$$
$$[(4 \times 8) + 2] \times [(10 - 6) \times 3] = 34 \times 12 \qquad = \qquad 408$$
$$[4 \times (8 + 2)] \times [10 - (6 \times 3)] = 40 \times (-8) \qquad = -302$$
$$\{4 \times [(8 + 2) \times 10]\} - (6 \times 3) = \{4 \times 100\} - 18 = \qquad 382$$

and so on.

The conventional rules which avoid all this confusion are:

1. First calculate anything in parentheses.
2. Multiplication and division next. (*Repeated* operations (powers and roots) precede single operations. They are explained in a following section.) A sequence of multiplications and/or divisions is performed in order from left to right.
3. Addition and subtraction come last, working from left to right.

The 'right' answer to the given sequence can now be found, without ambiguity, to be 34.

Fractional numbers. Between the *integer* numbers that we have been using lie the *fractions*, which may be expressed either as uncalculated division statements, e.g. $2\frac{9}{10}$, $\frac{25}{687}$, $33\frac{1}{3}$, or as the results of the divisions with the *decimal point* separating the integer part from the fractional part, e.g. 2.9, 0.036390102 . . . , 33.3333 . . . . Sometimes the decimal form is shorter and sometimes much longer than the fractional form; each has its advantages and disadvantages.

Fractions are unaffected if both top and bottom are multiplied or divided by the same number. Thus $\frac{4}{6}$ may be divided above and below by 2 to give $\frac{2}{3}$, the same value.

Since division is the opposite of multiplication, division by a fraction is replaced by multiplication by the opposite fraction (which is the same fraction with top and bottom numbers interchanged.) Thus

$$6 \div \tfrac{2}{3} = 6 \times \tfrac{3}{2} = \tfrac{18}{2} = 9$$

'Of' means 'multiply'. For instance,

$$\tfrac{2}{3} \text{ of } 6 = \tfrac{2}{3} \times 6 = \tfrac{12}{3} = 4$$

A *percentage* is a fraction multiplied by 100. To find 20 as a percentage of 70, multiply the fraction $\frac{20}{70}$ by 100.

$$\tfrac{20}{70} \times 100 = \tfrac{2000}{70} = \tfrac{200}{7} = 14.2857\%$$

P as a percentage of R is $\dfrac{P}{R} \times 100$ or $\dfrac{P \times 100}{R}$

Fractions, decimals and percentages, like any other numbers, may be positive or negative according to the case. The usual rules for calculation still apply.

Repeated multiplication. A number may have to be multiplied by itself several times over. So common is this that a special short notation—*indices*—has come into use for it. The number being repeatedly multiplied is called the *base*; the number of times it is used is the *index*. The base is written normally, with the index as a small figure above and to the right of the base. Thus

$$4 \times 4 \times 4 \times 4 \times 4 = 4^5 = 1024$$

or, with unknown quantities, $d \times d \times d \times d = d^4$. d multiplied by itself m times is d^m. We say that d^4 is the fourth *power* of d, and read it as 'd to the fourth'. Similarly, 1024 is the fifth power of 4, read as 'four to the fifth'.

To avoid the repeated calculations each time, rules for working with indices have been established absolutely by using letters or unknown numbers as bases and indices, pretending they are known and seeing what happens. This is a technique used widely in maths, since relationships that hold good with unknown numbers are quite generally true; they must hold for *any* numbers, including known ones.*

Examples:

1. $a^m \times a^n = \underbrace{a \times a \times a \ldots \times}_{m \text{ factors}} \underbrace{a \times a \times a \ldots \times a}_{n \text{ factors}}$

   The multiplication signs are all identical, so we have a multiplied by itself $(m + n)$ times

   Hence
   or

$a^m \times a^n = a^{m+n}$
To multiply powers of the same base, add the indices.

   e.g. $2^4 \times 2^6 = 2^{4+6} = 2^{10} = 1024$

2. $a^m \div a^n = \dfrac{(a \times a \times a \ldots \times a), \; m \text{ factors}}{(a \times a \ldots \times a) \qquad n \text{ factors}}$

   If $m > n$, cancel n factors to leave 1 at the bottom and $(m - n)$ factors of a at the top. This leaves a^{m-n} divided by 1, or a^{m-n}.

   If $m < n$, $(m - n)$ is of course a negative number. By the above argument

   we may cancel m factors (m is the smaller of the two) to leave $\dfrac{1}{a^{n-m}}$. But

   this is $\dfrac{1}{a^{-(m-n)}}$ by the rules for negative numbers, and this expression perfectly fits the rule found above, (that we subtract indices when dividing powers of the same base) provided we interpret negative powers as *reciprocals*.

   Definition: The reciprocal of a number is 1 divided by that number.

---

*An exception is zero. Due to its peculiar properties some of the rules do not apply if zero is involved. Which ones? Those which give absurd results with zero—try it and see.

If $m = n$, $m - n = 0$. To preserve our 'subtract-the-indices' rule we would have $a^m \div a^n = a^{m-n} = a^0$.

But a^m is the same as a^n, so $a^m \div a^n$ must be 1.

This exhausts all possibilities, and leaves us with these rules in all cases:

or

> $a^m \div a^n = a^{m-n}$
> To divide powers of the same base, subtract the indices.

or

> $a^{-p} = \dfrac{1}{a^p}$
> A negative power is the reciprocal of the same positive power.

or

> $a^0 = 1$
> Any number raised to the power *zero* gives *one*.

3. $a^m \times a^m \times a^m \dots \times a^m$ with n factors of a^m is, by our shorthand notation, $(a^m)^n$ or a^m raised to the nth power. By the addition rule, this must be $a^{m+m+m} \dots {}^{+m}$ with n terms in the index, which is $a^{m \times n}$ or a^{mn}.

Hence
or

> $(a^m)^n = a^{m \times n} = a^{mn}$
> To raise a power to another power, multiply the indices.

4. Consider the last case in reverse. What number will, when multiplied by itself 3 times, give a^m? Clearly, $a^{m/3}$, since $(a^{m/3})^3 = a^{m/3 \times 3} = a^m$.

This is the third *root* (or *cube root*) of a^m.

In general terms,

or, in notation

> The nth root of a^m is $a^{m/n}$
> $\sqrt[n]{a^m} = a^{m/n}$

As a special case,

or

> The nth root of a number K is $K^{1/n}$
> $\sqrt[n]{K} = K^{1/n}$

Definition: the nth root of a number, multiplied by itself n times, gives the number in question.

5. Decimal powers, such as $2.4^{3.6}$, are readily understood if the index is replaced by its fractional form, in this case $(2.4)^{36/10}$, which simplifies to $(2.4)^{18/5}$. This is the 5th root of $(2.4)^{18}$ or $\sqrt[5]{2.4^{18}}$. The calculation may be horrifying, but the concept is not difficult. The decimal nature of the base makes no difference except to the labour of the arithmetic.

Powers of 10. Since $10^2 = 100$, $10^3 = 1000$, $10^4 = 10\,000$ and so on, we see that for positive integer powers 10^n is written as 1 followed by n zeros. 10^0 is 1 like any other zero power, and fits this rule.

10^{-1} is $\dfrac{1}{10}$ or 0.1, 10^{-2} is $\dfrac{1}{100}$ or 0.01, 10^{-3} is 0.001 and so on. So for negative

integers, 10^{-n} is a decimal point followed by n digits, the last being 1 and the rest zeros. This allows brevity in writing very large or very small numbers. Thirty-eight and a half millions or 38 500 000 may be put as 385×10^5 or 38.5×10^6. Thirty-eight and a half milliards (American billions) are 38 500 000 000 or 38.5×10^9. Thirty eight and a half microns (thousandths of a millimetre) are 0.000,038, 5 of a metre, or 38.5×10^{-6} metre.

Factorials. Another kind of repeated multiplication involves the integers 1, 2, 3, etc. multiplied together in sequence. For brevity this product is called the factorial of its largest factor. Thus the factorial of 4 is $1 \times 2 \times 3 \times 4$ or 24, the factorial of 7 is $1 \times 2 \times 3 \times 4 \times 5 \times 6 \times 7$ or 5040. By definition there is no factorial for a fractional or negative number. The factorial of zero must conveniently be taken as 1 although it does not fit into the straightforward definition.

The notation for the factorial of A is to write A with an exclamation mark, $A!$; thus $7! = 5040$. Note that dividing one factorial by another enables cancellation of all the terms of the smaller factorial from the larger one, e.g. $28! : 25! = 26 \times 27 \times 28$, since all factors from 1 to 25 cancel out.

Series. Many repetitive situations, when translated into mathematical language, give rise to a number of items that must be added together, each item having some fixed relationship with the preceding one. A simple example of such a series is the old trick problem of an uncle giving his newborn nephew a penny and promising to give each day his yesterday's gift plus a penny more. What will the gift amount to by the child's first birthday or any other date?

On day 1 the total number of pence is   1
On day 2 the total amounts to $1 + 2$ (the day's gift is 3p)
On day 3 the total amounts to $1 + 2 + 3$ (the day's gift is 6p)
So on day r it is $1 + 2 + 3 + \ldots + r$.

The point of the problem is that the gift can rapidly amount to a large sum: on the first birthday it will be £671.61 and on the second £2675.46, ignoring leap years. As a series however, the relationship of each term to the last one is clear: one adds the next integer.

Some series go on endlessly, others are finite. Infinite series do not necessarily total to infinity, though the fortunate nephew's one obviously does. For instance consider the infinite series

$$100 + 10 + 1 + \frac{1}{10} + \frac{1}{100} + \frac{1}{1000} + \cdots$$

One can always add a bit more but the total is nevertheless finite, as is seen by putting the terms in decimal form:

$$100 + 10 + 1 + 0.1 + 0.01 + 0.001 + \cdots$$

which obviously adds up to $111.11111\ldots$ or $111\frac{1}{9}$.

The exponential series. This is an infinite series which is important in management studies:

$$1 + x + \frac{x^2}{2!} + \frac{x^3}{3!} + \frac{x^4}{4!} + \cdots + \frac{x^r}{r!} + \cdots$$

which is called e^x for short, with e being a constant that can be found by putting

$$x = 1 \text{ in the series to give } e = 1 + 1 + \frac{1}{2!} + \frac{1}{3!} + \frac{1}{4!} + \frac{1}{5!} + \cdots = 2.71828\ldots$$

Here I have produced e and e^x out of the blue; in practice they arise naturally from certain studies in differential calculus which also prove that the series really does give powers of e.

Because repeated multiplication by a negative number gives alternately negative and positive answers,

$$e^{-x} = 1 - x + \frac{x^2}{2!} - \frac{x^3}{3!} + \frac{x^4}{4!} - \cdots$$

The values of e^x and e^{-x} are usually included in books of mathematical tables and appear in this volume as Appendix I on page 261.

Graphs. Pictorial methods of expressing relationships sometimes bring out what happens in a very clear way. For example, numbers may be represented by lengths, as in Figure 1.1. Negative numbers come out quite naturally to the left of the zero starting point, as can be seen in Figure 1.2. Relationships between two distinct types of quantity need two dimensions, i.e. they fit on axes

Figure 1.1

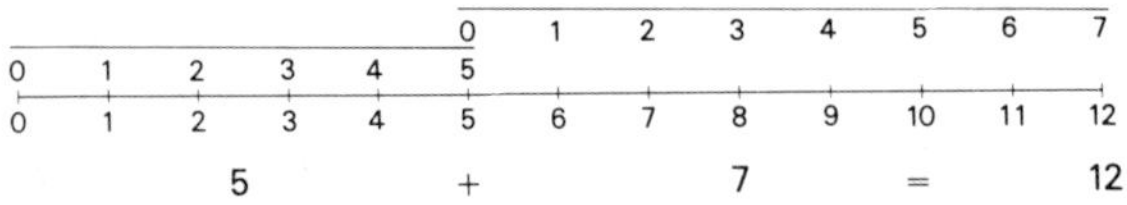

as in Figures 1.3 and 1.4. In this way it becomes possible to exhibit a whole range of relationships at once. For instance, how many wheels are there on any number of tricycles? If we label the axes Tricycles and Wheels as in Figure 1.4 we soon find points for 1 tricycle → 3 wheels, 2 tricycles → 6 wheels, etc. Any point is named according to its horizontal distance from the vertical axis and its vertical distance from the horizontal axis, in other words the distance to the right, then up, to reach it from the crossing of the axes (called the *origin*).

Leftwards and downwards each become negative. The two distances are called the *co-ordinates* of the point and may be written, for example (2, 6). To avoid ambiguity, the agreed convention is, as stated, horizontal distance before vertical distance.

Figure 1.2

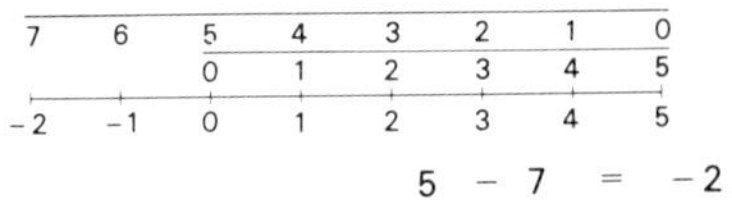
7 6 5 4 3 2 1 0
0 1 2 3 4 5
−2 −1 0 1 2 3 4 5
5 − 7 = −2

Having found various points for the tricycle/wheel relationship, the obvious progression is to join them with a line; Figure 1.4 then lets us read off 24 wheels for 8 tricycles and so on. There is also the absurd possibility of 16 wheels for $5\frac{1}{3}$ tricycles; this reversal makes more sense in a situation like changing currencies, where 3 units of one are worth one of another and it is possible to change

Figure 1.3 Axes.

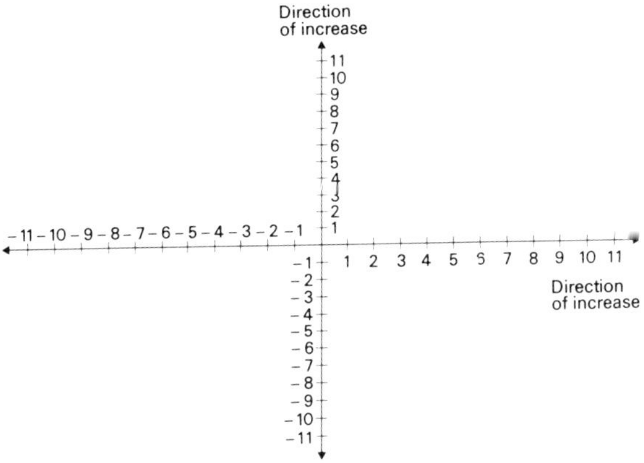
Direction of increase
11 10 9 8 7 6 5 4 3 2 1
−11 −10 −9 −8 −7 −6 −5 −4 −3 −2 −1
1 2 3 4 5 6 7 8 9 10 11
Direction of increase
−1 −2 −3 −4 −5 −6 −7 −8 −9 −10 −11

any amount of either into the other. The line may be read either way. If 3 for 1 is the wrong *rate*, another line will readily be drawn with an appropriate *slope*; the slope of the line indicates the rate of the relationship. Having spotted that a straight line is involved, we realize that we need only 2 points on it, for example, the origin (0, 0) and any one other known or calculated exchange; the line is drawn through the two points.

Suppose I am changing £ sterling into French francs at £1 = Fr 11.25. The graph in Figure 1.5 shows what I will receive for any number of pounds within its range, which can be whatever I please if my paper is large enough. In the more general relationship number of pounds = 11.25 × (number of francs) or, in short, $P = 11.25 \times F$ or $Y = 11.25 \times X$, or whatever letters we please. If the money-changer deducts Fr 5 for each transaction, we see that £1 brings in Fr 6.25 and £5, Fr 51.25. Drawing the line through these points gives Figure

Figure 1.4

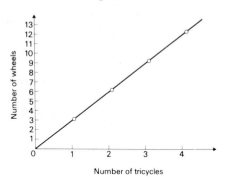

Number of tricycles

1.6, in which the straight line is always 5 below that of Figure 1.5. In other words it represents the relationship

$$P = (11.25 \times F) - 5$$

A straight line will always arise from a relationship where all the *variables*, the letters representing unknown quantities that may take any value, are present simply by themselves or associated only with known numbers. Roots, squares, cubes and any other power or function of the variables bring in curved lines. The *linear* relationship which gives rise to straight lines is $Y = mX + c$, where m (the multiplying factor) gives the slope and c the distance above the origin where the line cuts the vertical axis.

To plot a curved line on a graph, values must go on being calculated from the relationship concerned and marked in as points, until the shape of the line is

Figure 1.5

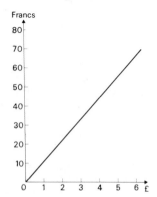

apparent. For example, the curve for e^x will show its value for different values of x if we insert the latter in the series and calculate (or save work by looking the answers up in tables); we plot e^x on the vertical scale against x on the horizontal scale to give Figure 1.7. The curve rises very slowly at first, then increasingly rapidly, as the value of x increases. As a matter of interest, if the

Figure 1.6

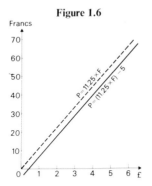

exponential curve is imagined to be rotated around the horizontal axis, travelling below and above the page, the 3-dimensional shape generated would be a tube that belled out rapidly at one end. This shape is the most efficient at transferring into the atmosphere all energy put in at the small end, for example, as a bugle or posthorn. A horn of any other shape would make less noise for a given amount of puff.

The example illustrates the limitations of graphs. They are fine for two dimensions, like the paper they are drawn on, but 3 dimensions must either be imagined as I have suggested, or drawn in perspective in 2 dimensions, which really means half-imagined. As soon as a relationship involves more than 2

Figure 1.7   Graph of e^x.

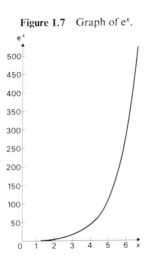

variables there is difficulty with graphs, while with more than 3 variables graphs are impossible. If we find that comfort for our workpeople depends, as far as can be ascertained, on temperature, humidity, lighting intensity and pay, we cannot express in graphical form the complex way in which a mixture of suitable values of any 3 factors might help to compensate for inadequacy in the fourth. However, the letter/number method of stating the relationship is practical for any number of variables.

Logarithms. The index rules allowed a multiplication, e.g. $5^3 \times 5^{17}$, to be replaced by a mere addition, 5^{3+17}. Similarly, division becomes subtraction and raising to a power becomes multiplication. Logarithms take advantage of this.

Since $10^0 = 1$, $10^1 = 10$, $10^2 = 100$, $10^3 = 1000$ and so on, 15.7 can easily be seen to be 10 raised to a power between 1 and 2, i.e. it is '10 to the 1-point-something', while 157 is '10 to the 2-point-something'. These 'somethings' must be exactly the same, for $157 = 10 \times 15.7$, i.e. $10^1 \times 10^{1 \cdot \text{something}}$, which is $10^{2 \cdot \text{something}}$ by the rule of adding indices. So a single table of index values (or logarithms) covering all numbers from 1 to 10 will suit every number. We simply add 1 to the logarithm for every time the table number must be multiplied by 10 to get the actual number, and subtract 1 for each corresponding division by 10.

We shall not look at how to use log tables as an aid to calculation (though the student is strongly urged to revise the technique if necessary); we merely note that the logarithm to base 10 of a number A is the index, such that

$$10^{\log A} = A$$

and the process of calculating with logarithms therefore follows precisely the index rules which were reviewed above.

Logarithm tables with e as base instead of 10 can be compiled with theoretical ease but arithmetical hard labour from the exponential series for e^x. If values from, say, 0.0001 upwards in steps of 0.0001 are inserted for x in the series, as many values of e^x will be found. (With more speed but less accuracy they could be read off the *graph* of e^x.) Each value of x, being the power to which e is raised to get its own e^x, is by definition the logarithm of that particular value of e^x. For example, inserting 1 for x and finding that $e^1 = 2.71828$ shows that 1 is the log (base e) of 2.71828, and similarly 1.57 is the log (base e) of 4.8066 which is $e^{1 \cdot 57}$. For this reason e is the base of *natural logarithms*, the first ones calculated by Napier in the seventeenth century. (They are also called *naperian* logarithms.) It is really quite easy to convert from natural logs to those of any other base, such as 10. The important point to note, however, is that logarithms are the inverse of exponentials because of the 'natural' relationship

$$e^{\log_e A} = A$$

in which $\log_e A$ means the logarithm of A to base e.

This inverse relationship, together with the cyclical repetition of logarithms (to base 10) over 1 to 10, 10 to 100, and so forth, enables us to use *logarithmic graph paper* as a means of taming the runaway increase of exponentials, as seen in Figure 1.7 (p. 11).

Normal scales on the axes of a graph are kept uniform, with the distance from the origin being proportional to the value represented. Semi-log paper instead has these distances on one of the axes proportional to the logarithms of the values, like the vertical scales in Figure 1.8. These scales, like logarithms themselves, change faster for small numbers than for larger ones; this is the opposite of what happens with exponentials. Thus if we graph on them some relationship which is exponential we shall get a straight line. Other relationships which give straight lines on log paper involve uniform rates of growth where one variable is multiplied by a fixed amount for each uniform increase of the other. For example, the demand for electricity approximately doubles itself every 10 years, as Table 1.1 shows. Another instance of a uniform rate of increase might be inflation at a steady annual rate.

Figure 1.8 shows the graph for e^x and also the electricity consumption figures of Table 1.1. Different scales have had to be combined on the same graph; this is a common procedure.

Figure 1.8

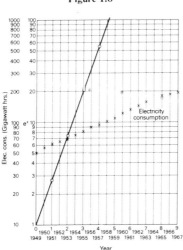

An easy way to check whether a rate of growth or decline is constant is to plot the data on semi-logarithmic graph paper and see whether a straight line results. The rate of growth (or decline) may also be found from the graph; for example, the change in the uniform variable for one cycle of change in the log variable is obvious.

This type of graph paper is available with 1, 2 (as shown) 3, 4, 5 and sometimes other numbers of cycles of the log scale. This enables the numbers concerned

Table 1.1

Year	1949	1950	1951	1952	1953	1954	1955
Electricity consumption	50.2	56.1	61.1	63.5	66.9	74.3	81.5
Year	1956	1957	1958	1959	1960	1961	1962
Electricity consumption	88.4	93.4	100.9	107.5	121.4	130.3	144.5
Year	1963	1964	1965	1966	1967	1968	
Electricity consumption	156.9	165.4	178.2	184.8	191.7	205.1	

Consumption figures in Gigawatt Hours $= 10^6$ Kilowatt Hours.

to vary by a factor of 10 per cycle, e.g. if numbers from 2 to 2000 have to be included, at least 3 cycles of log scale are needed.

Graph paper with logarithmic scales on both axes (log-log paper) is also available in 1 or more cycles. Among its uses are:

1. Situations in which very large ranges of numbers have to be included on paper of reasonable size, but more attention must be focused on the smaller numbers because percentage changes are important.
2. Situations in which a uniform rate of change of one variable is associated with a uniform rate of change of the other.

Log-log paper gives a straight line instead of the long, almost unreadable, slow curvature found on normal graph paper. For example, in a factory learning situation it has been established that a definite percentage improvement in a trainee's hourly output goes with a doubling of the total number of items he has produced. On normal graph paper this gives the learning curve of Figure 1.9; on log-log paper it becomes a straight line, as in Figure 1.10.

These graphs show the time taken to do a task reducing by 8%, that is to 92% of its previous figure, with each doubling of experience. Hence the output

Figure 1.9   Learning curve.

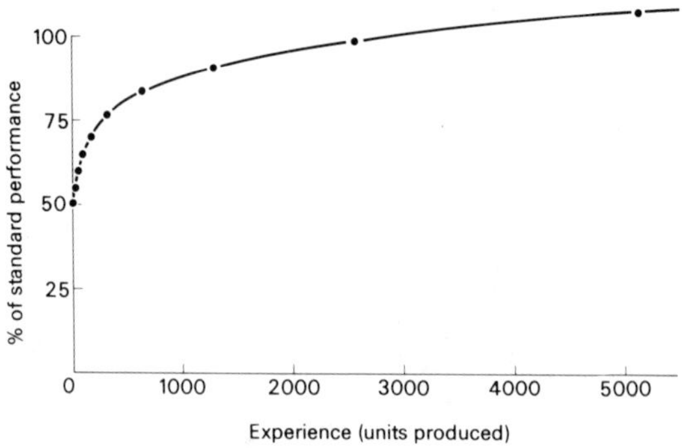

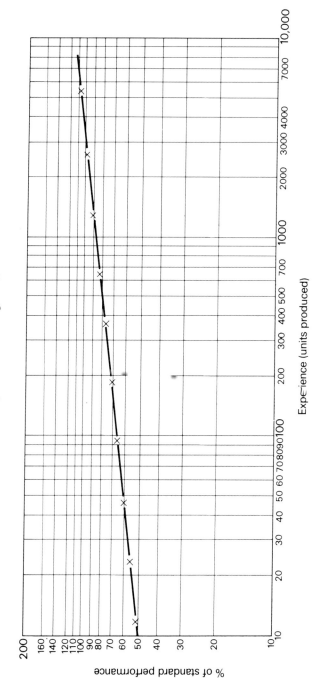

Figure 1.10 Learning curve.

per unit time (or rate of work) rises to $\frac{100}{92}$ or 108.69% of its previous value. A learner's work rate thus increases rapidly at first, then rises more slowly as he becomes more proficient. Very often the accepted work rate of a fully-trained operator is taken as 100%, and Figures 1.9 and 1.10 adopt this convention. For the reasons just given, these are called 92% learning curves.

Permutations and combinations. The number of choices involving arrangements of several things can be very large: permutations and combinations are concerned with finding the total numbers of possibilities. Unfortunately they cannot point to the best one; this must be decided on other than numerical grounds.

If a car manufacturer offers a model with a choice of 3 engines, manual or automatic gearbox, 2 body styles, 8 colours of paintwork and 3 colours of interior trim, how many different possibilities does the customer choose from?

Whichever engine is chosen it will have all the other possible types of car to go with. Since there are 3 engine options, the total number of possibilities is

3 times (possible choices excluding the engine)

Half of these remaining choices must involve a manual gearbox and half the automatic. The total number of possibilities is thus

$3 \times 2 \times$ (choices excluding engine and gearbox)

If we continue in this manner, we reach a final total of $3 \times 2 \times 2 \times 8 \times 3$ or 288. (Figure 1.11 is an illustration of this choice sequence.) This is how, with only a few variables incorporated in mass production, car makers offer what seem to be wide choices of the same model. The example illustrates the result

> The number of ways of moving through a sequence of A choices, B choices, C choices . . . is $A \times B \times C$ . . .

In how many ways can the seating plan for 6 workpeople (or the arrangement of 6 machines) be devised once the locations are fixed?

Since no-one has yet been seated, the first place (which is any of them) may be filled in 6 different ways. With one person and one place now settled, the second

Figure 1.11

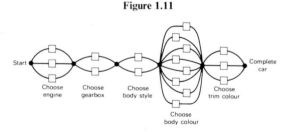

position (any of the remainder) may be filled with one of 5 choices. Then the third place may be filled in 4 ways, the fourth in 3, the fifth in 2 and there is only 1 possibility for the last one. In all therefore, the people or machines may be arranged in $6 \times 5 \times 4 \times 3 \times 2 \times 1$ or 6! or 720 ways. In general, R people or things may be arranged in $R!$ ways; of course each item is different from the others, so all arrangements are visibly distinct.

> The number of ways in which R different items may be arranged among themselves is $R!$

In how many ways may R items be arranged among themselves if T of them are identical?

There are $T!$ arrangements of the T items, but these are indistinguishable from one another. Any named arrangement of the remaining items would appear, in the total $R!$ arrangements of the whole lot, with each of the $T!$ repetitions. Only one of these should count, so there are $T!$ times too many arrangements in the $R!$ total. The result is as follows:

> The number of different arrangements of R items among themselves when T of them are identical is
> $$\frac{R!}{T!}.$$

The same argument is easily extended:

> The number of different arrangements of R items of which S are alike of one kind, T of another, V of another and so on is
> $$\frac{R!}{S!\,T!\,V!\ldots}$$

In how many ways may we choose 8 items from 52 if the order of choosing them must be preserved, i.e. if the list Smith, Jones, Williams is considered different from Williams, Smith, Jones?

There are 8 places to fill. The first has 52 choices, the second 51 and so on; the last may be filled in 45 ways. The total number of ways is therefore

$$52 \times 51 \times 50 \times 49 \times 48 \times 47 \times 46 \times 45$$

which is quite a large number as well as lengthy to write in this form. It is like 52! but with all the factors of 44! omitted so it is clearly 52!/44! or 52!/(52−8)! We can readily see that this argument gives in the general case the result

> The number of ways of choosing R things out of N, preserving the order of choice, is
> $$\frac{N!}{(N-R)!}$$

The ways where the order of choice must be maintained are called *permutations*. The last result is the number of permutations of R things from N and is sometimes abbreviated to ^nP_r, so that

$$^nP_r = \frac{N!}{(N - R)!}$$

When choosing a team of workpeople or picking matches from a list for football pools, it is usually the identity of the people or things chosen which is the only important result; the exact order in which they were picked is normally irrelevant. Arrangements in which the order is ignored are known as combinations; the football industry is wrong in calling them perms. Since ABCDEFGH is now to be considered the same as, say, HGFEDCBA, whereas before they were different, there will be fewer combinations than permutations where the same range of choices is involved.

Ignoring order, in how many ways may 8 items be chosen from 52? The number of permutations is $^{52}P_8$ or 52!/44! as we have seen. Any named list of 8 will also appear with its members in all possible arrangements among themselves, i.e. 8! times, so there will be 8! times more *ordered* arrangements throughout than we now need. The number of combinations is therefore $\frac{52!}{8! \times 44!}$, which is shortened to $^{52}C_8$. For the general case we can now say the following:

The number of ways of choosing R items from N where order is unimportant is

$$^nC_r = \frac{N!}{R! (N - R)!}$$

This is also the number of ways of choosing $(N - R)$ items from N. After all, choosing R is the same as picking $(N - R)$ for rejection.

$$^nC_r = {}^nC_{(N-R)}$$

Algebra. We have already been looking at algebra, but have not said so. It is merely arithmetic performed with unknown numbers instead of known ones, i.e. it is *generalized* arithmetic. If the results of operations are correct with unknowns, then they are valid for all numbers and we may substitute any quantities we please (namely, those relevant to our problems) in the algebraic results.

Algebra has followed two main paths:

1. A generalized look at *operations* on quantities.
2. A generalized look at *relationships* between quantities.

The first approach has produced a library of operations and their results, namely formulae. Substitution of the known quantities of any problem in the appropriate formulae then converts the situation back to the familiar arithmetic one with ordinary numerical calculations. The second approach allows problems to be solved by comparing their unknown quantities with known ones. Algebra has provided a set of rules for operating on these comparisons (in the form of *equations* or, less commonly, *inequalities*), so that the only possible sizes of the unknown quantities must emerge.

Formulae

Below is a summary of the formulae and rules for tackling equations or inequalities, in their logical order.

1. $A + A = 2A$
2. $B + B + B + \cdots + B$ (m terms) $= m \times B$ or mB
3. $A \times B = B \times A$; $AB = BA$
4. $A(B + C) = AB + AC$; $RS + RT = R(S + T)$
5. $A(B - C) = AB - AC$; $RS - RT = R(S - T)$
6. $(A + B)(C + D) = A(C + D) + B(C + D) = AC + AD + BC + BD$,
   i.e. multiply the second bracket through by each term of the first.
7. $(A - B)(C - D) = A(C - D) - B(C - D) = AC - AD - BC$
   $+ BD$
8. $(A + B)^2 = (A + B)(A + B) = A^2 + AB + BA + B^2$
   $$= A^2 + 2AB + B^2$$
9. $(A + B)^3 = (A + B)(A + B)^2 = (A + B)(A^2 + 2AB + B^2)$
   $$= A^3 + 2A^2B + AB^2 + BA^2$$
   $$+ 2AB^2 + B^3$$
   $$= A^3 + 3A^2B + 3AB^2 + B^3$$
10. Substituting $(-B)$ for B,
    $$(A - B)^3 = A^3 - 3A^2B + 3AB^2 - B^3$$
11. Extending this approach we have the general relationship
    $$(A + B)^n = A^n + {}^nC_1 A^{n-1} B + {}^nC_2 A^{n-2} B^2 + \cdots$$
    $$+ {}^nC_r A^{n-r} B^r + \cdots + B^n$$

    where ${}^nC_r$ is the number of combinations of r things from n,

    $$\frac{n!}{r!(n - r)!}$$

12. As we build up from $(A + B)^2$ to $(A + B)^3$ to $(A + B)^4$ to the nth power, we can spot a pattern in the coefficients that could save us from working in detail with the ${}^nC_r$ formula. The coefficients look like the following:

					1				
2nd power				1	2	1			
3rd power			1	3		3	1		
4th power		1	4		6		4	1	
5th power	1	5		10		10		5	1
6th power	1	6	15		20		15	6	1
7th power	1	7	21	35		35		21	7	1

and so on where, apart from the 1s at the outsides and the 2 in the 2nd power, each figure is the sum of the 2 immediately above it, e.g. each 35 in the 7th power is the sum of the 15 + 20 (or 20 + 15) above. A more extended table of this Pascal's pyramid is given in Appendix A on page 250.

13. $(A + B)(A - B) = A^2 - AB + BA - B^2 = A^2 - B^2$;
$R^2 - S^2 = (R + S)(R - S)$

14. $\dfrac{1}{1 + A} = (1 + A)^{-1} = 1 - A + A^2 - A^3 + A^4 - A^5 + \cdots$

15. $\dfrac{1}{1 - A} = (1 - A)^{-1} = 1 + A + A^2 + A^3 + A^4 + A^5 + \cdots$

Relationships

The formulae above all include the $=$ sign. Its meaning is equivalence; inevitably the values on the left-hand side are identical with those on the right and either side may replace the other.

Equations. Here again we have the $=$ sign separating two sides in a relationship. It is concerned, however, with equality; there is nothing inevitable about the identical nature of the two sides. For instance, consider the relationship

$$A + B = 4$$

The $=$ sign means that, for purposes of our own such as the circumstances of our current problem, we insist that the sum of A and B must be 4 precisely. This of course limits the possible values that A and B can have. If A is 2 then B can only be 2; if B is 3.7 then A must be 0.3. This equation, simple though it is, can be solved only if a definite value is given to one of the letters, leaving one of them unknown. There must be as many equations as unknowns for solution to be possible.

Since we insist that both sides of an equation shall be equal, any operation performed on one side must also be made on the other. We may do anything we like as an operation to both sides, on two conditions:

1. We must not divide by zero or by an expression which amounts to zero.
2. If we take square roots we must not forget that there are two possible results, one positive and one negative, (e.g. $\sqrt{4}$ is either 2 or -2). It may be convenient to ignore one of them, but it is wrong to do so.

The object of altering both sides of an equation is simply to manoeuvre the unknown into isolation on one side, with only known quantities, linked by operations, on the other. The knowns can then be operated on as specified, to produce a value which must equal the other side of the equation, and which we have ensured is just the unknown. This process is called solving the equation.

In real life, equations rarely come simply and even more rarely, singly. Solution then becomes a matter of skill in choosing the quickest techniques and manipulating the equations with them. Fortunately, the manager need not acquire these skills since two extremely powerful techniques (graphs and the computer) are within his grasp and can provide all the answers desired, to any required degree of accuracy. Solutions can even be found in cases too difficult for 'correct' mathematical treatment. Both methods will be examined here and for full comparison we should now look at the theoretical solving of equations.

1. First set up the relationship(s) in mathematical form. This is the area of problem solving, the trickiest part of the mathematics but the closest to managers' ways of thinking.

2. Isolate one of the unknowns in one of the equations so that it is exposed solely in terms of others and their operators. If there is only one equation, only steps 4 and 6 will apply from here onwards.

3. Use the principle of substitution, i.e. that since the two sides of an equation are to be equivalent, either can replace the other wherever it appears. At this stage we replace the isolated unknown by the expression which does not include it, thus reducing the number of unknowns (and equations) by one. This process continues until only one equation and one unknown are left.

4. While this equation may be very complicated, a numerical value can somehow be found for its unknown which is henceforth a 'known'.

5. Then reversing the process we work back, substituting each new known in turn for its unknown until all have been found.

6. The task is complete when we relate the calculated values to the terms of the problem.

Looked at without examples, this procedure may seem complex. Since it outlines the powerful work of the mathematician tackling equations, this should not be surprising. However, on re-reading the very first part of this chapter one sees that we have just

1. Set up a model of the situation as a set of equations.

2. to 5. Used the rules of the modelling language (mathematics) to analyse the model.

and it remains only

6. To interpret the analysis in the language of the situation.

Graphical solution of equations. As we have seen, a line or curve on a graph is also a model of a relationship and it shows, if enough of it is drawn, all possible values of the relationship. Figure 1.12 shows, for example, the graph of

$$y = 2x^3 - x^2 - 10x + 7$$

drawn after calculating y for certain values of x:

x	-3	-2.5	-2	-1.5	-1	-0.5	0	0.5	1	1.5	2	2.5	3
y	-26	-5.5	7	13	14	11.5	7	2	-2	-3.5	-1	7	22

Now consider the following relationship, i.e. equation

$$2x^3 - x^2 - 10x + 7 = 0$$

Figure 1.12 Solving $2x^3 - x^2 - 10x + 7 = 0$ by graphs.

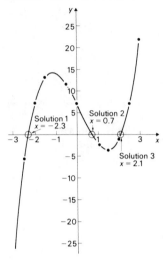

If this arose as the mathematical model of a situation, the solution would be difficult by algebra but easy by graphs. The equation is just like the graphical relation in Figure 1.12, except that y is replaced by zero. Therefore the graph represents the equation wherever, but only wherever, y on it has the value zero. As before, replaceability means equality. The points where $y = 0$ are all on the x axis, the horizontal axis, so the solutions of the equation are at the intersections of the curve and this axis, namely at about $x = -2.3$, $x = 0.7$ and $x = 2.1$.

In practice some theoretical solutions may be physically impossible and should be ignored; negative values of x might, for example, not be feasible and attention would then be focused only on the other mathematical possibilities.

The graphical method is not merely easy; it also lets the manager see just what is hidden in the behaviour of his model, e.g. where the peaks and troughs are (maxima and minima). The use of graphs in all possible circumstances, whether equation solving or not, cannot be too strongly recommended. The only possible drawback is some loss of accuracy, the solutions were 'roughly' the values stated. However, this is easily overcome. We draw the relevant parts of the graph as exactly as we please (without wasting time on the remainder), by extending the little table of values in the (feasible) regions where y is around zero. Inserting values of x, we find the values of y as follows:

1.

x	0.7	0.75	so try	0.73	and the solution is about $x = 0.725$
y	0.196	−0.22		−0.055	

2.

x	2.1	2.05	so try	2.09	and the solution is about $x = 2.091$
y	0.112	−0.47		−0.009	

If this is not yet accurate enough, the process may be continued as long as necessary.

Note that while we spoke of drawing the graph more exactly, we have found our solutions without needing to do so; the table alone is often sufficient when refining the solutions, though the first sketch of the curve is still essential.

Pairs of simultaneous equations are solved graphically by plotting both curves on the same diagrams. Figure 1.13 shows the graphs for

$$4x + 6y = 17$$
$$\text{and} \quad 3xy = 8$$

Figure 1.13   Graphical solution of simultaneous equations.

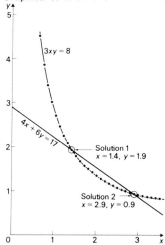

The first is a straight line, the second a commonly-met type of relation with two equally strong factors interacting.

Since the relationships must both be true at the same time, the same solutions must fit both simultaneously. The curves have identical values of x and y only where they cross each other, so the intersections (2 of them in this case) provide the solutions; we read off the pair of x, y values at each crossing to find

$$x = 1.4, y = 1.9 \quad \text{as one}$$
$$\text{and} \quad x = 2.9, y = 0.9 \quad \text{as the other.}$$

Greater precision may be obtained by trial, as before. This time the aim is to bring $y = \dfrac{17 - 4x}{6}$ and $y = \dfrac{8}{3x}$ to the same value simultaneously.

When solving equations graphically it is impossible to avoid limiting all graphs to 2 dimensions. Three or more simultaneous equations cannot, then, be solved graphically, but they still yield to solution by trial if somehow a set of guesses of the unknowns can be approximated to the true answer. This is often quite easy, since the equations model a situation about which there is usually some sort of practical knowledge. Lest it be thought that trial-and-error is hardly mathematics. I would remark that to us, mathematics is for solving management problems and not a study for its own sake. Indeed, the computer works out many (though not all) of its answers by systematic trial, the process of *iteration*. It works so much faster than we can that it appears to produce the answers almost at once and we do not notice the many steps on the way to finding them.

Inequalities. School maths teaching so concentrates on equations and equality that it almost ignores the far greater field of inequality. In graphical terms, the infinitely thin curved line in Figure 1.13 shows where $3xy = 8$, but there is an infinitely large area above and to the right of the line in which $3xy > 8$ and also the infinitely large area below and to the left where $3xy < 8$. To see which way they are, try any point off the line, e.g. $x = 4$, $y = 4$. This is above the curve and, of course, $3xy = 3 \times 4 \times 4$ which is greater than 8. There is no single solution of $3xy > 8$, nor of any number of inequalities simultaneously unless the case is exceptional.

In management the inequality very often represents the truth. 'We must sell at least 10 000 units to make a profit' imposes the mathematical relationship $S \geqslant 10\ 000$. In words, S is greater than or equal to 10 000. 'Our production is limited to 800 tons per week' implies $P \leqslant 800$. A whole series of such inequalities represents the constraints under which management must operate and, let us repeat, there is usually no single set of values which provides the complete mathematical solution of the managers' problems.

Once again the graph provides a clear picture if there are not too many factors. Drawing all the limiting curves, e.g. $S = 10\ 000$ and $P = 800$, on the same diagram and inspecting to see on which sides lie feasibility, one can see the total scope that the constraints allow or even (as does happen) that there is no solution within every constraint. In Figure 1.14, if our constraints are $3xy > 8$ and $4x + 6y < 17$, the feasible area is both below the line and above the curve, i.e. the little segment between A and B. However, if there is a further restriction that $y \geqslant 3$ (y is at least 3), then this horizontal line at height 3 does not meet the other two criteria simultaneously and the situation is seen to be impossible. Where there is feasibility and thus many possible solutions, a 'best' one in some sense (greatest profit, least idle time, etc.) may be sought. The section on linear programming in Chapter 16 discusses some ways of finding this.

Problem solving

All too commonly, students learn to perform standard mathematical routines adequately, but when faced with a problem in ordinary language they cannot solve it. They fail to identify the relevance of any of the techniques they have learned; the difficulty is one of re-formulation in mathematical language. While practice is the only sure way to achieve facility in this, a systematic approach can help.

1. Is the problem expressed in quantitative terms? If there are no quantities, maths cannot help. A problem like 'Our labour turnover is too high' is not susceptible to our treatment as nothing in it is quantified.

Figure 1.14

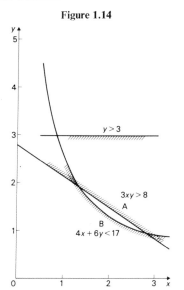

2. Identify the factors which are quantifiable or already quantified (e.g. the number of people leaving in a month, the total labour force, etc.).

3. Express the situation as briefly as possible, as one or a series of verbal statements involving the factors: for example, our total labour force should be 486; 20 people left in January, 6 in February . . . ; fortunately these are not our best people but the accountants say that it costs £78 to train each of these leavers and each replacement.

4. Decide which of the factors are knowns and which are unknowns. Label the unknowns. If no unknowns can be identified, then the problem has not yet been stated in quantitative terms.

5. Express the statements, using the labels, as mathematical relationships; the requisite operators will be declared in the statements.

6. If possible, sketch graphs to illustrate the relationships. The insight that even a rough drawing provides may be startling.

It will often be realized by this stage that there is not enough information, and that some factors have not been considered at all. As their nature becomes apparent they may themselves be the solutions, for not all problems are mathematical. In other cases they may lead to questions ('How long do people stay with us, i.e. what proportions last under a month, 1–3 months etc.'), which may entail more research before they are elucidated and rewritten as further statements and relationships. A point will be reached at which the non-mathematical answers will appear, or a set of mathematical relationships to which the rules of maths can be applied. If an approximate set of values for the unknowns can be discerned, this is an added bonus as it provides a check on any theoretical solutions.

PART II THE COMPUTER IN MANAGEMENT
II
WHAT THE COMPUTER IS

In the management context today 'the computer' is the electronic digital computer, a machine that is much maligned through lack of understanding. At the present time the computer can be seen in two different formats, which indicate distinct origins. There are the machines which require a special staff and which must be installed in air-conditioned rooms; these represent investments of at least £250 000 and perhaps several millions. On the other hand, there are machines the size of a desk which work happily in any office, operated by the normal office staff and needing only an electric point for power supply. The first category is descended from the giant calculators of the early 1950s, while the latter has grown out of the mechanical accounting machines long familiar to business. Development of these big machines is steadily making them smaller, faster, more reliable and less demanding, thanks to ultra-miniaturization of their components. This same fact has made possible the increase in power of the small machines, by using the same components, until the point has been reached where the two types merge, with no clear borderline. We can already see the spectrum of computer power as complete, machines being available to suit tasks of any size. Moreover these machines are adaptable; their units are interchangeable to suit various needs. One step remains, which is urgently being worked on; add-on units built by the different manufacturers are not yet compatible with each other. Generally speaking, the larger makers who can offer complete installations of their own design prefer that only their own products should be used. Customers and specialist makers of add-on units would prefer more compatibility between brands so that an installation could contain the elements judged best for the end use, regardless of make.

As a calculator, the computer is extremely fast. Thousands or even millions of arithmetic operations may be performed every second. Comparing it with the traditional desk calculator, the 'whirring time' employed on the calculating is reduced effectively to nothing, and if the computer were used in the same way as the old calculator it would spend the whole of its working life awaiting the next input of data or instructions. This is not the case, of course. The store in which the computer keeps its data and its answers is also used to hold the instructions that tell it what to do; this feature is one which distinguishes the computer from any other calculator, whether mechanical or electronic.

Storing its instructions makes the computer particularly valuable for repetitive work such as stock control or invoicing or payroll preparation; the same instructions are used over and over again until all the new figures have been processed and the task is complete. Switching from one piece of data to the next (e.g. to the next item of stock, the next invoice or the next employee on the payroll) is done at computer speeds without human intervention. All that is necessary is:

1. To get the instructions (called the program) infallibly correct.
2. To get the current raw data put into the computer without errors.

The machine cannot make mistakes unless it breaks down, a rare event nowadays. Errors in the answers are therefore due either to faulty programming, i.e. inadequate or erroneous program preparation, or to wrong data being fed in. The latter is much more common, since fresh data is required all the time whereas programs once developed are simply re-used without alteration. The problems of data accuracy are such that they have given birth to the term GIGO, made of the initial letters of garbage in—garbage out. As we shall see, special effort must be devoted to making data entering the computer as accurate as possible.

Some of the smaller types of computer are worked exclusively on single tasks and therefore need just one program each. However, this is unusual, and it is extremely unlikely for a larger machine to be used in this way except for process control. More commonly, a computer has a large number of different tasks to perform, with the separate programs being on call as required. A computer installation therefore consists of two parts:

1. The machinery itself—the *hardware*.
2. All the necessary programs—the *software*

The hardware is almost certain to be an assembly of standard products available to all from the manufacturers. The software, however, must be prepared to suit precisely the needs of the firm concerned. Many procedures, such as payrolls and stock control, are more or less standard and programs for them may be modifications of a standard *package* available from the hardware manufacturer. Other procedures will be unique to the firm in question and their programs will have to be specially written.

Bearing this in mind, a rule of thumb is that the investment in software in all but the smallest installations will about equal that in hardware. In other words, when looking into installing a computer beyond the desk-type, one must expect to double the apparent cost of the proposed equipment. Alternatively, the cost of keeping up with new program requirements will be about the same as the cost of renting the hardware.

The hardware: a general view

A computer contains a number of main units, as shown in Figure 2.1. The arithmetic unit does the work, removing data from storage, processing it and returning it to storage or to output under command of the control unit. The input and output units are, as their names suggest, the means of communication between user and machine. Commonly the control unit, the arithmetic

Figure 2.1 The main units of a computer.

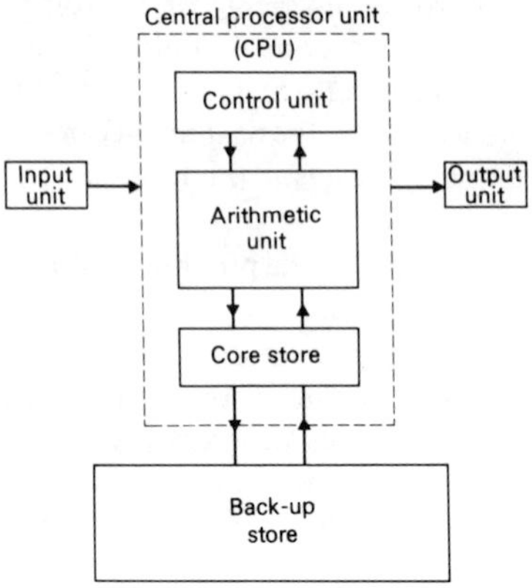

unit and the internal store are combined in a single cabinet (the spectacular one with flashing lights) and called the *central processor unit* or CPU.

The working speed depends partly on the speed of internal operation of the arithmetic and control units and partly on the speed of information transfer along the links shown as arrows in Figure 2.1. Within the central processor these speeds have risen in such dramatic jumps, due to technical changes, that computers are classed in *generations*:

1st generation	(1946 to mid-50s)—used electromechanical relays and electronic valves: unreliable, slow, large and with heavy power consumption.
2nd generation	(1950s)—used electronic valves: considerably faster but still unreliable and with high power requirements.
3rd generation	(1960s)—used transistors: huge gains in speed and reliability, far smaller and less power-consuming.
4th generation	(late 60s and early 70s)—used integrated circuits: still tinier and enormously more reliable, some gains in speed and power consumption.

At the time of writing (1975), there are rumours of a coming 5th generation in which the action takes place in individual molecules of certain plastics. If this is even half-true then the size will be reduced still further, speed yet again enhanced, reliability will be virtually total and power requirements trivial.

The transistors, etc. are used essentially as switches capable of extremely rapid repeated operation. The circuits which contain them perform addition and subtraction by means of pulses of current which switch them on or off; multiplication and division are carried out as repeated addition or subtraction respectively, with counters to control the number of repetitions. Other types of circuit perform logical operations; they compare two numbers and can cause differing actions depending on whether one or the other is greater, or they are equal.

The switch circuits are, of course, either on or off. A single circuit can there-fore represent only two states of affairs, zero and not-zero. A chain of linked circuits working in sequence can, however, represent any number within its capacity by means of codes in the on-off-on . . . sequence. Sequences may also be used to represent letters of the alphabet or any other symbols such as mathe-matical signs and the computer can therefore deal with either numbers or words. For example if it is programmed to regard A, B, C, D . . . as being successively larger, its logic circuits could sort a list of words into alphabetical order.

Storage

Some of the power of a computer will derive from the size and number of its chains of linked circuits, since longer chains can deal with bigger numbers or words while more of them can cope with more data simultaneously. Another and perhaps even more important factor in the power is the size of the store or *memory* and the speed with which data can be put into or taken out of it. Some memory is transient; switching off or a power failure destroys the information held in it. Examples are the circuits used as *registers* to receive data from the input units before passing it into a more permanent location. Other types of transient memory, particularly for mass storage, have become obsolete because undesired loss of memory can be so expensive. Permanent storage usually depends on magnetism. Tiny magnets are magnetized either this way or that to correspond to a switch being on or off: they therefore match the electronics precisely. In this context permanent simply means remaining until changed; the devices can be remagnetized at will and so the contents of the memory may be changed whenever desired.

If the magnets are in the form of tape, like domestic recording tape but of much more uniform quality, the cost is very low, but reading the stored data, or recording more without erasing what is already there, involves winding the tape through to find the right place. This is *serial access* to data and can take quite a time if the point needed is at the far end of the tape; serial-access memory is useless as the main, internal storage of a computer. However, magnetic tape has been widely used as secondary or back-up storage for the many jobs in which data is to be processed serially, such as weekly payroll work or invoicing or stock control, where it is perfectly satisfactory always to deal with the employees, customers or items stocked in the same order. Another important use is to store programs *off-line*, i.e. out of the computer assembly itself. The computer operator selects and loads the correct reel of tape when it is needed; this slight inconvenience is far outweighed by the low cost of the method.

Where *on-line* storage with *random access* is needed, i.e. every item stored is to be found equally (and very) quickly, the memory unit has tended to be much more expensive. The most widely-used form consists of tiny ring magnets placed at the intersections of a wire mesh so that each magnet has an 'address' corres-ponding to its co-ordinate on the wire grid. Currents sent along two grid wires are arranged to be strong enough when combined, at their intersection, to magnetize the ring there but weak enough to have no effect on the other rings through which they pass singly. A third wire, threaded through the rings in a special way, enables the magnetization of any individual ring (i.e. the information it contains) to be read at will. This type of memory has had to be hand-made and was very expensive; despite this it is used because it works reliably and at computer speeds. Relatively small *core stores* of this type have therefore been built into central processors as instant containers for the current program and current data only, with a larger, slower but cheaper back-up memory trying to keep pace with the needs of the CPU. It is obvious that large core stores offering random access provide high power for computers, and much work is being done on building them by machine instead of by hand. There has been some success and core storage is now becoming comparable in cost with some of the faster types of back-up store next to be described.

If serial access memories could only be made fast enough their major disadvantage would be overcome. Attempts to provide improved speed have included magnetic drums and magnetic disks. Both consist of rapidly rotating, fairly large surfaces covered with magnetic material, with *read/write heads* that can be moved quickly to the desired position to extract or insert data. The disk seems to be winning; a stack of say 8 or 10 on a common spindle, working with a pair of read/write heads for each disk so that all 16 or 20 faces are accessible simultaneously, almost converts serial into random access and is ample in size for mass memories. Several such *disk drive units* may be attached to a single CPU. The cost is appreciably higher than magnetic tape, but has been lower than core storage; whether this will continue remains to be seen. The term *direct access* describes the method of using disk storage.

The cheapest and by far the slowest memories are completely external to the computer; punched cards and punched paper tape. Even the so-called high speed readers and punches operate at far below the speeds of magnetic devices and the stored material is much less compact than, say, magnetic tape. However, cheapness and relative immunity from damage make the paper forms useful as memory in some cases.

The main distinction between what I have called desk-type computers and the large type is in the mass memory. Generally speaking, the desk-types do not have this feature: they produce visible records such as ledger cards or invoices (being known for this reason as visible record computers) and any further work to be done on a document involves the manual transfer of data from it to the core store via the machine's typewriter keyboard and the operator's eyes and fingers. Modern trends have introduced a magnetized strip mounted on the ledger card to contain the latest data and avoid manual transfer with its low speed and high error rate; also there is a movement towards simultaneous production of visible documents and a punched paper tape or a magnetic tape. Another distinguishing feature of the visible record computer is that the entire machine—input/output units (typewriter, calculator keyboard and perhaps magnetic read/write devices), arithmetic and control units and the small core store—is in a single cabinet, usually arranged like a desk for convenience. But the day of plug-in extras has already arrived, and by the time a powerful visible record machine has been augmented with add-on core store, tape or disk back-up memory and so on, it resembles a small 'large' computer very closely indeed, both in appearance and power.

Input units

The input to a computer consists of instructions (programs) and data. Some programs, especially those used regularly, will be held in the secondary storage but even these, like rarely used programs, will have been input at some stage.

In their original form both programs and data are likely to be written or printed for human reading. So far computers cannot read as we can and a conversion process is needed. One is via punched cards. The type of card shown in Figure 2.2 is very common. It contains 80 punchable columns and can therefore hold up to 80 characters in coded form. The preparation is done on a *card punch*, a sort of typewriter which punches the hole code instead of printing on to paper. The card punch may also be able to *interpret* afterwards, i.e. read the punched holes and print their meaning along the top margin, for visual reference or checking. Remembering GIGO, garbage in—garbage out, we realize the need to eliminate errors at this stage so far as we can, since the computer will blindly accept what is fed in. Cards punched by one girl are therefore *verified* by another who puts each newly punched card into a verifier and goes through the same motions as the punch operator, using the same data. The verifier resembles the punch, but instead of producing holes it senses their presence. If both girls press the same keys in the same order the verifier will simply detect that the holes agree with the verifier operator's keying. Where a depressed key does not match the holes the machine locks and the operator must check whether she, or the punch girl or both, were wrong. Unfortunately, errors of punching will not be detected if the verifier girl makes the same mistake as the punch girl. The likelihood of this is reduced by insisting that no one verifies her own punching, for individuals may tend to repeat certain mistakes such as misreading a character or word in the original document. Nevertheless the chance of undetected errors remains and is a major bugbear in any computer operation. Good programming might sometimes make the computer detect and reject some types of error that can slip through, such as impossible wage rates or stock levels. However, there are those errors that escape even this screen, and give rise to the gas bills for £1 000 008 and similar spectacular items; in such instances the computer is usually blamed, not the people who provide the data.

Stacks of punched and verified cards are fed through a *card reader* into the computer. This device reads all 80 columns simultaneously and with cards passing through at several hundreds per minute, the work of many punch/verifier teams can be accommodated by a single card reader. However, the computer is many times faster than even the quickest card reader and can lose potential working time while receiving input.

Input on punched paper tape is produced and verified on machines similar to those for cards apart from the format of the material: *paper tape readers* are the input units. These read only one character at a time, and tape is even slower

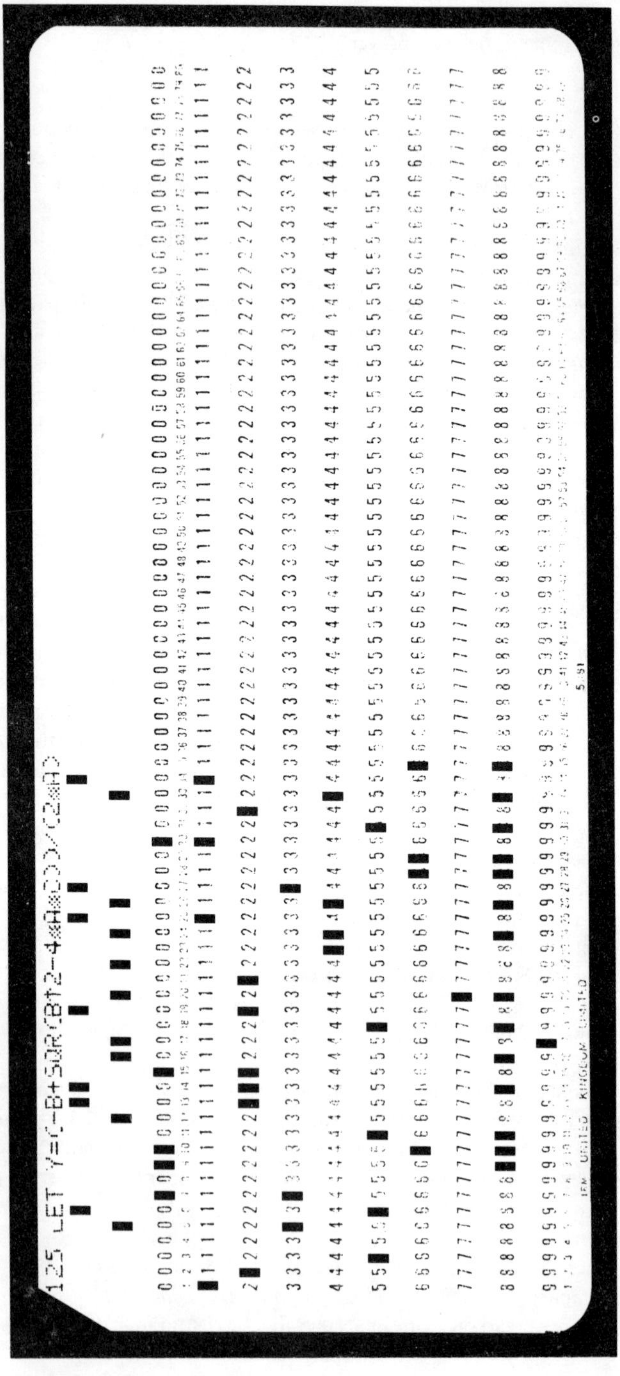

Figure 2.2 An 80-column punched card.

than cards. As compensation, paper tape and its machines are cheaper than the card equivalents.

Punched cards or tape are sometimes produced as by-products of the process to be computerized. For example:

1. Time clocks which punch instead of printing the time produce time-cards that may be passed directly to the computer for payroll calculations.

2. In shops where the little price-tags on every item are suitably hole-punched, the cashier is instructed to remove all tags as the goods are sold. Daily bundles of tags, representing the day's total transactions, are fed through a suitable reader for rapid computer analysis by money, rate of turnover of each class or even line of stock, comparison of different shop performances and so on.

3. Where simple records have to be kept on a process (for example, occasional numbers might need to be recorded) it is possible to use suitably printed 80-column cards on which the appropriate printed numbers are marked with a soft pencil. *Mark sensers* detect the presence and locations of graphite and automatically feed the corresponding data to the computer.

4. Visible record computers or the less pretentious accounting machines producing, for example, invoices, may at the same time generate a paper tape containing the salient data for later analysis either on itself (with a different program of course) or on a larger machine, perhaps amalgamated with the tapes of other small units.

To avoid some of the delays inherent in punched cards or paper tape, and also the costs of high-quality paper items often useless after one passage through their readers, data is sometimes recorded magnetically on tape or disk directly from the keyboard. These records feed into the computer at their usual high speeds and of course the tapes or disks themselves may be re-used repeatedly. The disadvantages are mainly in the area of error correction, which can involve serious problems with such vast amounts of data stored so compactly.

For special purposes there are special input units. Magnetic ink character recognition or MICR is used, for example, with cheques processed by a clearing bank's computers. The cheques are pre-printed in magnetic ink with the bank, branch and account numbers; a keyboard machine adds the amount in the same ink. Everyone will be familiar with the special typefaces that enable the MICR reader to distinguish between characters that are also legible to us, and pass the data speedily into the computer. *Optical* character recognition or OCR is more unusual still, but works for the same or similar special alphabets at similar high speeds. Unfortunately humans, unlike machines, get tired of seeing the same things and these typefaces are certain not to be brought into universal use. The problem of reading all typefaces or, worse, handwriting, directly into the computer has not yet been solved.

Designers and others working with drawings may be computer-aided via a cathode-ray tube that presents a picture of the design stored in the computer and which may be altered throughout using a *light pen* on the screen. Thus the light pen is an input unit.

The *teletype terminal* can feed into the computer the characters typed on the keyboard. This device is much like a typewriter and does produce a typed copy of the input, but its main function is to generate at each key depression a coded electrical pulse that goes to the computer. Of course, only human typing speeds can be achieved using this means. However, the teletype can alternatively make a punched paper tape which is either transferred to a high-speed tape reader for input, along with the tapes of many other teletypes, or else can be fed back through the teletype itself and input at 10, 15 or 30 characters per second according to the model used. But the teletype is not just an input unit; the computer can also print its output through it.

Output units
First comes the teletype terminal. The computer drives it to produce both typed output and, if a punch is fitted, paper tape, at 10, 15 or 30 characters per second. This averages a line of output (max. about 80 characters) in about 1 to 4 seconds. With very high-speed terminals at around 90 characters per second, times are correspondingly lower and costs higher. As a two-way input/output unit the teletype is of great and growing importance despite its low speed; it is among the cheapest units in the entire computer field.

For printed output where the teletype is too slow the *line printer* is widely used. This prints a complete line at a time, up to 160 characters wide and at 300, 600, 1200 or even more complete lines per minute depending on the machine. Even these speeds are incomparably below the capabilities of the central processor. Often, therefore, the computer's own output unit is the magnetic tape drive or its disk drive, and the printing is done off-line from tape or disk by the line printers, several of which are kept fully loaded by a single computer. These magnetic records will possibly be re-used as input on the next run of the same program. They may for instance be the updated stock balances.

Card punches and paper tape punches may be computer-driven where cards or tape are suitable forms of output. Sometimes these are used off-line to generate printed copy, but documents for human reading are by no means always necessary.

If a permanent copy is not needed, the cathode-ray tube or *visual display unit* (VDU) produces extremely fast responses in transient form. Airline reservation systems use them in conjunction with special keyboard input units to check on current seat availabilities. We have also met the VDU in conjunction with the light pen in design work.

For appropriate applications there are *graph plotters* which draw curves directly under computer instructions.

III
WHAT THE COMPUTER DOES

In short, the computer does precisely what it is told, no more and no less.

Since in essence a central processor is an assembly of devices (switches or magnets) that are stable in either of 2 states, all instructions must be in a 2-state form, as must all numbers, letters or symbols that it handles. This 2-state form is known as a *binary code* and the two elements that it uses may conveniently be represented by the symbols 0 and 1, which may correspond to numbers zero and one, or to switches being off or on, or to magnets being magnetized this way or that. The exact codes used are chosen by the machine manufacturers and are usually different for each type of computer. In the early days, therefore, programming a machine involved an intimate knowledge of the way it worked; every program consisted only of a sequence of zeros and ones, was excessively tedious to write and was quite incomprehensible to anyone else. Worst of all, a program worked only on the model (and sometimes only on the very machine) it was written for; changing computers meant the entire re-programming of all work. It is not surprising that programmers were scarcer than gold-dust and correspondingly priced.

Inside a computer all that happens is that sequences of electric pulses corresponding to 0s and 1s are altered, shifted, removed, mixed, examined and compared at speeds of millions per second. If the sequences are codes for numbers, the activity usually amounts to *calculation*; if they are letters or words, perhaps mixed with a few numbers as with payrolls, the term is *data processing*. In both cases it occurred to programmers that a limited number of small routines would suffice, when suitably combined, to produce any desired program. By means of a dictionary of such sub-routines the computer itself can be made to produce its own ultimate program in 1s and 0s; this is called *machine language*. Multiplication of 4 × 3, for example, might involve a programmer writing something like

$$
\begin{array}{lll}
\text{I} & 4 & 164 \\
\text{I} & 3 & \\
\text{M} & 164 & 200 \\
\text{O} & 200 &
\end{array}
$$

The meaning of this is:

Program			Meaning
I	4	164	Input 4 and store in location 164.
I	3		Input 3 and store in a temporary register.
M	164	200	Multiply the contents of the register by the contents of location 164 and store the result in location 200.

Program	Meaning
O 200	Output (i.e. print or whatever) the contents of location 200.

Thus M is translated by the machine into the complete sequence of instructions for multiplication (in fact by repeated addition); the programmer need no longer know the machine intimately, but must still appreciate what can and cannot be done in each available location. This program has been written in a sort of *assembly language;* the machine translation process performed each time the program runs is called *assembly*.

Further thought will show that the machine itself can allocate correct locations as well as produce the right binary coding if a suitable set of instructions is provided. Multiplying 4×3 or any other two numbers might, for example, only require

$$\text{READ B, C}$$
$$\text{A} = \text{B} * \text{C}$$

as two lines of program. With its inbuilt dictionary, called a *compiler* or compiler program, the computer prepares coded instructions for reading the values 4 and 3 for B and C from the data we provide. It can then generate their binary codes and store them, operating on them with the binary sequence for multiplication, storing the result and labelling it so that it will be produced whenever letter A next appears in the program, perhaps to print its value as output or perhaps for use in further work.

The obvious value of writing programs in something near a normal language (with mathematical elements) is so great that several such *high-level languages* have become widely accepted and each hardware manufacturer, while free to use whatever binary codes he likes for his machines, now has to offer compilers for each major high-level language, for every model. So programming has become easy, programmers are plentiful and command reasonable instead of exaggerated salaries, and the same program may be used on a range of machines if it is compiled for each. This need be done only once per machine type and the program is stored in compiled form (as a deck of punched cards, a paper or magnetic tape, on disk or drum or in the core store) for use whenever required. In computer terminology, the program as written is the *source program*; compilation creates the *object program* from it (see Figure 3.1). This in turn is married to the data on each run to generate the current output.

High-level languages sound so obviously right that one may wonder why the simplification does not proceed to the ultimate, with a single high-level language and perhaps a single binary coding too. Just one compiler would then suffice for every machine and every user. There are various reasons why this has not come about. Many people have had, and are continuing to have, new ideas of what the universal language should do and should offer for ease of both programming and compilation. Unfortunately these ideas, while good and useful, are all different. Only those which are backed by the manufacturers (adding to or replacing what was offered before) can possibly become wide-

Figure 3.1

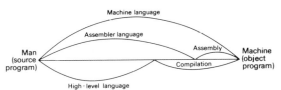

spread, and the situation remains confused. In the data processing field the US Government, as the world's biggest user of computers, imposed some order by insisting on having COBOL compilers available for every central processor purchased; this name comes from Common Business Oriented Language. Today COBOL is almost the only language encountered in the data processing field. In the scientific or calculation field there are still several popular languages, each offering particular ease in programming for certain types of work. COBOL is almost useless here as it is mainly concerned with easy programming for storing, retrieving, sorting, screening (i.e. searching through), re-arranging, merging and controlling the output format of large masses of alphabetic or alpha-numeric data. Calculating the orbit of a satellite around Venus uses none of this. FORTRAN (from FORmula TRANslator) has become widely used for calculations, partly because it is efficient and not hard to learn, and partly through the powerful backing of IBM, who dominate the hardware industry in the western world. Other scientific languages are ALGOL and PL/I, with BASIC (from Beginners All-purpose Symbolic Instruction Code) as a fairly widespread, FORTRAN-like language that is extremely easy to learn and also offers much of the data-handling capability of COBOL. Any manager, for example, could quickly learn to write his own programs in BASIC. PL/I is said to be suited to both scientific and data processing work. Further languages, each with its claimed advantages, continue to appear every year.

Machines use different internal binary codes partly because they really have different needs and partly because manufacturers naturally like to offer something unique to their equipment, with certain advantages over each other product. Having to write their own new compilers for each new model is considered a small price to pay for this. Incidentally, the different facilities offered on the various models mean that even COBOL, FORTRAN and BASIC may have variations in their finer points for different machines, though the fundamentals of the languages are universal.

Generally speaking, the visible record computer is too small to store the compiler for a high-level language. Instead it uses a *machine code* that rather resembles an assembly language and must be learned for each type of machine. Fortunately, these computers are normally used on a limited range of routine tasks so that a dozen or so programs are all that will ever be required by a single user. The manufacturers offer one or more programs as part of the initial cost of the installation and will produce and, more importantly, *de-bug* any further programs for a moderate charge. For this reason most organizations using these machines do not bother to include a trained programmer in their staff: a range of programs is even available 'off the shelf' since many, if not all, office routines are common to most firms.

Off-the-shelf programs or *packages* also exist for tasks performed on the larger machines. These tasks include stock control, payroll, survey analysis, vehicle scheduling, linear programming, statistical analysis, critical path analysis and discounted cash flow: all are jobs that can be done in exactly the same way no matter which firm or organization is involved.

Whether using packages or special programs, it is normal for a single computer to have to tackle a wide range of work in the course of a day. As we have already seen, the speed of the central processor is so much higher than that of the *peripherals* (all the ancillary devices) that if the changeovers from job to job were to be performed manually after each was completed, the central processor would be nearly always idle, awaiting instructions. Thus a most important part of the software is a set of programs for making the computer itself do all the internal re-settings necessary for the changeovers. These *supervisory programs*, supported by *utility programs* that might, for example, clean a disk for re-use, will be specially prepared to suit the work routines to be followed. It is obvious that much thought must be given to the daily, weekly and monthly work patterns both when commissioning a new computer installation and also once it is running in what might be considered a satisfactory manner. This latter is not always done, but can pay well.

Anyone watching a computer at work under the control of a good *operating system* such as we have just outlined cannot fail to be impressed by the smoothness of the rapid work flow as the operators continually load and unload tapes or stacks of cards, occasionally pressing buttons on this or that piece of hardware. The operators and the peripherals are indeed kept busy. But the pace of activity inside the central processor leaves the rest so far behind (computers are said to be peripheral bound, limited in speed by their peripherals) that efforts are always being directed to finding ways of piling yet more work into the same central processor to fill its spare time between jobs. With the operating time costing upwards of £200 per hour this is not surprising. Two different approaches are proving successful, namely *multi-programming* and *time-sharing* or *multi-access*.

We have been considering what is called *batch processing* work, in which the computer tackles one job at a time, completing it as a single batch before proceeding to the next individual job. Many single tasks will demand the full capacity of the hardware available, but many more will be relatively small, using only a portion of the available space in the computer. The idea of multi-programming is that several such small jobs may be processed simultaneously instead of queueing one behind the other for the machine's undivided attention. Of course, they must not interfere with one another in any way, and multi-programming depends for its success on very critical and complex software that appropriately allocates storage space and sequential time to each task. Thus one part of the computer may be controlling the output of program A while another is calculating for program B and yet a third part is receiving the input for program C. Naturally there will have to be enough input and output units on-line to suit the multiplicity of work being handled.

With all batch processing, including multi-programming, the owners of the hardware, by their ultimate control over the operators and operating systems, can determine what goes through the machine and when. This makes for efficient use of the computer's time but involves inflexibility. For example, if I want to know my bank balance promptly at the end of business today I cannot discover it. The best my bank can do is to tell me the amount when the balances of all their customers were last printed out. This was probably last night, with yesterday's closing balance, and I must wait until tomorrow for today's figure. Since this question is put to the bank by a significant number of customers every day, one of the daily routines of the bank's computers is to output all the current balances, whether they will be requested or not; this is a very large task indeed. In other circumstances, where the routines do not happen to include daily printouts of the latest data, a current position is totally unobtainable until the next printout is due. This is a cause of much dissatisfaction with computers, although of course the fault really lies with the system in which the machine is run.

A way of gaining flexibility and at the same time a high utilization of the central processor is known as time-sharing or multi-access and also as the *real-time* system (see Figure 3.2). A computer is arranged to work simultaneously with a number of completely independent input and output units. These are usually teletypes, each having its own channel (usually a telephone line via a *Modem* or *Modulator/demodulator*, which converts the teletype actions into pulses suited to the line) linking it to a *multiplexor* connected to the central processor. Computer jargon has changed the name of this device to *front-end*; in essence the front-end is a little computer offering a set of little stores, one per channel, buffered to react with both main computer and peripherals at their own speeds. Communication between multiplexor and central processor is under the control of a supervisory program that allocates chunks of time in

Figure 3.2 Schematic diagram of a time-sharing computer.

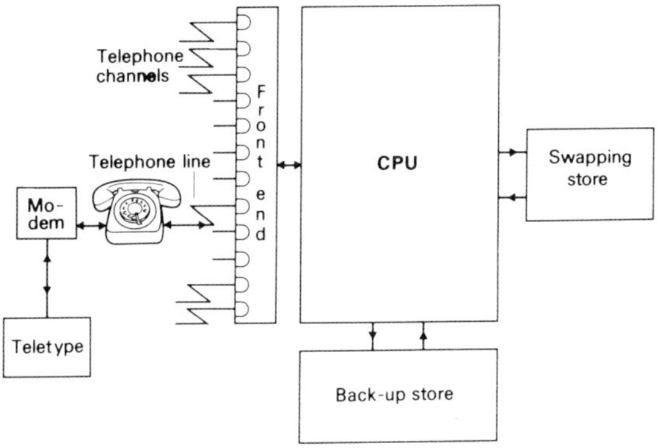

sequence to each channel, according to predetermined priority rules. These will involve the nature and size of the work demanded, the number of channels in use at the moment and the identity of the channel users (for example, the chairman may be given higher, or lower, priority than one of the production controllers). In typical use a teletype operator will take several seconds to type out a command. If it is one to which the computer can respond immediately by the nature of the program concerned, the teletype will normally begin to print out the reply at once. In the tenth of a second that it takes for the unit to output the first character (at 10 per second) the computer will have come round to this channel, processed the command, fed the answers back into the buffered store, and very likely have gone on to 2 or 3 totally different jobs for other channels. The teletype user will therefore have the impression that he has the total power of the computer at his sole disposition, with instant response. Thus if I were able to ask the bank's computer for my current balance on a real-time system I would have it at once. Time-sharing systems are used within single organizations and are also offered as a public service. Below are some examples of the former:

1. Some airlines operate a seat reservation system in which all the seating capacity offered for a year ahead is stored in a large central processor, which may be 'interrogated' by booking clerks in many locations. These are equipped with terminals (often with VDU output) linked in over the telephone network. Tapping out the correct code will produce any desired seat information for the booking clerk; by keying other code sequences he can also reserve seats in the travellers' names, which will be stored in the computer.

2. Some large engineering firms place terminals at the disposal of their designers, who can contact the central computer through them for all their calculations. Others use computerized production control systems in which the production workers themselves can update the computer's information on the work situation through terminals located on the factory floor.

3. Larger banks are indeed keeping the customers' balances on real-time systems. For the sake of security, terminals are accessible only to authorized bank staff. The cost of the system is partly offset by eliminating the daily printout of all balances, most of which would not be asked for in any case.

Public systems are offered by a number of firms. Subscribers use special telephones on which they dial the number of the computer: they must then type their own *log-in code* on the terminal before the system accepts their work. Charges are based on the amount of connect time used and might be of the order of £4 to £10 per hour as against up to £200 per hour for a computer dedicated exclusively to a user. The difference, of course, is in the amount of CPU time actually taken, which is likely to be only a few seconds per hour of connect time. The remainder is sold by the system owners to other subscribers on-line simultaneously. All public systems offer a wide range of package programs in their 'libraries', as well as facilities for subscribers to store their own programs and data on the system using a range of languages. Library programs are naturally available to all users; the others may only be accessible through the log-in code under which they were originated. Of necessity, the operator can examine anything stored on his system; security depends on the integrity of the firms offering the service, and of their employees. So far this has raised no problems.

Apart from the terminals located at the users' premises, time-sharing systems need additional hardware for batch processing systems. In addition to the multiplexor and possibly a small computer to administer the supervisory program, very large rapid-access back-up storage is needed so that any subscriber can have access to his material without delay whenever he wants it. In batch work there is no problem in waiting while the operator finds and loads data stored off-line on reels of magnetic tape, but in real-time this will not do. In addition, the special software needed to operate the system is very large indeed. As a result, public networks tend to use very powerful computers, involving huge investments. All this can be made available through terminal equipment costing (in 1975) less than £900, or rentable for around £30 or £35 per month, plus connect time of only a few pounds per hour. And in one hour a great deal of work can be done. It is therefore not surprising that real-time usage is increasing very rapidly.

One other type of computer work has not yet been mentioned. This is *process control* in which, as the name states, a computer is dedicated solely to ensuring that any changes in the process (often a chemical one such as oil refining) are instantly corrected by appropriate means. Every such system will involve especially designed sensors that both monitor the process and communicate with the computer. Output will be of a nature suited to the process, such as computer-operated valves that adjust flow rates, possibly supplemented by printouts to report on what has happened. Each process control system will of course be purpose-designed, although the field has grown to the point where some manufacturers offer CPUs intended purely for process control. Allied to this work are numerically-controlled machine tools, by means of which a small computer translates draughtsmen's data directly into the movements of a tool cutting metal.

Process and machine-control by computer, important though they are, are nevertheless mere sidelines off the main track of computer possibilities. Management in particular is deeply affected by this latest type of labour available to industry and commerce.

IV
HOW THE COMPUTER JOINS THE MANAGEMENT TEAM

The first question is: Should the computer join the team? All too often this is not asked. Instead the chief accountant or the managing director decides to look into computers, calls in a hardware manufacturer for advice and it is only a matter of time before the computer arrives. Three hectic years then elapse before it is realized that an extremely expensive mistake has been made.

Ignoring the scientific work of the computer, which the research or engineering departments will usually evaluate properly, the machine should be used for simple, repetitive but enormous tasks like invoicing or stock control, and for screening the masses of data in its memory to generate management information. The speeds of operation and of output are such that managers can readily be showered with more information than there is time to look at, which could nullify the entire project. It is essential instead to study carefully what is really needed and a discipline called *systems analysis* has arisen to do this. The analysts examine the entire management information systems, which of course includes the invoicing, stock control and other procedures, to make them more effective. Systems analysis has become bound up with computers but the relationship should not be an exclusive one; if the best system in a particular firm is a manual one, the analyst should say so. For this reason alone, the systems analysts should be called in before the acquisition of a computer is undertaken: it has been seriously suggested that one or even two years earlier is not too soon. Unfortunately this rarely happens. The computer is bought (perhaps not the best one for the purpose) and then the analysts have to work under tremendous time pressure so that the expensive white elephant begins work immediately after its arrival. It is impossible for them to produce the optimal solution in such circumstances, and there are many other, equally significant reasons for analysis before commitment.

Manual systems are slow but flexible: computer ones are very fast but immensely rigid. The old manual payroll system, for example, could easily allow for the gatekeeper to receive 75p weekly for cleaning the chairman's wife's car if the wages clerk was told once about it. However, the computer's payroll program will merely multiply hours worked × hourly rate for the gatekeeper as for everyone else unless provision is made for this exception (and for every non-standard item) when the program is written, and appropriate data is fed in each week. This is harder to do than it sounds, and the ill-will generated by such inflexibility, where errors must wait until next week for correction, can hardly be exaggerated. One could almost say that the payroll, which demands ready response to variation above all things, should be the very last task to be computerized; instead it is often the first.

Systems analysts will review all paperwork procedures in the organization, comparing their performance with the ends they are intended to achieve: they will then proceed to design new systems and, inevitably, new forms and other paperwork to be used in them. The analysis will have clarified the question of whether or not to computerize; if the decision is affirmative then the new documents will be designed to facilitate both the punch operators' and the computer's use of them, in converting and printing out data. Systems programming follows the systems design and may indeed continue for the entire working life of the computer, as the systems should continually be reviewed in the light of the organization's changing needs.

If computerization is chosen, the hardware to be used may be obtained in several ways:

1. *Purchase* is straightforward, but apart from the sheer cost, especially of major installations, there is the severe disadvantage of rapid obsolescence through technical advances. One might be tempted to go on using an old computer years after real savings could be made by going for a newer one, just to avoid further capital expense.

2. *Leasing* overcomes this problem, for after 5 or 7 years of the contract one is free to re-negotiate for the newly-developed equipment while the large initial capital cost is of course avoided. The manufacturers will lease their computers, but are happy also to work through leasing specialists. These firms buy outright from the makers, then offer the user lower annual rentals, but over a longer minimum period. The makers need the rapid cash flow to support their operations, while the leasing firms do not as they have no other operations.

3. *Buying secondhand* can be much cheaper but has the obvious drawbacks associated with old equipment. Now that computers have been in use for some time a secondhand market is developing, but it is mainly restricted to firms where low cost outweighs reliability. An exception to this is the case of a firm acquiring a second or third CPU secondhand, to increase an installation in which the hardware is no longer current; this avoids having to change systems to suit a newer model of computer. However, makers are now tending to construct their new models to be compatible with their older ones, which may make this situation disappear.

4. *Buying time* on someone else's computer can be useful if one does not need an installation full-time. This can be arranged on a neighbouring firm's hardware (there are brokers who will put buyers in touch with nearby sellers of time), or by using a computer bureau, an organization that runs a computer like a taxi, selling its services to all comers. In either case, data preparation and systems help may or may not be provided along with the processing time. The main disadvantages are delay and inconvenience while our own work queues up, and lack of security as our

secrets are seen by others. However, the advantages of no capital outlay or rental costs are often overwhelming; we pay only for our usage.

5. *Time sharing*, discussed in Chapter III, enables the full power of a large computer to be available at any time to anyone at low prices. The main disadvantages are the security risk and the low input/output speeds if one limits oneself to the cheap teletype. Where there are large amounts of input or (more probably) output, a high-speed teletype, line printer or visual display unit is essential though much costlier.

The software may also be obtained in various ways. The hardware suppliers are almost bound to help in the first instance and later the firm may employ its own analysts and programmers. The alternative is to use the services of a specialist software house, one of the many firms who offer expertise in these areas, for a fee.

Whatever the method of acquisition chosen, the input of its first computer will have great and perhaps unexpected effects on an organization. Obviously, the systems analysts will be very apparent to many people in the early days. These continual reminders that the machine is faster and more accurate than people, and does not get tired or go on strike, may arouse feelings of insecurity in a firm's reliable, existent staff, who may decide to leave while the going is good. Threats of redundancy are felt even if they are neither present nor intended. There are serious risks of sabotage to the new systems, though probably not to the hardware: small delays in providing data, for example, can disrupt an entire operating timetable, with disastrously costly results. The de-bugging of the systems programs is bound to take longer than expected so that *parallel running* (old-style and new simultaneously) is needed at great expense. The pay-packet problems like forgetting the gatekeeper's 75p will cause serious ill-feeling even among the majority whose jobs are not thought threatened by the monster. Entirely new types of staff come in; where do computer operators, key-punch operators, programmers, etc. fit into the existing pay-and-status structure? To what extent should existing staff be re-trained to run the computerized systems? There used to be no alternative to converting one's own people, but there are now plenty of computer specialists; as the hardware becomes simpler to run it is now as easy, or easier, to get a computer manager from a manager instead of from a computer specialist. Existing staff know the organization (i.e. its former systems) and its people but not the computer computer specialists know about the new techniques but little else: the choices are not easy.

Under the traditional manual systems, any manager needing the odd fact can ring Jenny in the office and, at the cost of taking her from other work for a few minutes (a high cost, but one which is hard to quantify and is therefore taken as zero), can have his information. She need only look up the correct document This is totally impossible under a computer regime, as current data is stored magnetically and invisibly. One must await the next routine printout or make do with the last one. It is not realized how much one depends on Jenny until the systems are computerized; this is one of the main reasons for the use of real-time systems under which, at a higher cost in hardware and software, any data files can be interrogated through teletypes at any time. But this in turn might mean security risks, since only authorized people should have access to the organization's files. One solution is to have 'locks' built into the software, so that a demand for information is met only if a correct password 'key' is fed into the teletype with the request. The passwords may be changed as often as necessary and there may be several levels of keys so that some facts are more closely protected than others.

There are also security risks involving fraud. Centuries of business practice have evolved means of preventing and detecting frauds in manual systems, but the invisible records of the computer make possible new types of malpractice, as the newspapers and computer security consultants frequently remind us. It should not be forgotten that frauds were not eliminated by the traditional protection; they merely failed to hit the headlines unless they were big or involved some new angle. Frauds involving the computer, or rather the computerized system, still have an intrinsic news-value and are thus bound to be publicized. There are probably fewer people sufficiently qualified to embezzle with the computer's help than capable of executing an old-style fraud, but ultimately it is still necessary to depend on the honesty of the individual. As the novelty of computerized systems wears off, protective measures will become more normal and the whole matter less frightening. Since the fault is not with the machines but with people and systems, there are obvious precautions that should be taken. Those who design and program the systems, for example, should never be left to run them. Analysts and programmers are as honest as anyone else but are also just as susceptible to temptation. In fact the operation of the computer should be divorced as far as possible from the material which passes through it, to minimize the risks of collusion. The hardware manufacturers will always give sound advice on these matters.

The auditing of the firm's accounts presents another problem. The auditors can no longer send their boy along to look at the books; all he could see would be reels of magnetic tape. Audit methods, including the preferred sampling techniques, must be accommodated in the systems design and the auditors must therefore be fully involved from the start. Large firms of accountants employ their own systems analysts, to enable the closest liaison with their clients in this matter. A typical outcome is a special program written and held on mag-tape by the auditors, which when run on the client's computer will provide the necessary access to all files for audit purposes. However, many accountants and auditors operate as small firms or even one-man businesses and were professionally trained before the advent of the computer. Some of them must find it very difficult to change their techniques and try to preserve the old methods as much as possible, e.g. by insisting that the computer prints out all the firm's accounts in traditional styles and formats, down to the double-underlining of totals. Even without this final absurdity, this subtle form of resistance makes nonsense of the computer's ability to get through a great deal more work through following different, though equally effective, techniques in accounting.

All in all, it seems to take about two years for a firm's first computer installation to settle down, clear all bugs and become one of the standard tools of management. At this stage, when it can be seen in true perspective, the value of the computer is recognized as lying in its rapid but meticulous attention to detail. Because it can run through the entire production control data daily, planning can be updated and progress monitored effectively, with potential as well as actual trouble-spots highlighted for attention and with stocks and work-in-progress substantially reduced. This is an immediate saving which helps pay for the computer. Because the machine can store and sort the sales and purchase ledger data so easily, the production of invoices, statements and reminders, with the associated forecasting and control of customer credit, cash flow and profits, is made easy. As by-products, financial statements and sales analyses by region, type of customer or any other desired classifications are no trouble to produce, giving the basis for much better financial and sales decisions by management. It is now also possible, thanks to the combination of calculating power and mass storage, to construct mathematical models of the market so that alternative sales strategies can be simulated and the consequences forecast without the risks and delays of real life. In brief, so much new, useful management information now becomes available that managers are able to devote more time to improving the firm's future and less to fighting yesterday's and today's fires. Even the payroll runs settle down in the end, to everyone's satisfaction.

Looking ahead a little, it is possible to predict developments in many directions:

1. As computers become smaller, cheaper and simpler to run, their use will extend into smaller organizations. Already mini-computers have spawned micro-computers.

2. Time-shared or real-time systems will find ever wider applications in organizations of all sizes.

3. Firms with powerful computers will rapidly adopt and extend the use of market modelling techniques.

4. With growing data-banks about themselves in their computers, firms will try to model themselves in relation to their environment. This extension of market modelling has not succeeded too well so far, but it is bound to improve.

5. As education with and about the computer spreads down into the schools, fear of it will disappear. It will even become normal for managers to solve their simultaneous equations on the teletype terminal.

PART III STATISTICS

V

WHAT STATISTICS IS ABOUT

Many people are comforted by regarding the world as something fixed and unchanging, or at least as something which changes in a regular, ordered way. Any kind of unpredictable behaviour is seen as disquieting and to be avoided or at least disregarded. Life however, is full of deviations from the desirable norm. For example:

1. Each living species comes in many sizes and displays little uniformity. Makers of parrot cages, where the fit need not be too exact, are not troubled by unusually large or small parrots, but the mass-production clothing industry for humans has to take variability seriously into account.

2. The seaside holiday industry in Britain has to plan for a normal season every summer. If the weather one year is sufficiently bad to deter people from going to the coast resorts for their holiday, then there is much surplus capacity and consequent losses.

3. The takings in a shop, or the orders obtained by a salesman, can fluctuate widely and unpredictably from day to day. How are the buyers or planners to prepare for future sales?

4. A machine set up to make identical items in fact yields a range of dimensions; tolerances have to be admitted to accommodate the variation.

5. Absenteeism, while known to follow seasonal trends, is nevertheless impossible for management to predict precisely, day by day. A snowstorm, a big football match or the imminent expense of the Christmas season may be known to have an influence in one or other direction, but by just how much on a given day? Similar remarks could be made about labour turnover.

6. The response of individuals to training, selection tests or many other standard procedures is itself far from standard. Just how should the variation be allowed for if the very best use is to be made of all the human resources?

The cynic was undoubtedly right who said that the only constant factor in nature is its eternal variability. Efforts to impose some kind of order on this chaos have led to the science of statistics, which may be defined as the study of variability. This science helps us to understand the variation as the first step to imposing our will on it, but it cannot take us beyond this first step.

There is, of course, the other definition of statistics as a collection of data which exhibits the variation we have been discussing. The word is commonly used in this sense when a person is trying to show what statistics 'prove'. All too often such statements are false, besides which the figures alone can prove nothing. The science of statistics should help us by acting as an analytical and interpretive tool on the data, extracting conclusions with a measurable and stated degree of justification.

The raw material of the science of statistics is the data. There are two distinct methods of attacking the variation revealed or concealed by the data:

1. Where the data is complete, for example a census has been carried out or all the measurements from a finished production run are available, the figures are examined to try to discern the presence of a pattern in them.
2. Where only incomplete data is available, i.e. only samples can be examined, calculations are carried out to try to fit some standard pattern to the partial data. It is then assumed that this pattern will hold good for the unobserved individuals. However, this involves obvious risks of error and further calculations discover how big these are. The theory of probability, commonly known as the laws of chance, underlies these calculations.

If a pattern can be found (and it usually can), we may then speak of the pattern itself as a single entity with known characteristics that represents the behaviour of the group as a whole. The individuals comprising the group have made their contributions to the overall pattern and will no longer be considered singly. After all, they represent variability, while the group behaviour is the pattern and represents regularity.

Those who believe that the individual matters may find this idea disconcerting, but the following example will show why such fears are unnecessary. If a maker of television sets knows from sample studies that about 5% are likely to break down under guarantee, he need neither know nor care who are the unfortunate individual owners. He must naturally face up to his responsibility to provide sufficient service facilities for the 5%, but he would also be wrong to provide too much service, for its cost must add to the price of all the sets and thus adversely affect every owner. The point is that so long as the pattern of receiver performance (5% break down and 95% work) is matched by the pattern of service facilities, then the best possible solution is found. There remains the problem of reducing the 5% breakdown figure, but this is a technical one that the science of statistics cannot cure unaided. In more complex matters, such as the provision of housing to suit family needs, the matching pattern can again be fully satisfactory without the need to build houses individually for specified families; the problems which arise tend to do so mainly if the data examined omits factors that turn out to be important.

Most statistical work is concerned with samples rather than complete data, mainly because of the cost of collecting facts. Since we are reaching conclusions about individuals who have not been examined because they were not part of the sample, the most important part of the results is not the main conclusions, but the chance of their being wrong. Statistics is an uncomfortable science; as soon as it produces something to grasp in a sea of variability, it seems to snatch it away again. But this is not the fault of the science; the trouble is surely our search for absolute certainty where none can exist. Instead we should become accustomed to the statistical ways of thinking as our best guide to safe conclusions in an uncertain world. A commonly-met instance will illustrate this. Suppose a pre-election opinion poll shows candidate A with 49% support and B with 51%. Who will win the election? Newspapers usually quote these bare figures and opt for B, especially if they agree with his politics. But the percentages are only of the people sampled; the vast majority were not asked their views and will give them only on polling day. In theory it is possible for every one of them to support A, though this is of course an extreme case. However, if we know the sample size we can calculate the probability that the result on election day will or will not bear out the sample poll's apparent conclusions, i.e. the probable margins of error; if any business decisions must be taken ahead of election day that could be affected by the result, the true nature and size of the risk will be known to us.

The science of statistics, then, is about reaching valid conclusions with known margins of error. Commonsense and experience will indicate whether or not it is safe to put the conclusions into practice: for example, how much real money should one wager on B's victory in the above example; should one drop or persevere with a line of merchandise whose sales are fluctuating; should one reset a machine or leave it alone? Statistics is a measuring tool for managers, bringing a measure of certainty into uncertain situations.

VI
DESCRIPTIVE STATISTICS

Few people, if any, can look at a mass of figures and quickly get a clear idea of what they are about. For example, a manager concerned about the effectiveness of his job training scheme for assembly-line workers chose 100 employees and found from the records of the quality control department the number of times that faulty work had been ascribed to them in the previous year. The information is given in Table 6.1. It is highly unlikely that any sensible conclusions could be reached by looking at the data as it stands.

Table 6.1

0	2	6	2	6	5	22	3	1	10
2	5	1	45	4	9	7	25	9	48
10	16	15	5	7	8	3	26	6	18
5	0	6	22	8	11	23	8	5	9
15	0	6	11	13	1	7	32	2	18
9	8	5	9	17	7	29	5	9	12
5	17	13	18	8	37	8	27	7	13
7	20	1	9	4	6	23	9	6	11
7	7	22	71	17	41	11	28	1	44
53	14	55	2	62	6	11	3	34	56

Descriptive statistics comprises ways of reducing such an indigestible mass into forms which can be clearly appreciated: in other words, it makes the figures convey more vividly the information they represent. In one respect the figures have already lost something, the identities of the people to whom they are attached. This is characteristic of statistical methods and it helps us to focus on what is being studied, in this case the overall response of people to the training scheme.

There are two complementary approaches in descriptive statistics:
1. We can represent the data by a picture which brings out any pattern that may be present.
2. We can calculate from the data a single figure which summarizes it all in some way. Since most of the information will be lost in such a drastic condensation, two or three such single figures may be needed, looking at the data from different points of view.

Pictorial methods
No matter which of the many possible pictures is to be used, we must first reduce the data to suitable groups and simply count how many items fall into each group. It is not always easy to decide on the most appropriate groups and

the grouping operation may have to be repeated until a satisfactory, i.e. clear, picture emerges. In the extreme case, each possible result forms a group in itself; with the above data the group table would be as Table 6.2.

Table 6.2

Faults	0	1	2	3	4	5	6	7	8	9	10	11	12	13	14
Employees	3	5	5	3	2	8	8	8	6	8	2	5	1	3	1

Faults	15	16	17	18	20	22	23	25	26	27	28	29
Employees	2	1	3	3	1	3	2	1	1	1	1	1

Faults	32	34	37	41	44	45	48	53	55	56	62	71
Employees	1	1	1	1	1	1	1	1	1	1	1	1

A *frequency table* like this gives us a much better idea of what has happened. Clearly most workers make few faults, but some make a lot. The frequency table can be converted into a picture with bars for the groups of heights proportional to the frequencies concerned; Figure 6.1 is one such *bar chart*.

Figure 6.1   Frequency of faults made by workers in a year (bar chart).

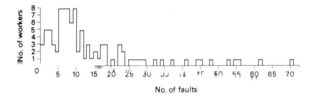

Even in this form there may be too much detail in the information for full clarity. For example, if the manager is interested merely in the number of workers who average more than one error per fortnight, he does not need to know that one individual made 32 faults and another 53. So one guide to the best method of grouping is to ascertain the features of most interest. Table 6.3

Table 6.3

Faults	0–2	3–5	6–8	9–11	12–14	15–17	18–20	21–23	24–26	over 26
Employees	13	13	22	15	5	6	4	5	2	15

shows another grouping from the same data: Figure 6.2 is the corresponding bar chart. The original 72 classifications have been reduced to 10 which makes the information easier to grasp. However, this is counterbalanced by a loss of detail, including one group (over 26) which is open-ended. I have no special justification for closing this group where I did, but if we do not have the

Figure 6.2 Frequency of faults made by workers in a year (bar chart).

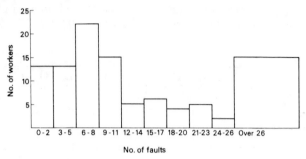

original, raw data there is no special justification for any particular closure. Note the huge apparent size of the 'over 26' group. All the other groups are 3 units wide, but this one is not. Wherever unequal intervals are used, a bar-chart can be quite misleading.

Where the number of groups is small, other kinds of picture may be drawn, such as the *ideograph* of Figure 6.3 or the *pie chart* of Figure 6.4. These types of diagram are popular because they are so easily understood. Any number of groups could be included in them, but for the sake of clarity the fewer groups the better.

When a pictorial presentation is needed, but without too much loss of accuracy, a graph is the best answer. The bar chart is a kind of graph and if

Figure 6.3 How many faults do workers make in a year? (ideograph).

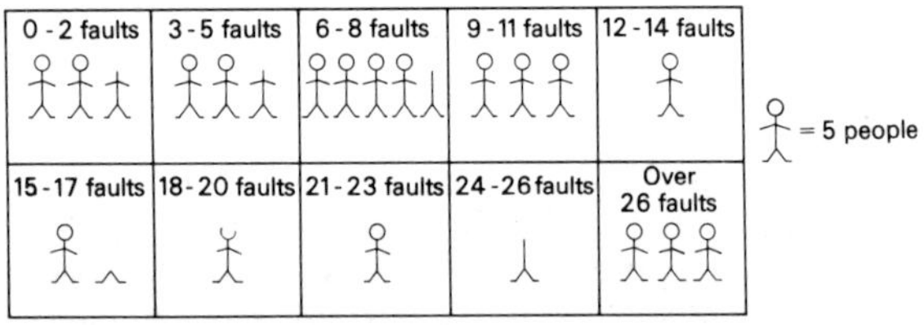

0 - 2 faults	3 - 5 faults	6 - 8 faults	9 - 11 faults	12 - 14 faults
👤👤👤	👤👤👤	👤👤👤👤👤	👤👤👤	👤

👤 = 5 people

15 - 17 faults	18 - 20 faults	21 - 23 faults	24 - 26 faults	Over 26 faults
👤	👤	👤	👤	👤👤👤

Figure 6.4 How many faults do workers make per year? (pie chart).

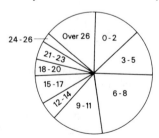

figures are included on both horizontal and vertical scales, quite a lot of accurate information is available from it. Other graphical presentations include the *frequency polygon* such as Figure 6.5 and the *histogram* of Figure 6.6 which is like a bar chart but with the quantities represented by areas and not heights. The histogram will present a truer picture than the bar chart where the group widths are unequal, but there is the problem of how to draw the area of an open-ended group. One possible solution has been used in Figure 6.6.

Other ways of presenting the same data appear in Tables 6.4, 6.5 and 6.6 and in the corresponding Figures 6.7, 6.8 and 6.9. These use cumulative data, i.e. the figures have been added appropriately to show, for example, how many

Figure 6.5   Frequency of fault work produced in a year (frequency polygon).

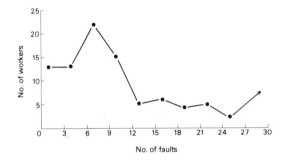

Figure 6.6   Frequency of faults produced by workers in a year (histogram)

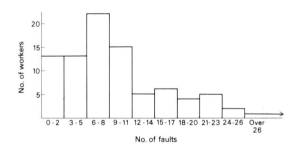

workers make more than 26, not more than 26 or less than 26 faults in a year. Both straight and cumulative data have their uses, depending on what is required.

It is now obvious how to prepare any other tables and graphs required. Having been presenting different aspects of the same story, we realize that while telling the truth it is possible to present a picture giving a slant and creating an untruthful impression. Compare the graphs in Figures 6.10 and 6.11 for instance. Which shows the faster-growing company?

Table 6.4   Number of employees not exceeding the stated number of faults in a year

Faults	2	5	8	11	14	17	20	23	26	29	35	45	55	65	75
Employees	13	26	48	63	68	74	78	83	85	88	90	94	97	99	100

Figure 6.7   Cumulative frequency polygon.

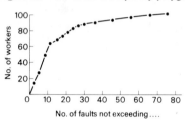

Table 6.5   Number of employees exceeding the stated number of faults in a year

Faults	2	5	8	11	14	17	20	23	26
Employees	87	74	52	37	32	26	22	17	15

Figure 6.8

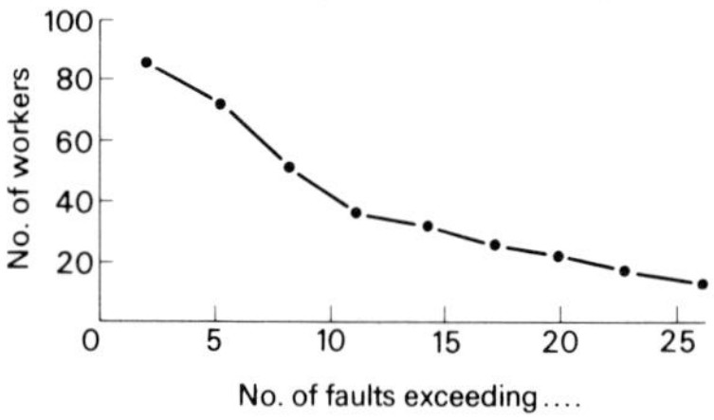

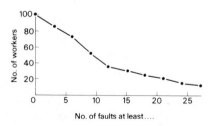

Figure 6.9

Table 6.6 Number of employees making the stated number of faults or more in a year

Faults	0	3	6	9	12	15	18	21	24	27
Employees	100	87	74	52	37	32	26	22	17	15

Figure 6.10 Increase of company A's turnover.

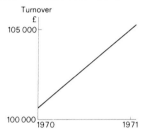

Figure 6.11 Increase of company B's turnover.

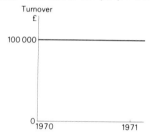

Unfortunately, prejudicial presentation of information is frequently encountered, but two points should always be borne in mind:

1. Any slanted pictures may be redrawn to present a less biased view.
2. In presenting one's own data in a real-life setting, it will pay first to consider the true story which is required and then to choose the picture which tells this story most clearly.

Numerical methods

Looking again at Figure 6.1, we realize the problems in condensing the whole picture into just a single number. However, it is evident that:

1. The picture sits at a definite position on the horizontal scale. If each worker had happened to make just 100 more faults than was the fact, the identical picture would appear just 100 units to the right of its present position. This characteristic (of position on the graph, or of typical size of the data itself) can be summarized by a number which is representative of the data size such as a middle figure, a *measure of central tendency*.
2. The variations in the data are seen as a spread or scatter in the picture. Some *measure of dispersion* could indicate the extent of the spread, irrespective of any of the graphical tricks for creating false impressions.

In some circumstances the fact of symmetry in the data may also be important.

One cannot measure symmetry itself but the extent of departure from it, the *skewness*, can be expressed as a single factor.

Not surprisingly, there are several ways of deriving measures of central tendency and dispersion. Each must be true, since it is derived from established data strictly according to formula. However, since the compression of any information into a single number has to leave out more possibilities than it includes, the various measures will be more true or less true according to the circumstances and it is vital to choose the most appropriate measure in each case. It was probably this plethora of choice that led Disraeli, a man of words but an incompetent with numbers, to cry despairingly that 'there are three kinds of lies: lies, damned lies and statistics.'

Measures of central tendency

(a) The mean
This is the ordinary average found by adding every item of data and dividing the total by the number of items. In mathematical notation, where the symbol $\sum_i$ is shorthand for 'addition over all the *i*s', if there are N items of data that are respectively $X_1, X_2\ X_3 \ldots X_n$, the mean is

$$\bar{X} = \frac{\sum_i X_i}{N}$$

and the bar over a symbol, such as $\bar{X}$ (read 'X bar'), is standard notation for the arithmetic mean of, in this case, the Xs. Another standard name for the mean is μ, the Greek lower-case M, pronounced 'mew' and sometimes anglicized to 'mu'.

So to find the average number of faults per worker from the data in Table 6.1, we add up all the faults and divide by the number of workers:

$$\bar{X} = \frac{0 + 2 + 6 + 2 + \cdots + 56}{100} = \frac{1432}{100} = 14.32$$

This is a very tedious operation with large amounts of data, and is shortened by using grouped data. Table 6.2 gave the frequencies of occurrence of each item and, multiplying each number of faults by its frequency,

$$\bar{X} = \frac{(0 \times 3) + (1 \times 5) + (2 \times 5) + (3 \times 3) + \cdots + (71 \times 1)}{3\ +\ 5\ +\ 5\ +\ 3\ +\ +\ 1} = \frac{1432}{100} = 14.32$$

In symbols, where f_i is the frequency of occurrence of observation X_i, we have

$$\bar{X} = \frac{\sum_i X_i f_i}{\sum_i f_i}$$

This is a much shorter procedure, but can still be tedious. The accuracy and the answer are precisely the same since every item of data has been included at its observed value. More condensed grouped data like that in Table 6.3 is quicker to work with, but at the cost of some accuracy; the techniques of handling it are described later in this chapter.

(b) The median

If all the items of data are arranged in order of size, the median is the middle one. Odd numbers of items have just one middle one; with even numbers there are two middle items and the median is defined as the mean of these two.

Our standard example has 100 items so the median is the mean of the 50th and 51st after they are ranked in order. Table 6.2 is easily modified into Table 6.7 to do this for us:

Table 6.7 Cumulative frequencies of faults per worker

Faults	0	1	2	3	4	5	6	7	8	9
Workers actual	3	5	5	3	2	8	8	8	8	8
Workers cumulative	3	8	13	16	18	26	34	42	48	56

There is no need to go further. Both the middle items are 9 and so, therefore, is the median. It does not matter whether the ranking is in ascending or descending order; the middle items are inevitably the same.

There is no serious calculation in finding the median, and frequently none at all, but the ranking process can take a very long time.

(c) The mode

What is in the mode is fashionable; the most 'fashionable' number in a set of data is the one which occurs most frequently and this is defined as the mode, or the modal value.

In our example (see Table 6.2) 5, 6, 7 and 9 faults all occur most frequently, with 8 appearances each. They are all modal values, therefore. With the grouping in Table 6.3 it is clear that the modal group is 6–8 faults. So there may be several modes or even none at all, as when all items or groups occur with equal frequency and none is most frequent. A pack of cards has no modal value, for instance.

(d) Other measures

Fortunately, the mean, median and mode so predominate that there is no need to consider in depth any of the many other measures of central tendency. It will suffice briefly to mention two more.

The *geometric mean* of N items is the Nth root of the product of all N items

$$\text{geom. mean} = \sqrt[N]{X_1 . X_2 . X_3 \ldots X_N}$$

If any items are zero then this mean must be zero. If an odd number of the items are negative then the product will be negative and there will be no root if N is even. These conditions restrict the use of the geometric mean, but it is found in the *Financial Times* Share Index where share prices are never negative and rarely zero.

In general, the geometric mean is relevant where it is the percentage change in the data that is important. The arithmetic mean is concerned with actual changes, not percentages.

The *harmonic mean* is more complicated still. It is the reciprocal of the arithmetic mean of the reciprocals of all items.

$$\text{harmonic mean} = \frac{N}{\dfrac{1}{X_1} + \dfrac{1}{X_2} + \dfrac{1}{X_3} + \cdots + \dfrac{1}{X_N}}$$

Its use is to find the true mean where the data consists of rates of change, such as velocities. Thus if a journey from A to B is performed at 30 km/hour and the return at 60 km/hour, the average speed is

$$\frac{2}{\dfrac{1}{30} + \dfrac{1}{60}} = 40 \text{ km/hour}, \textit{not } \frac{30 + 60}{2} = 45 \text{ km/hour}$$

To check this, assume that A and B are 30 km apart and work out the total time for the 60 km return trip; then find the overall average speed. (The actual distance does not matter.)

(e) Comparing the mean, median and mode

All are in the same units as the data; in our example the units are faults per year. Thus they are directly comparable with the data itself. The mode requires no calculation, the median little or none though the ranking must be done, and the mean always needs some and possibly heavy calculation.

The mode may not exist or may not be unique, but where it does exist its value or values must be actual pieces of data. The mean and median will always exist and be unique, but may not be actual or even possible data items. Our mean number of faults per worker is 14.32, so the average worker cannot exist. However, we do understand the implications of such a value. Our median number happens to exist but might easily have been, for example, 8.5 faults had the data been slightly different.

The significance of the median is that half the workers made the median number of faults or more, and half made the median or less. We note that the median would not be changed if the greatest number of faults observed had been 171 or even 71 millions instead of 71; the median ignores all the sizes except the middle one(s). The mean, on the other hand, is affected by the sizes, especially if very extreme values are involved. (Try what happens to the mean if the top number of faults is 71 million.) So we can judge how typical a worker is by comparing his performance with the median, but we have no idea from the median of the repair load that management must plan for; it has focused on the people, not the work. The mean concentrates on the work and not the people. The repair workload is easily found by imagining that every worker produces the average number of faults.

The choice between mean and median will depend on the aspect of most interest and it may be necessary to specify both. The clash of viewpoint becomes prominent whenever there is a well-publicized strike over pay. Management's figures for average pay are always higher than those of the unions. Leaving aside questions about before or after tax, which each side will take care not to specify before being challenged to do so, both parties are telling the truth. The unions are concerned with the typical worker and quote the median, management with the size of the payroll and quote the mean, which may be inflated by a few individuals with high earnings.

Where the pattern of the data is symmetrical, as happens with many human characteristics such as height or intelligence, the mean, median and mode are all identical and in the middle (Figure 6.12). However, where the data is not symmetrical but skewed, and with only a single mode (incomes, for example) as in Figure 6.13, the median will always lie between the mode (the summit value) and the mean, which in this example is dragged towards the long tail by the high values in it. While this is not a law of nature, it happens surprisingly often that the median is about a third of the way between the mean and the mode, being nearer the mean.

Figure 6.12

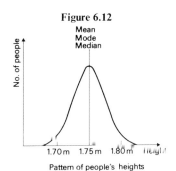

Pattern of people's heights

Figure 6.13

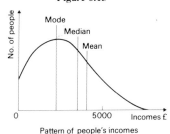

Pattern of people's incomes

From this point as we develop statistical theory we shall almost exclusively use the mean as the preferred measure of central tendency. The reason has nothing to do with the merits of mean, median and mode already discussed; it is because the mean is the easiest with which to perform further calculations. For instance, if our manager takes a further sample of workers' records, the mode or median of the new sample will not mix with the already established mode or median. The frequency table or the ranking must be prepared afresh from the combined samples before the most frequent one(s) or the middle one(s) can be found. The overall mean, on the other hand, is easily calculated without merging the data:

$$\bar{X} = \frac{N_1 \, \bar{X}_1 + N_2 \, \bar{X}_2}{N_1 + N_2}$$

where the 1s and 2s refer to the first and second samples respectively. The formula is instantly extended to cope with any number of samples. This is the true reason for the predominance of the mean in statistical work.

(f) Off-centre measures of position

The median divides the data equally into two parts and the question of finer subdivisions arises. These are used particularly in economics.

1. The *quartiles* divide the data into quarters, as the name implies. The lower quartile has 25% of the observations at or below it and 75% at or above it; the upper quartile reverses these percentages. The median is, of course, an intermediate quartile.
2. The *deciles*, with corresponding definitions, divide the data into 10% groups. Thus the 4th decile splits the data 40/60 and the median is the 5th decile.
3. Where still finer graduations are needed the *percentiles* are spread 1% apart. The quartiles are the 25th, 50th (median) and 75th percentiles.

Figure 6.14 shows the deciles and quartiles for our hundred workers. We can hardly include percentiles as there are only 100 observations.

Figure 6.14   Deciles (numbered) and quartiles.

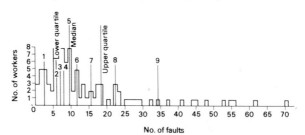

Measures of dispersion

(a) The range

This simplest measure of spread is the difference between the smallest and the largest items in the data. In our example the minimum is 0 and the maximum 71, so the range is 71. Calculations are trivial and this overall spread does give a slight picture of the variability, but the range ignores all but the extremities. For this reason it is sometimes quoted together with the median, which ignores all but the middle, to give a succinct description of a set of data.

(b) The mean deviation

It would clearly be advantageous to measure the spread in ways that involve every item of data, just as the mean measures the middle. A simple method is to consider how far each observation lies from the overall mean. In our example with mean 14.32, each 7 lies 7.32 below the mean and each 20 is 6.68 above it. The deviations are thus −7.32 and 6.68 respectively. Totalling all such deviations and dividing by their number gives their average. However, the positive and negative quantities will cancel each other out, for this is what places the mean where it is, and the total of these deviations will always be zero. The average deviation is therefore not a measure of spread alone. To isolate the spread we could ignore the negative signs, averaging the deviations regardless of direction away from the mean. Doing so gives us the *mean deviation*.

With 100 deviations to calculate and average, the work is tedious by hand, but the computer quickly shows that it is 10.7552 in our example. By itself this tells us very little. We cannot visualize the faulty work spread out to the extent of 10.75 in the same way that we could see the average of 14.3 faults per worker. The value of the mean deviation lies in comparisons. If another group had a mean deviation of 16.8, we would recognize that it contained a more variable set of workers than our sample. Economists, continually comparing data, use this measure of spread freely because it is easy to calculate and does become meaningful in their work.

A formula for the mean deviation must indicate that the value of each deviation $(X - \bar{X})$ is to be taken as positive. Putting vertical bars on either side of the quantity concerned is the symbolic way of expressing this absolute value thus:

$$\text{mean deviation} = \frac{\sum |(X - \bar{X})|}{N}$$

(c) The variance

Economists may be quite happy with the mean deviation, but mathematicians point out that it is illegal to ignore minus signs just because they are inconvenient (a bank balance of −£150 may not be treated as equivalent to one of £150, may it?) and doing so makes it impossible to pool the mean deviations of two samples without pooling all the data and re-calculating from the start. Since it is important to be able to mix samples, we need a measure that keeps its negative signs or at any rate gets rid of them in a mathematically legal way.

The simplest such way is to square each deviation, since $(-2)^2$, like $(+2)^2$, is 4. Totalling and averaging the squared deviations then gives us a legal measure of spread, the *variance*.

$$\text{variance} = \frac{\sum (X - \bar{X})^2}{N}$$

The calculations are still more tedious, but the computer immediately gives us 216.018 as the variance of our 100 workers' faulty performances. As is the case with the mean deviation, this value is not self-explanatory.

It is in fact even more remote from reality. While the measures of central tendency, the range and the mean deviation are expressed in the same units as the observations (in this case in faults-per-worker) the variance is in the square of the units. We understand, for example, square centimetres as an area, but what is the meaning of squared grams or squared £ or squared faults-per-worker?

(d) The standard deviation
For those unhappy with the idea of working in nonsense units, the alternative is to take the square root of the variance. There are of course two square roots, of equal magnitude but respectively positive and negative. The positive one is defined as the *standard deviation*, usually given the Greek symbol σ (sigma, the small letter)

$$\text{standard deviation} = \sigma = \sqrt{\frac{\sum(X - \bar{X})^2}{N}}$$

Engineers will recognize this as an exact analogue of the RMS voltage or current. Thus even in symmetrical frequency patterns (like symmetrical alternating currents) the spread has a defined value which is not zero.

As with other measures of spread, the meaning of the standard deviation's value (14.6975 faults-per-worker in our example) emerges from comparisons.

(e) The inter-quartile deviation
Economists already using quartiles have found that the distance between the lower and upper quartiles is a measure of spread both easy to find (by mere subtraction) and useful to them. As seen from Figure 6.14, the inter-quartile deviation of our sample is 13.

(f) Using the measures of dispersion
For reasons that we have seen, the range's very simplicity limits its usefulness for serious statistical analysis of data, though it is widely used in statistical quality control. The economist's various measures are straightforward and usable in their circumstances, but are of doubtful mathematical validity and do not allow several samples to be pooled easily for greater accuracy.

With the mean, the variance and the standard deviation are the manager's main weapons in the use of statistics, and it must be admitted at once that the awkwardness of calculating them, combined with their lack of instant meaning, make them rather inaccessible at first. However, familiarity cures the latter problem and the former can be eased.

I feel sure that the multi-access computer will shortly do away with all need for serious statistical calculation by the manager. As in Figure 6.15, he will call up the package program, type in the data and out will come the answers. He can then devote himself to his real task, using the results to interpret his managerial situation and to guide him in formulating his decisions. At the moment, where there is not yet a computer at hand, the small electronic calculators now available take the sting out of the necessary but tedious calculation.

Figure 6.15

```
GET-CONSTA
RUN
CONSTA  1356

NUMBER OF ENTRIES ?100
?0,2,6,2,6,5,22,3,1,10
??2,5,1,45,4,9,7,25,9,48
??10,16,15,5,7,8,3,26,6,18
??5,0,6,22,8,11,23,3,5,9
??15,0,6,11,13,1,7,32,2,18
??9,8,5,9,17,7,29,5,9,12
??5,17,13,18,8,37,8,27,7,13
??7,28,1,9,4,6,23,9,6,11
??7,7,22,71,17,41,11,28,1,44
??53,14,55,2,62,6,11,3,34,56


    FREQUENCY TABLE

        0           3
        1           5
        2           5
        3           3
        4           2
        5           8
        6           8
        7           8
        8           6
        9           8
       10           2
       11           5
       12           1
       13           3
       14           1
       15           2
       16           1
       17           3
       18           3
       20           1
       22           3
       23           2
       25           1
       26           1
       27           1
       28           1
       29           1
       32           1
       34           1
       37           1
       41           1
       44           1
       45           1
       48           1
       53           1
       55           1
       56           1
       62           1
       71           1


    NUMBER OF VALUES IS       100
    SUM IS                    1432
    MEAN IS                   14.32
    MEDIAN IS                 9
    MODE HAS FREQUENCY        8     AND IS  5     6     7     9

    RANGE IS                  0    TO 71   I.E. 71
    MEAN DEVIATION IS         10.7552
    VARIANCE IS               216.018
    STANDARD DEVIATION IS     14.6975
    STD. ERROR OF MEAN IS     1.46975

    DONE AT 1401
```

By expansion of $(X - \bar{X})^2$ the standard deviation formula may be rewritten as

$$S = \sqrt{\frac{\Sigma(X^2)}{N} - \left(\frac{\Sigma X}{N}\right)^2}$$

(i.e. the mean of the squares minus the square of the mean is under the root sign), which is much easier to calculate as long as the machine accumulates both the sums and the sums-of-squares of data items entered on its keyboard. Once both totals are divided by N on the machine, the rest is just squaring, subtraction and square rooting. Most instruction booklets show how to use the machines for standard deviations.

Where even this fails and we are reduced to pencil and paper, the formula itself shows what should be written down, the data items and their squares, in columns for adding up. For the first 10 items of our data, for instance (to do all 100 is tedious and liable to cause error without a machine) we have

X	X^2
0	0
2	4
6	36
2	4
6	36
5	25
22	484
3	9
1	1
10	100
57	699

Hence the mean $\dfrac{\Sigma X}{N} = 5.7$

and the variance is $\dfrac{699}{10} - (5.7)^2$

or $69.9 - 32.49$

or 37.41

and the standard deviation is $\sqrt{37.41}$ which, from tables, is 6.12.

The question remains, why bother with these calculations? What are the results, the numerical descriptive statistics, for? The answer lies in the fact that we have taken a sample for the purpose of predicting into the *population* from which it was drawn. As we shall see, the mean and standard deviation are the keys to working out both the predictions and their accuracy or inaccuracy. This subject is discussed further in Chapter 9.

(g) Calculating with grouped data

If we were given the data in Table 6.3 without the underlying individual scores, we would not know whether each observation lay high, low or central within its group. To calculate we must therefore make an assumption, usually that all data lies in the centre of its group, at the *class mark*. For this reason, grouped data is likely to be less accurate but it has the advantage of requiring a small amount of arithmetic. Another problem is that one class, over 26, is open-ended, so we cannot fix its class mark without a further assumption to close it, which involves a further possibility of error. Realism shows that 50 or 70 would be quite feasible upper *class boundaries*, but the ability to calculate easily depends on all classes being of equal width, the *class interval*. This stringent requirement makes us close the class at 29, which we know to be hopelessly short of the truth; this demonstrates clearly the disadvantage of grouped data, especially if open-ended.

The formulae to use become, with C as the class interval, D as the class mark and F as the observed *frequencies of occurrence* in each class:

$$\text{mean} = \bar{X} = \frac{\sum(F \times D)}{\sum F}$$

$$\text{and standard deviation} = S = C \times \sqrt{\frac{\sum(F \times D^2)}{\sum F} - \left(\frac{\sum(F \times D)}{\sum F}\right)^2}$$

and the calculation proceeds as follows:

Observations X	Employees F	Class mark D	$F \times D$	D^2	$F \times D^2$
0– 2	13	1	13	1	13
3– 5	13	4	52	16	208
6– 8	22	7	154	49	1078
9–11	15	10	150	100	1500
12–14	5	13	65	169	845
15–17	6	16	96	256	1536
18–20	4	19	76	361	1444
21–23	5	22	110	484	2420
24–26	2	25	50	625	1250
27–29	15	28	420	784	11760
$\sum F = 100$			$\sum(F \times D) = 1186$		$\sum(F \times D^2) = 22054$

So the mean is 11.86 and the standard deviation is $\sqrt{3 \times (220.54 - 11.86^2)}$, or $\sqrt{3 \times (220.54 - 140.69)}$, or $\sqrt{3 \times 79.85}$, or 17.31. These compare with 14.32 and 14.69 for the original data, demonstrating the higher speed and lower accuracy of grouping the data, with enforced equal class intervals.

(h) A definition

The term *statistic*, in the singular, is used to refer to any single number which has been condensed out of a set of data items by arithmetic. Thus a mean is a statistic, as is a range or indeed any of the measures we have discussed.

VII
SAMPLING, PROBABILITY AND THE LAWS OF CHANCE

A coin is tossed and it comes down heads on 7 occasions and tails on 3. Is it biased?

If my wife and I have 4 children, all girls, is this evidence that we are unlikely to produce a boy if we try again?

All applicants for management positions in a certain firm are given psychological tests. The last 6 successful candidates with IQs below 130 have stayed at least 2 years; the last 6 with IQs of 130 or more have left in less than 2 years. Does this give the personnel department any clues to future selection procedures?

In statistics the word *population* is used to represent the whole of the data in any given situation, whether or not it refers to people. Most populations involving management data contain plenty of variability, and we almost always try to judge the population that interests us by looking at a *sample* drawn from it. Sometimes this is obviously so, sometimes not. Here are two examples:

1. We may check the quality of output of a machine by looking at a handful of its product. Theoretically the machine could go on for ever, so this sample could conceptually come from an infinite population.
2. A balance sheet is a view of a firm's financial situation frozen at a single moment. Since the life of a firm is an infinite sequence of moments, each balance sheet represents only a sample of the continuous picture. Moreover, the data included is only a sample of the many aspects that could be examined.

These are perhaps two extreme instances. In the first case it is obvious that a fair picture of the current product demands a random sample, which is defined as one in which every available member of the population has an equal chance of being selected. In the accounting situation the sampling is definitely not random; the data is always taken as at December 31st (or whenever) and the aspects examined are always the same, for very good reasons based on accounting experience. The luck of the draw may have a profound effect on the contents of the samples, either through the number of defects in the machined product, or in the cash positions on the balance sheet: 1 day later and £51 764 of debtors may have settled up, the exact moment of receipt being outside our control because of postal vagaries.

So we are subject to two levels of variability, one inherent in the population we are examining, the other introduced through sampling. Since the first is trouble enough, why do we have to make things worse by taking samples? The answer is that looking at the whole population is either too expensive or totally impossible. It is simply not worth checking every screw that a machine produces, or preparing a balance sheet five times a day. There are also products such as flashbulbs, seeds and gelignite which cannot be tested without making them unusable afterwards. Sampling is unavoidable. We therefore have to study the variable effects of sampling if we wish, as we must, to reach justified conclusions about a population. We are in the area of the chance of this or that turning up in the sample, and we shall use words like chance, likelihood and probability as all having essentially the same meaning.

Members of a population may have many characteristics, some of which are measurable (height; diameter; shelf life), which are called *variables*, and others which are merely classifiable (male or female; acceptable, re-workable or scrap quality; Conservative, Labour, Liberal or Don't Know), called *attributes*. Variables may be reduced to attributes, for example, by splitting actual incomes into round groups like wealthy, medium and poor. The obvious loss of detail here shows that measurements, where they can be found, provide more accuracy than classifications; in other words, for a given level of reliability we shall need larger samples for attributes than for variables. On the other hand, it is usually much cheaper and easier (where there is a choice) to classify than to measure.

The probability that the next member of our sample will (according to circumstances)

> be heads or tails
> be male or female
> have a sensitivity of better than 10 microvolts

must depend respectively on the ratio of heads to tails that can be obtained in tossing a coin, on the sex proportions of the group concerned, and on the pattern of sensitivities in the batch of equipment. Note that we have a theory about the coins; the chances of a head or a tail should be equal at 50/50 or 50%. We have no such prior ideas in the other cases, though if we know from experience that 20% of all the instruments we make have a sensitivity better than 10 microvolts, we can see that the chance of a random choice having this measurement is 20%, or 1 in 5, or 4-to-1-against. Our concepts therefore work by associating probability with proportion or *relative frequency* where we have no prior knowledge, and by assuming that our past experience will continue until we have evidence to the contrary. If, then, we know the chance of something occurring at the next trial, whether from laws of nature or from experience, we can go on to develop the chances of whole sequences of occurrences. This is of course a theoretical exercise; unless one is gambling and concerned with something like the chance of drawing 3 hearts, the problems do not present themselves like this. As in the examples at the beginning of this chapter, we usually start with a sequence of events that has actually occurred, and somehow we have to draw conclusions from it.

This is not an easy task. The method is to study sequences in general as if they are agglomerations of single events and, so to speak, file away the many conclusions for reference. Then when an actual situation arises we compare it with our files and find the (possibly several) conditions which could have led to our situation. These give the probability picture underlying it and enable us to reach our conclusions. This subject is discussed further in Chapter 9.

So we must begin with the theoretical exercise after all, and ask ourselves how to define probability. From considerations above we realize that it could be something measured on a scale from 0 to 100%, or alternatively from 0 to 1 as a decimal or fraction, as in Figure 7.1. Thus 1 or 100% represents certainty, e.g. the probability that I will die one day, and 0 represents impossibility, e.g. the chance that I will live forever. Between these extremes, 0.5 or 50% applies to the situation where the event could equally well occur or not, e.g. a head or a tail in tossing a coin. If 9 out of 10 film stars truly do use Brand Z toilet soap, the probability that a star chosen at random will use Brand Z is 0.9 or 90% while the chance that he/she will not is 0.1 or 10%. If 13% of 100-watt lamp bulbs last at least 1500 hours and 5% over 2000 hours, the probability that my next lamp will exceed 1500 hours is 0.13 or 13%, with 0.87 or 87% that it will die sooner, and 0.05 or 5% that it will be very long-lived (over 2000 hours).

Figure 7.1 Probability.

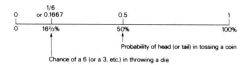

We are dealing with attributes in the above examples. Either the lamp will burn out before 1500 hours, or it will last 1500 to 2000 hours, or it will exceed 2000 hours. The film star will either use Brand Z or will not. The coin will give either head or tail. In each case there is bound to be a result, i.e. the probability of a result is 1. Thus, using the probability symbols,

$$\text{Pr (head \textit{or} tail)} = 1$$
$$\text{Pr (Brand-Z-user \textit{or} not-Brand-Z-user)} = 1$$
$$\text{Pr (short life \textit{or} medium life \textit{or} long life)} = 1$$

But since Pr (head) = 0.5 and also Pr (tail) = 0.5, we see that

$$\text{Pr (head \textit{or} tail)} = \text{Pr (head)} + \text{Pr (tail)}$$
$$= 0.5 + 0.5 = 1$$

In general we notice that we have the probability of one of the alternatives by adding the separate probabilities. Thus we have the *addition law of probabilities*

$$\boxed{\text{Pr (A \textit{or} B)} = \text{Pr (A)} + \text{Pr (B)}}$$

which can also be extended to

$$\text{Pr (A } or \text{ B } or \text{ C } or \ldots) = \text{Pr (A)} + \text{Pr (B)} + \text{Pr (C)} \ldots$$

This law is generally true provided that A, B, C . . . are mutually exclusive, i.e. that if any one of them occurs it prevents the occurrence of all the others. If we get a head from a coin, we could not possibly have a tail at the same time. A counter-example, for which the addition law would not be true, might occur if we chose one person from a group and spoke of the chance of that individual being *either* female *or* under 40. One characteristic does not exclude the other in this case.

Note that, as a consequence of the addition law, with the probability of something either occurring or not making a total of 1,

$$\text{Pr (not-A)} = 1 - \text{Pr (A)}$$

For instance, Pr (not-user-of-Brand-Z) = 1 — Pr (user-of-Brand-Z)

If we go on to look at more than one event at a time, for example, toss 2 coins or test 3 lamp bulbs, then 2 or more results must occur together and we shall have to speak of the chance of A *and* B *and* C, etc. The simplest case, that of tossing 2 coins, will illustrate what happens. There are four possible results:

Coin 1	Coin 2
Head	Head
Head	Tail
Tail	Head
Tail	Tail

Since one of them must occur, the combined chance of all four must be 1, i.e. Pr(HH *or* HT *or* TH *or* TT) = 1. But for reasons of symmetry, the 4 results are all equally likely, so the probability of each is $\frac{1}{4}$ or 0.25. Of course the chance of each head or tail separately is 0.5, so we realize that the probability of two of them together is found by multiplying the separate chances. In other words, for our coins

Pr (head *and* head) = Pr (head) × Pr (head), since 0.25 = 0.5 × 0.5

In general,

$$\text{Pr (A } and \text{ B)} = \text{Pr (A)} \times \text{Pr (B)}$$

and by extension

$$\text{Pr (A } and \text{ B } and \text{ C } and \ldots) = \text{Pr (A)} \times \text{Pr (B)} \times \text{Pr (C)} \times \ldots$$

This is the *multiplication law of probabilities* and is valid so long as A, B, C . . . are independent of each other. There can be no question of mutual exclusivity, for all of these events do occur together. An example of non-independence might be in the chance of picking at random an individual who is both female and over 6 feet, or 1.83 metres, tall. Since height and sex are by no means independent the law will not apply.

The addition and multiplication laws of probability are often spoken of as the laws of chance. With them one can calculate probabilities in many complicated situations. However, they also demand great clarity of thinking. The theory of probability was developed, primarily to meet the demands of eighteenth century gambling aristocrats, by some of the best mathematicians ever, such as de Moivre, Laplace and Gauss. Even men of this eminence had to correct one another's errors of thinking, and their correspondence on elementary probability problems is amusing and instructive even today.

At the heart of the calculations lies the premise we met earlier, that the probability of an event is effectively the same thing as its proportion of all events. Thus, if in the UK 106 boy babies are born for every 100 girls,

$$\text{Pr (boy)} = \frac{106}{206} \quad \text{and} \quad \text{Pr (girl)} = \frac{100}{206}$$

The denominators refer to all births; out of every 206, 106 are boys and 100 are girls. By the multiplication law, the chance of two girls in succession should be $\frac{100}{206} \times \frac{100}{206}$, or 0.236, just under 1 in 4. The chance of 4 girls in a row, if each baby has its sex determined just by chance, should be $\frac{100}{206} \times \frac{100}{206} \times \frac{100}{206} \times \frac{100}{206}$, or $\left(\frac{100}{206}\right)^4$, about 0.0555 or 1/18.

However, the law is valid only if the sexes of successive births are independent of one another; in simpler terms, it is only valid if the parents do not have a bias in favour of one or other sex, and the sex of one birth does not influence in any way the sex of the next. Does the fact of a 4-girl family provide any evidence of lack of independence? Since there are hundreds or thousands of 4-child families in the country, at the rate of 1 in 18 quite a lot of them will consist of 4 girls. The parents of such a family may or may not find it delightful, but something as common as 1 in 18 is not especially surprising, nor can it prove anything one way or the other about independence. To test for independence we should have to see whether, over the whole country, the proportion of all-girl 4-child families is 1 in 18 or not. We shall return to this topic in Chapter 10 and meanwhile note that, if there really is independence, the chance of a boy next time is still $\frac{106}{206}$, regardless of the past. It is open to question, though, whether the parents would believe it.

What about the chances of 3 girls out of 4, or 2 of each kind, or 3 boys and a girl, or 4 boys? It is easy to show that they cannot be merely the separate probabilities multiplied together (i.e. respectively $\left(\frac{100}{206}\right)^3 \times \left(\frac{106}{206}\right)$, $\left(\frac{100}{206}\right)^2 \times \left(\frac{106}{206}\right)^2$, $\left(\frac{100}{206}\right) \times \left(\frac{106}{206}\right)^3$ and $\left(\frac{106}{206}\right)^4$), for the total of these and the 4-girl case comes to far less than 1. Yet it must in truth be 1 since these 5 possibilities are the only ones. Where is the discrepancy?

It is in the fact that there are several ways of building mixed families. For instance, the birth orders BGGG, GBGG, GGBG and GGGB all give 3 girls and one boy. Thus the probability element for the 3 girls/1 boy situation must be multiplied by 4, which is the number of different ways of arranging 3 of one kind and 1 of another among 4 things. Similarly, the other mixtures of boys and girls will have their probabilities multiplied by the number of orders in which they can occur. How many will this be in each case? This can be found easily from the general case, the number of ways in which N things may be arranged if r are of one kind, the remainder are of another and the order does not matter. This is the combinations situation discussed in Chapter 1; the answer is $^{N}C_r$ or $\dfrac{N!}{r!(N-r)!}$. Thus for 2 children of each sex in a family of 4, $r = 2$ and $N = 4$, and the number of arrangements is

$$^{4}C_2 = \frac{4!}{2!\,2!} = \frac{4 \times 3 \times 2 \times 1}{2 \times 1 \times 2 \times 1} = 6$$

and for 1 girl and 3 boys, $^{4}C_1 = \dfrac{4!}{1!\,3!} = 4$, the same as for 3 girls and 1 boy.

Of course, there is only 1 way for no girls, namely BBBB, and $^{4}C_0$ is indeed 1.

So we have the following results:

Number of girls	Number of arrangements	Probability of any one arrangement	Probability of all arrangements
4	1	$\left(\dfrac{100}{206}\right)^4 = 0.0555$	0.0555
3	4	$\left(\dfrac{100}{206}\right)^3 \times \left(\dfrac{106}{206}\right) = 0.05885$	0.2354
2	6	$\left(\dfrac{100}{206}\right)^2 \times \left(\dfrac{106}{206}\right)^2 = 0.0624$	0.3744
1	4	$\left(\dfrac{100}{206}\right) \times \left(\dfrac{106}{206}\right)^3 = 0.06615$	0.2646
0	1	$\left(\dfrac{106}{206}\right)^4 = 0.0701$	0.0701
			1.0000

and the total probability is 1, as it must be where we have included all possible alternatives. Thus if the sexes at birth are truly independent, we would expect about $5\frac{1}{2}\%$ of all 4-child families to have all girls, $23\frac{1}{2}\%$ to have just one boy, $37\frac{1}{2}\%$ to have two of each, $26\frac{1}{2}\%$ to have just one girl and 7% to have all boys. These percentages, too, should be checked in real life to verify or disprove independence.

Our calculations have taken it for granted that all arrangements of the same mixture (e.g. 2 of each) are equally likely. Assuming independence at each birth, this is something to be accepted as obvious. However, the independence is easier to assume where we are less emotionally involved, as when tossing coins. At the start of this chapter I asked whether a coin was biased if it gave 7 heads and 3 tails in 10 tosses. The answer will lie, of course, in the likelihood of such a sequence occurring on a 50/50 basis at each toss; if the probability is reasonably high, we cannot conclude that there is bias. Using the laws of chance with $^{10}C_7$ different (but equally likely) arrangements to take into account, the probability is

$$^{10}C_7 \times [Pr(head)]^7 \times [Pr(tail)]^3$$
$$= {}^{10}C_7 \times 0.5^7 \times 0.5^3 \text{ or } {}^{10}C_7 \times (\tfrac{1}{2})^{10} = 0.1172$$

So, in nearly $11\tfrac{3}{4}\%$ of trials where a coin is tossed 10 times, we may expect 7 heads. A result which can occur as frequently as this cannot be considered at all surprising, hence it is in no way proof of bias.

If we look at any sequence of heads and tails we see that the chance of each result in turn is 0.5, whether head or tail. Thus the probability of H T H T H T H H H H, for example, is $(0.5)^{10}$ or $\dfrac{1}{1024}$, about 0.001. So also is the chance of 10 heads, or 10 tails, or any specified sequence. All possible results are equally likely or unlikely, and the reason for 7 heads being quite common is simply that there are 120 specific ways of them resulting, out of a total of 1024 arrangements.

In these analyses we have begun to see the emergence of patterns of frequencies. The consequences of these are studied in the next chapter. Meanwhile, it is impossible to have too much practice at working with the laws of chance, for they underlie a surprisingly large number of management situations.

VIII
PATTERNS OF VARIATION

As we saw in Chapter VII, the laws of chance allow us to find the probability of a given set of results if we know the separate chances for the separate members of the set. This is all very well, but statisticians, like managers, prefer if possible to have rules that apply to many situations rather than have to calculate from first principles every time. Thus we must look for overall, general behaviour.

If we were somehow able to find a generalized probability formula to cover all possible cases of a situation, we would have a *probability distribution function*. But since probability is associated with proportion or relative frequency we may (and usually do) speak instead of the *frequency distribution*, of which we have the formula. Strictly speaking the frequency distribution will be the pattern of observed data expressed as the numbers of items in each class or each measurement. Any set of data will thus have its own frequency distribution that may be seen, for example, in the bar chart of the data. Many such frequency distribution patterns, like that in Figure 8.1, are special, occurring only in a particular situation and therefore not worth general study: each case is dealt with on its merits. However, three distribution patterns are found so widely and are so relevant for managers that they must be looked at in some detail. These are the Binomial, Poisson and Normal (or Gaussian) distributions. Since they are concerned with proportions of a population, they are probability distributions and our statistical work with them will be mainly concerned with fitting the theoretical patterns to frequency patterns observed in real life, so that predictions can be made on theoretical grounds.

Figure 8.1 Age distribution of a DMS class.

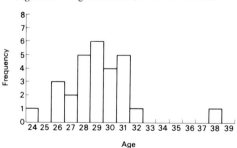

The Binomial distribution

In Chapter VII we distinguished attributes from variables by terming them classifications and measurements. Very often we are faced with just two attributes or classes, either because only two exist (for instance, male or female employees; good or reject product quality), or because we are interested in only one of several possible classes and may lump all the rest into a single other class (for example, green or other colours). We looked in Chapter VII at specific numbers of each class in a definite sample size (3 girls and 1 boy in a family of 4), but what about any number of a kind in any size of sample? In a more mathematical statement of this problem:

If there are 2 kinds of item in a population, in the proportions p and $(1 - p)$, what is the probability that a sample of N items will contain r of the first kind and hence $(N - r)$ of the other?

As a specific illustration of this general statement, if a batch of invoices includes 5% with errors and 95% correct ones (i.e. the proportion of wrong invoices is 0.05), what is the chance that a dozen invoices picked at random from this batch will include 2 (or 1, or any other number) containing errors? The answer is easy to establish, employing the arguments used in Chapter VII.

1. The total number of ways of getting r of one kind and $(N - r)$ of the other is $^N C_r$.
2. The probability of any one arrangement of the r and $(N - r)$ things is $p^r \times (1 - p)^{N-r}$.*
3. We multiply the probability of one desired arrangement by the total number of such arrangements. (This follows from the addition law; the $^N C_r$ arrangements are mutually exclusive alternatives so their $^N C_r$ equal probabilities must all be added together.)

Hence

$$\Pr (r \text{ items out of } N) = {}^N C_r\, p^r\, (1 - p)^{N-r}$$

and it remains to make a small conventional abbreviation by putting q for $(1 - p)$, afterwards remembering that $q = 1 - p$.

Thus

$$\boxed{\Pr (r \text{ out of } N) = {}^N C_r\, p^r\, q^{N-r}}$$

Because N, p and r can be any appropriate numbers (N and r being whole numbers and p being between 0 and 1), this formula really does apply in all 2-class cases and is a probability distribution function, the Binomial distribution.

For just 3 girls in 4 children, N is 4, r is 3, p is $\dfrac{100}{206}$ and

---

* This is not strictly true, for if the batch size is 100 and only 5 invoices have errors, picking 1 of the 5 significantly reduces the chance of later choices containing errors. In this and in all other such examples we assume that the sample size is small compared with the batch, so that drawing an item for the sample does not significantly affect the subsequent chances.

$$\text{Pr (3 girls)} = {}^4C_3 \left(\frac{100}{206}\right)^3 \left(\frac{106}{206}\right)^1$$

$$= 4 \times \frac{100^3 \times 106}{206^4} = 0.3744$$

We make direct use of the formula, without needing to go back to first principles. For 2 wrong invoices and 10 good invoices in a dozen,

$$\text{Pr (2 wrong)} = {}^{12}C_2 (0.05)^2 (0.95)^{10} = 66 \times 0.0025 \times 0.5987 = 0.0988$$

The calculations, at least of $(0.95)^{10}$, become tedious but we arrived at once at the theoretical answer. With very large sample sizes, e.g. $N = 100$, calculations like $(0.75)^{99}$ have to be evaluated. The labour becomes excessive without a computer, but fortunately we can usually escape from the Binomial into approximations of the Poisson and Normal distributions, as shown later. There are some important points to note:

1. Of the infinite number of possible Binomial distributions, the two *parameters* N and p identify the particular distribution in a given instance.
2. The formula contains $(N + 1)$ possible answers, for r can be any integer from 0 up to N.
3. p and q are fixed in any Binomial situation and this distribution cannot apply in cases where the probabilities vary. An example is the chance of dealing 4 aces in a row from a shuffled pack of cards, for once an ace had been dealt (its probability is $\frac{4}{52}$ or $\frac{1}{13}$) the chance of an ace next time is only $\frac{3}{51}$ or $\frac{1}{17}$, as both an ace and a card have gone. The argument continues over the next two cards. The fixed chances in the Binomial imply sampling from a population of infinite size or, approximately, from a population so large compared with the sample that the small changes of probability can be ignored. This latter is true in many production situations and the Binomial finds wide application in quality control. Incidentally if each card is replaced and the pack shuffled before the next one is dealt, the chance of an ace is always $\frac{1}{13}$: *sampling with replacement* generates a theoretically infinite population.
4. Formula 11 on page 19 of Chapter I is known as the Binomial Expansion, being the Nth power of the sum of two quantities (hence the binomial part). If the two items added are respectively q and p we have

$$(q + p)^N = q^N + {}^N C_1 q^{N-1} + {}^N C_2 q^{N-2} p^2 \ldots$$
$$\ldots + {}^N C_r q^{N-r} p^r + \ldots + p^N$$

Now $q = (1 - p)$, so $q + p = 1$. Hence this is an expansion of 1^N which must always total to 1. Then, looking at the terms of the expansion, including the general (i.e. rth) term, we identify them respectively as the probabilities of finding in a sample of N items, zero, one, two . . . of the kind whose probability is p. Altogether there are $(N + 1)$ such terms and the total probability, for such it is, must be 1, since there must be *some* result. This is why the distribution is called the Binomial. Moreover, to avoid calculating ^NC_r in every case, we may get the value from Pascal's Pyramid in Formula 12 (page 19) and, more extensively, in Appendix A (page 250).

5. One can find tables of Binomial probabilities, but as these have first to be classified according to both N and p, and then all values of r from 0 to N listed, they get very bulky. Also, if (in the long run) 2.2% of our products have been faulty so that we need to enter the tables with $p = 0.022$, there is only a remote chance that our tables will contain our requirements. The preferred method is to calculate the probabilities each time from the formula and, if desired, with the help of Pascal's Pyramid.

6. The Binomial formula gives the chance of getting exactly 0 or 1 or 2, etc. of a kind in a sample of size N. If, as often happens, we are really after the chance of 'at least 3' or 'not more than 5' we add the individual probabilities. To save us this further work, some Binomial tables are already set out in *cumulative* form. However they still suffer from bulk and from the restricted range of p already discussed, and they add work if an individual chance is needed. For example

$$\text{Pr} (4) = \text{Pr} (4 \text{ or more}) - \text{Pr} (5 \text{ or more})$$

so subtraction is called for. Confusion is possible because cumulative tables are constructed either for 'r or more' or for 'r or less'; in the latter case

$$\text{Pr} (4) = \text{Pr} (4 \text{ or less}) - \text{Pr} (3 \text{ or less})$$

and we must check which way our tables work. Again, if a cumulative probability is needed, it is better to calculate from scratch, remembering that the total probability is 1, so

$$\begin{aligned} \text{Pr} (4 \text{ or more}) &= 1 - \text{Pr} (\text{less than } 4) \\ &= 1 - \text{Pr} (0 \text{ or } 1 \text{ or } 2 \text{ or } 3) \\ &= 1 - \text{Pr} (0) - \text{Pr} (1) - \text{Pr} (2) - \text{Pr} (3) \end{aligned}$$

which considerably shortens the work, especially if N is large. We must not forget the possibility of zero in the sample; this is the commonest error in this area.

7. The Binomial pattern of probabilities is neither smooth nor continuous, and is finite. The probabilities exist only for integer values of r from 0 to N; there is no chance at all of finding $3\frac{3}{4}$ males, nor 12 females, in a sample of 10 people. Graphs of two Binomial distributions (Figure 8.2) show this. It may be natural to visualize a smooth curve passing through and beyond the points shown, but it would be totally false. Only the points belong to the distributions. Note however that as the sample size increases, the points are relatively more closely packed; one can imagine that for large enough sample sizes we would come nearer to a smooth curve. We shall return to this later.

Figure 8.2 Two Binomial distributions.

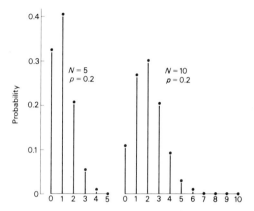

8. Although a frequency distribution is not a sample, it nevertheless has a mean and a standard deviation. The mean is, by definition, the average frequency we can expect to meet. Like all means it does not have to be feasible; one can have a mean of 3.5 yet would never see a sample with $3\frac{1}{2}$ males in it. The standard deviation measures the scatter of expected observations around the expected average. In a Binomial case, if 50% of a workforce is male and we take a random sample of 25 people from it, we expect on average 0.5×25 or $12\frac{1}{2}$ males in the sample. In the general case, by the same reasoning,

> The mean of a Binomial distribution is Np.

It is not so easy to get at the standard deviation, but

> The standard deviation of a Binomial distribution is $\sqrt{Npq}$.

9. Conveniently to remember, the chance of zero is q^n and the chance of all is p^n.

The Poisson distribution

We found the formula for the Binomial distribution from straightforward probability considerations. Unfortunately, there are no such simple sources for our other theoretical distributions; their formulae will have to be stated without explanation.

There are many situations in which events happen *at random*, i.e. one cannot predict precisely when each will happen, nor how many will happen altogether. Examples are road accidents; faults in a complex product like a car; telephoned orders from customers; arrivals of patients at a doctor's surgery if there is no appointments system to impose order. In a more scientific area, the decay of a radioactive substance illustrates the situation perfectly: nobody can tell which atom will disintegrate next, nor exactly when the event will occur.

Apart from all being unpredictable in the short term, these examples all have something in common which, rather surprisingly, is accurate predictability in the longer term. We can identify for each case some uniform opportunity in which the event may occur, for example, a definite stretch of road for a year, or a particular lump of radioactive material for 0.01 second.

Considering any one case, successive opportunities will yield either 0 or 1 or 2, etc. events. The exact number per opportunity may vary considerably, but over a longish period the average number of events per opportunity often proves surprisingly stable. When this is so a formula due to the French mathematician Poisson enables us to predict the chances of 0 or 1 or 2 . . . events in any one opportunity. In the long run the proportions of opportunities with 0 or 1 or 2 events having happened will be the same as these calculated chances. Therefore, the predictability is exact, but of a statistical nature: it works for the mass or for the long run but cannot tell us what will happen in individual cases.

If the long-run average number of events per opportunity is called a, the Poisson formula for the probability of c events in a given opportunity is

$$\Pr(c) = \frac{e^{-a} a^c}{c!}$$

e is, of course, the exponential 2.718 . . . , which we met in Chapter I. c must be a whole number, for we cannot find $2\frac{1}{2}$ defects in a motor car. However, the average a need not be integer. For example, if a small car-hire firm receives on average 6.7 requested bookings per day, how many cars should it operate? From the Poisson formula, with $a = 6.7$,

$$\Pr(0 \text{ bookings}) = e^{-6.7} = 0.00123$$
$$\Pr(1 \text{ booking}) = 6.7 \times e^{-6.7} = 0.00825$$
$$\Pr(2 \text{ bookings}) = 6.7^2 \times e^{-6.7} \, 2! = 0.02763$$

from which we see that on only 1 day in 1000 (or 0.001) should the firm expect no business at all, on 8 days in 1000 just one booking, and on 28 days in 1000 (0.0276) just two bookings. We shall continue this, but it is already clear that the cumulative form of the Poisson probabilities, featuring the chance of up to 3 or up to 8 or whatever, is going to be needed in many cases. There is no new formula; we simply add up to find the total probability to date, by the addition law.

Table 8.1 is the continued table for our car-hire firm. The basis for managerial decision is now complete. The only question remaining is the proportion of days on which the firm is willing to turn business away for lack of cars. Thus if they decide to satisfy demand on 98% of all days, 12 cars are needed since Pr (up to 12) is 0.98. On the other hand, since Pr (11) is 0.038, one car will be idle when 11 are in use, i.e. on 3.8% of all days. 2 cars will be idle when 10 are demanded on 6.2% of days, 3 cars on 9.2% of all days and so on. Idle cars cost money, just as turning away business costs money. The desired compromise can be chosen from Table 8.1, bearing both costs in mind. (Note that while a

Table 8.1

C	PR(C)	PR(UP TO C)
0	0.00123	0.00123
1	0.00825	0.00948
2	0.02763	0.03711
3	0.06170	0.09881
4	0.10335	0.20216
5	0.13849	0.34065
6	0.15465	0.49530
7	0.14802	0.64332
8	0.12397	0.76728
9	0.09229	0.85957
10	0.06183	0.92140
11	0.03766	0.95906
12	0.02103	0.98009
13	0.01084	0.99093
14	0.00519	0.99611
15	0.00232	0.99843
16	0.00097	0.99940
17	0.00038	0.99978
18	0.00014	0.99993
19	0.00005	0.99998
20	0.00002	0.99999

computer easily produced Table 8.1 to 5 decimal places, working to 3 as we have done is normally quite adequate.) Finally, there will probably be differing average demands at different times of year. If so, the level of car stocks should be seasonal too; the calculations would be repeated with each different average. This is not as laborious as it sounds, for the calculations are much easier than with the Binomial, and can even be avoided altogether, as we shall see.

Important features of the Poisson formula are:

1. It generates a genuine probability distribution (which we have so far taken for granted) because the total chance of 0 or 1 or 2, etc. events amounts to 1. It is quite easy to see this, putting 0, 1, 2 ... for c and then adding the results from the formula:

$$\text{total probability} = e^{-a} + \frac{a\,e^{-a}}{1!} + \frac{a^2\,e^{-a}}{2!} + \frac{a^3\,e^{-a}}{3!} + \cdots$$

$$= e^{-a}\left(1 + a + \frac{a^2}{2!} + \frac{a^3}{3!} + \cdots\right)$$

The series in brackets is the exponential series for e^a, so we have

$$\text{total probability} = e^{-a} \times e^a \text{ which is } 1$$

2. There is no theoretical maximum number of events that can occur. Whether the mean is large or small one could conceivably have thousands of road accidents per year on a given stretch, or multitudes of faults in a single car. However, the probabilities for these are extremely low. From Table 8.1, for instance, the chance of more than 20 demands in a day is less than 0.00001 and this covers all possibilities beyond 20, up to infinity. This example is graphed in Figure 8.3. from which we can see that the probabilities build up rapidly to a peak around the mean, then die away quite quickly, although there is no theoretical top limit.

Figure 8.3   Distribution of Poisson demand for cars: data of Table 8.1.

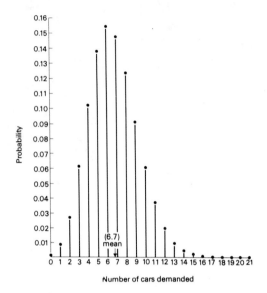

3. As with the Binomial, one can see only integer numbers; there is therefore no smooth curve through the points in Figure 8.3. However as the
   mean a rises, the distribution pattern gets wider and more symmetrical;
   if only a smooth curve were possible it would resemble the Normal
   distribution pattern discussed in the next section. In fact one rarely
   meets Poisson distributions with large means. Indeed, so uncommon are
   large quantities of random events that the Poisson is sometimes called
   the law of small numbers.
4. Although we can predict chances, we cannot predict occurrences.
   Random events do not occur uniformly; if they did they could not be
   random. It is therefore typical of a Poisson situation that the events
   appear to be clumped together, perhaps with fairly wide gaps between
   clusters. The belief that air crashes (or any other 'unlucky' events) occur
   in threes probably has its foundation in this statistical fact of life. Although the clusters may well be of twos or fours, the superstitious start
   counting again after proving their point at crash number 3 in the latter
   case, while in the former they wait as long as necessary for the next acci-
   dent to complete their sequence.
      The time between events in a Poisson situation is clearly a statistical
   variable in its own right, and its distribution pattern has been studied under
   the name *negative exponential distribution*. We need only note that there
   is a connection between the Poisson and the negative exponential; the

Poisson describes the pattern of numbers of events in a given opportunity while the negative exponential gives the pattern of intervals (usually times) between successive events.

5. The Poisson probability of no events is always e^{-a} where a is the mean. The chance of something happening is therefore $1 - e^a$. Both these results are quite commonly needed.

6. There is only one parameter with the Poisson, the average. It is therefore quite easy to find, and to use, tables of the Poisson distribution instead of calculating from the formula every time. We find tables either straight (giving probabilities of each number of events), or cumulative downwards ('c or less', or 'up to c',) or cumulative upwards ('c or more'). We must check which type of table we are using, but it is easy to find whatever we need with any type, since for example

$$\Pr(10) = \Pr(10 \text{ or more}) - \Pr(11 \text{ or more})$$

$$\Pr(10) = \Pr(\text{up to } 10) - \Pr(\text{up to } 9)$$

$$\Pr(\text{up to } 10) = 1 - \Pr(11 \text{ or more})$$

$$\Pr(10 \text{ or more}) = 1 - \Pr(\text{up to } 9) \quad \text{and so on.}$$

If in doubt about these relationships for a particular number, we write down the nearby integers in a row, then consider them in groups below, up to or above the chosen positions.

7. The Poisson distribution, in cumulative form, is also available on graph paper. Figure 8.4 shows its use with the car-hire example to find the chance of c or more given the mean and c. We first find the vertical line for $a = 6.7$, next see where it crosses the curve for $c = 8$ (for example) and go across from there to find $p = 0.36$, which is the chance of 8 or more cars being demanded. Table 8.1 gives the calculated chance of up to 7 as 0.64, so the calculated chance of 8 or more is $1 - 0.64$ or 0.36. The graph is thus quite good enough for most practical purposes.

As we see, the subtractions apply to graphs as much as to tables. A little practice soon familiarizes one with the use of the graphs and the many ways they can work. Here for example we worked from known a and c to find p, but we could start with any two of a, c and p to find the third. Then again, the graph paper can be used to check whether observed data fits the Poisson situation by working out whether the observed percentages of 1 or more, 2 or more, etc., fit reasonably where the curves cross the line of the average.

8. Like the Binomial and all other distributions, the Poisson has a mean and a standard deviation. The mean of a Poisson distribution is the parameter, a, which identifies it. The standard deviation is almost equally simple; it is $\sqrt{a}$. In other words, in a Poisson distribution the mean and the variance are equal.

Figure 8.4

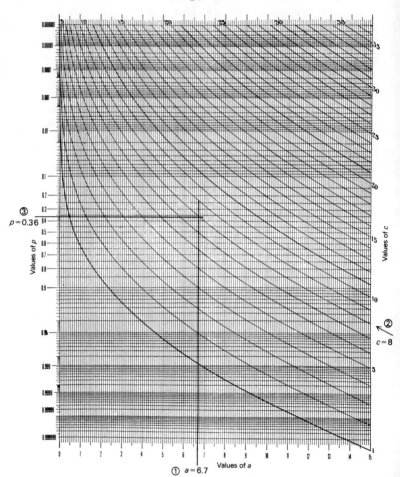

9. With only one determining parameter the Poisson is far easier to work with than the Binomial. For this reason we use the Poisson as an approximation to the Binomial whenever this is justified, i.e. whenever we have a Binomial which is awkward because N is large, and also has the mean about the same as the variance. With the Binomial mean at Np and the variance at Npq (standard deviation $\sqrt{Npq}$), q must be about 1 if the latter condition is to be approximately true. p will then be about zero, i.e. small. Since p and q are interchangeable in the Binomial situation we are left with three conditions in which the Poisson may stand in for the Binomial:

    N is large

Np is small, e.g. less than about 8 (law of small numbers!)

p is small or large, i.e. less than 0.1 or more than 0.9

and the appropriate Poisson distribution to use has the mean a = *Np*. Appendix B (p. 251) is a guide in this matter of approximation.

10. Generally speaking, Poisson will fit a situation if the events involved can be regarded as happening when they do accidentally. The occurrence of a production defect is clearly of this kind. Less obviously, someone placing an order with our firm has surely done so deliberately, but the exact moment of its arrival may have been affected by uncontrollable situations, such as delays in the post, and may therefore be 'accidental'. From the sales manager's point of view the exact number of orders in hand at the end of each day will have a random element about it. Bearing in mind the possibly random delays in filling the orders we have a queueing situation that may be analysed with Poisson. This subject is resumed in Part IV.

The Normal distribution

We have been looking at situations involving classifications. The observations were made by counting the number of occurrences of the item that interested us. There is also the variables situation involving making some measurement, and the observations can have any value that the measuring instrument can indicate. A bar chart showing the frequencies of each measurement may well show many groups, as in Figure 8.5. In this case we may fit the smooth curve that the eye detects because, in theory at least, the dimension concerned may truly take any value.

Figure 8.5 Distribution of earnings in a firm.

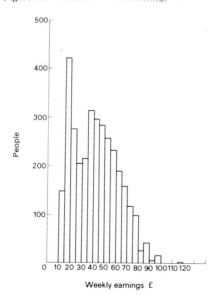

Weekly earnings £

There is one pattern which occurs so frequently where large numbers of people/things are involved that it is called the Normal distribution and also, sometimes, the law of large numbers. This pattern arises whenever the situation involves some overall average and the members of the population differ from the average and from each other in a random way. There will therefore be as many above average as below it and the pattern is symmetrical. The well-known *quincunx* demonstrates this. In it little balls fall centrally from a single source on to a pin, so that each might equally well be deflected either way. They travel on to other pins centrally in their paths, and so on. After the staggered array of pins, the tiny balls collect in columns where they chance to fall, forming whatever pattern arises naturally by random deflections. This has a symmetrical, bell-like shape, as seen in Figure 8.6.

Francis Galton, coiner of the word regression, which we shall meet in Chapter XII, was studying human populations. He assumed that people's heights, for example, departed from the overall average (if they did so at all) for random reasons. Even within a single family there are both upward and downward variations from the family average, each contributing (with all the other families) to the total picture. The overall histogram of heights at a given moment, then, might be imagined as generated by a sort of biological quincunx, in which an individual's height is determined partly by his origins (his parents' heights), his parents' origins, and so on, but with the whole sequence affected

Figure 8.6a The Quincunx.

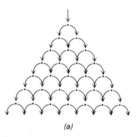

(a)

Possible paths for balls dropping squarely on to the top pin. A ball is more likely to bounce towards the middle (where more paths converge) than towards the extremities.

by chance changes at each stage. Galton found from measuring many people that the pattern was indeed symmetrical, bell-shaped and concentrated around the mean. This confirmed the earlier theoretical work of the greatest mathematician who has ever lived, Karl Friedrich Gauss, who had studied the large-numbers, random-deviations situation that we meet so frequently. Gauss discovered a formula for this Normal distribution, alternatively named the Gaussian distribution in his honour. His complicated formula is quite unusable for all but theoretical statisticians, but can nevertheless be found, for

Figure 8.6b   The Quincunx.

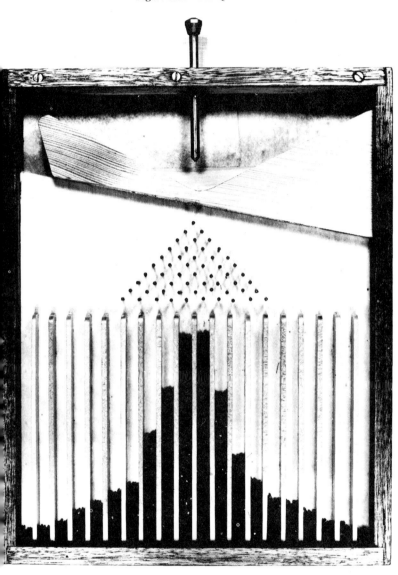

information's sake, in almost any statistics textbook, whether intended for managers or not. Fortunately we do not need it; for our practical use the formula has been converted into tables and graph paper.

The Normal or Gaussian distribution has two parameters, i.e. by specifying just two numbers we can state precisely which symmetrical, bell-shaped pattern applies to our situation. One parameter, of course, is the mean called $\bar{X}$ or μ (X-bar or mu). If we are speaking of a machine set to fill cans with just 500 grams of our product, the mean delivery, μ, from the machine will be 500 g. Not every can will contain precisely this amount; we know that there is some tolerance to allow for and if we are guaranteeing a content of 500 g we must set the machine above this figure. How much higher depends on the inherent inaccuracy of the machine. The second parameter we need to specify is concerned with just this: it is the standard deviation, σ (sigma). Figure 8.7 illustrates the case and we shall see shortly how the parameters are used in this instance.

Figure 8.7 Distribution of weights delivered by a packing machine.

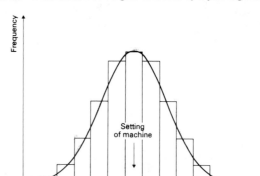

The Normal distribution appears in tables in terms of its two parameters and can therefore appear on a single, 2-dimensional page. The tables work in relative frequencies and answer the following question:

What proportion of the whole population lies beyond a desired number of standard deviations from the mean?

A table of the distribution is given at Appendix C (page 252). In it Z is a number of standard deviations distant from the mean, and A is the fraction of the population beyond the chosen Z standard deviations. Thus with $Z = 1$, $A = 0.1587$; for $Z = 2$, $A = 0.02275$; for $Z = 3$, $A = 0.00135$. Looking at the small diagram above the tables, we see that this refers to a single tail of the pattern and looking now at Figure 8.8(a) we recognize that the same fractions will also be in the other tail. Consequently, considering distances on either side of the mean we learn approximately that:

68% of the population is within ± 1 standard deviation of the mean

95% of the population is within $\pm 2\sigma$ of the mean

99.8% of the population is within $\pm 3\sigma$ of the mean

Figure 8.8a

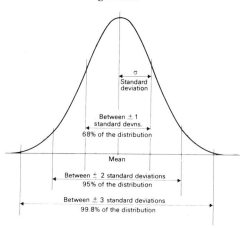

σ

Standard deviation

Between ± 1 standard devns.

68% of the distribution

Mean

Between ± 2 standard deviations

95% of the distribution

Between ± 3 standard deviations

99.8% of the distribution

Figure 8.8b

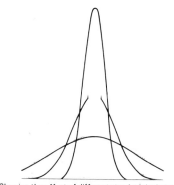

Showing the effect of different standard deviations

So only about 5% or $\frac{1}{20}$ of the population is more than 2 standard deviations away from the mean, i.e. 1 item in 40 is more than 2σ above the mean and 1 in 40 is more than 2σ below it. Only the tiny proportion of 0.2% lies outside 3σ limits, i.e. only 1 item in 1000 is more than 3σ greater than the mean and only 1 in 1000 is more than 3σ below it. Effectively, then, the Normal pattern is 6 standard deviations wide overall, though in theory both tails are infinitely long. A further theoretical point is that the proportion of the population *exactly* 2σ (or any other distance) away from the mean is *zero*. We have areas to represent fractions, and any exact value is represented by a line which has no thickness, and thus no area. In practice this is not the nonsense it may seem at first. What, for instance, is the proportion of the population exactly 1.80 metres (or 6 feet or anything else) tall, not approximately 1 m 80, e.g. 1.80 ± 0.001 m, but precisely 1 m 80? Once we get down to the niceties of measurement, we must recognize that we do in fact use bandwidths and there is of course a proportion of the population in the band $1.80 \pm .0001$ m, or in any other band we care to name. Looking back at Figure 8.7 with a mean of 500 g, if the value of σ is 3 grams then only 1 packet in 1000 would be underweight if the machine was set to 509 g, i.e. the desired 500 g is set to be 3 standard deviations below the mean. This much reduces the chance of prosecution for short weight, but on the other hand half our packets would contain over 509 g, and 1 in 1000 over 518 g. Should our pricing correspond to the cost to us of the average weight we are actually supplying or to the minimum we are (generously) claiming? This is a real, everyday problem for food or paint manufacturers, and it also illustrates the need to keep the machinery in good order, to reduce its inherent variability.

Remembering now that proportion *is* probability, we could equally well speak of the chance of 1 in 1000 that a can would contain less than 500 g, and so forth. The total area under the Normal curve therefore corresponds to 1 unit or 100% and the lesser areas, given in the table, to the probabilities of finding a member of the population with more than the stated dimension (converted into 'sigmas away from the mean'). Since the chance of finding an exact dimension is zero, the table contains the chances of finding a member with *the stated dimension or more*.

With the total area at unity or 100%, it follows that Normal curves for smaller values of σ must be drawn taller and more peaked, and curves for larger σ must be flatter and wider, as in Figure 8.8(b).

Before proceeding to examples of the use of the Normal, we should note that there is no standard form for its tables. Appendix C (page 252), to which we shall here always refer, shows the area in a single tail above a positive value of Z, as in Figure 8.9(a). The other diagrams in Figure 8.9 show the content of tables which give the areas: (b) beyond $\pm Z$ standard deviations in both tails, (c) between the mean and Z standard deviations in a single tail, (d) between $\pm Z$ standard deviations from the mean.

There are other possibilities which may readily be discerned from diagrams like these. It is therefore vital, when using a set of Normal tables for the first time, to check which way they work. There will usually be either a sketch or some explanation. Alternatively, we must look up $Z = 0$ in the table. If $A = 0.5$ we are dealing with a single tail; if $A = 0$ we have the area between the mean and Z but cannot yet tell whether in 1 or 2 tails. To find out, we look up $Z = 1$, i.e. 1 standard deviation from the mean. Do we get about 0.34 or 0.68 or 0.32 or 0.16? These correspond respectively to (c), (d), (b) and (a) of Figure 8.9. 0.84 corresponds to the unshaded part of Figure 8.9(a).

Conversions such as that from 'less than' to 'greater than' are also simple. If in our tables Z is, for example, 1.4 (i.e. we are interested in a dimension 1.4 sigmas above the mean) then A is 0.08076 (i.e. 8.08% of all the population are 1.4σ or more above the mean). Clearly, then, twice this or 16.16% are outside $\pm 1.4\sigma$ from the mean (as in Figure 8.9(b)); $1 - 0.08076$ or 0.91924 or 91.92%

Figure 8.9 Ways of tabulating the Normal distribution.

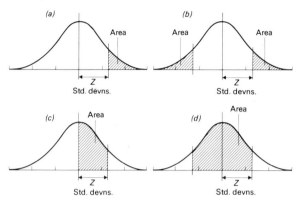

are less than 1.4σ above the mean (the unshaded part of Figure 8.9(a)); $0.5 - 0.08076$ or 0.41924 or 41.92% are between the mean and 1.4σ above it (Figure 8.9(c)), and so on.

To use the tables in a typical real-life case, let us revert to the can-filling example. The desired minimum weight is 500 g and σ is 3 g. (Incidentally, note the convenience of working with measures of central tendency and dispersion in the same units as the observations; refer back to Chapter VII if necessary.) With this μ and σ:

At what level should we set the machine if we are prepared to run (a) a 1% risk, (b) 1 chance in 500 (c) 1 chance in 800 of prosecution for short weight?

These probabilities are proportions, which we will find in the body of the table under 0.01, 0.002 and 1/800 or 0.00125 respectively. These give Z values of (a) 2.33, (b) 2.88 and (c) 3.02, i.e. we must respectively set the machine at these numbers of standard deviations above the desired 500 g minimum weight. (See Figure 8.7.) With $\sigma = 3$ the answers are thus: (a) set the mean to $\mu = 500 + 2.33 \times 3$ or 506.99 g, (b) set $\mu = 500 + 2.88 \times 3$ or 508.64 g, (c) $\mu = 500 + 3.02 \times 3 = 509.06$ g. Our earlier approximation of 1 in 1000 beyond 3σ is obviously not quite right, but it will do for most practical purposes; the difference between 1/800 and 1/1000 is only 1/4000.

If the mean is set at 515 g, what are the proportions of cans containing over 525 g, i.e. more than 25 g overweight, and below 500 g, i.e. underweight?

The standard deviation σ is still 3 g, being unaffected by the mean setting and merely describing the machine's inherent variability.

525 g is 10 g above the mean, i.e. $\dfrac{10}{3}$ or 3.333σ above μ. 500 g is 15 g below the mean, i.e. $-\dfrac{15}{3}$ or -5σ above μ. So we enter the table respectively at $Z = 3.333$ and $Z = -5$ ($+5$ will do; the tails are equal) to find $A = 0.00043$ and

$A = 0.0000003$ respectively. Note how Figure 8.10 helps. It pays handsomely to draw a sketch like this whenever working with the Normal distribution. Note also how we arrived at the figures for Z: we subtracted the mean from the desired value and then divided the difference by the standard deviation, e.g. $\frac{525 - 515}{3}$. In algebraic form we found $Z = \frac{X - \mu}{\sigma}$, which is the formula at the top of Appendix C and most other Normal tables. In my view it is best to

Figure 8.10

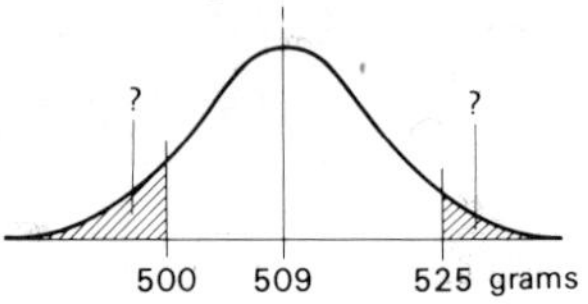

500   509   525 grams

think in terms of 'how many σs away from μ' rather than becoming involved with formulae, but everyone must decide for himself.

Sometimes one hears of a standardized Normal distribution. This has a mean of zero and standard deviation of unity and so can easily be tabulated. In working, as we have been, with the number of standard deviations away from the mean, we are in effect using the standardized pattern and there is no need to go deeper into this concept.

We have been working with the straight Normal distribution. There is also the cumulative form which shows the total probabilities (or proportions) from $-\infty$ up to the desired value of Z. These correspond to the unshaded parts in Figure 8.9(a), or to subtracting from 1 each of the figures in our table. If graphed, as in Figure 8.11, we see a slow rise at each tail but quite a rapid rise in the middle, as one must expect from the Normal shape where most of the mass is in the middle. This type of curve is called an *ogive*. Its value to us is that, if it is distorted into a straight line by appropriate changes of vertical scale, it gives us a form of graph paper* (Normal probability paper), that avoids even the simple use of Normal tables, and also lets us check quickly whether data we have is Normally distributed. The paper is used in Figure 8.12, to solve the following problem:

The salaries of 3337 people in a firm are shown in Table 8.2. Do they fit the Normal pattern?

Table 8.2

Salary range £	10–15	15–20	20–25	25–30	30–35	35–40	40–45
People in range	148	56	29	54	40	173	198

Salary range £	45–50	50–60	60–70	70–80	80 +	Total
People in range	223	482	981	606	347	3337

* The special graph papers mentioned in this chapter are available from stationers as part of the Chartwell range, or from Wightman, Mountain of, 12 Artillery Row, London SW1.

Figure 8.11 Cumulative Normal distribution.

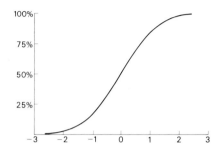

If the answer is affirmative, then the cumulative data will fit a straight line on Normal probability paper. To get the cumulative form, we simply add up the data step by step, then find percentages (see Table 8.3) and finally plot the % figures against the salary figures on Normal paper. The top of each range has to be used in the cumulative form, for we really do mean all those up to, and including, the highest figure in each step.

Table 8.3

Salary up to £	15	20	25	30	35	40	45	50
Total people	148	204	233	287	327	500	698	921
% of total	4.44	6.11	6.98	8.60	9.80	14.98	20.92	27.60

Salary up to £	60	70	80	100
Total people	1403	2001	3000	3337
% of total	42.04	71.44	89.60	100

Looking at the pattern of crosses in Figure 8.12, it is clear that they lie far from a straight line, so the Normal does not apply. (Incidentally, there is no reason why salaries should fit, since salary levels are not random deviations from an overall mean.)

Where the Normal does fit, i.e. where we can draw a straight line nicely through the cumulative percentages, it is easy to read off the mean and the standard deviation:

1. μ is the value with a cumulative probability of 50%, i.e. half the population is below (or above) the mean.

2. Since 95% of the population lies within $\pm 2\sigma$ of the mean, σ is one-quarter of the gap between the value with $2\frac{1}{2}$% probability and the one with $97\frac{1}{2}$% probability.

The Normal distribution works for us as managers in four main areas:

(1) Where our work concerns the natural characteristics of large numbers of people, e.g. their clothing sizes, we can learn all we need to know about which sizes to make or stock (and in what relative quantities) by measuring a sample

Figure 8.12

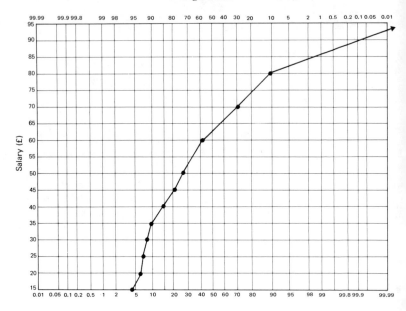

of a few hundred people, fitting the appropriate Normal distribution with probability paper and then deducing (from the paper or from tables) the fractions of the population in each size range. Another example is in grading people's suitability for jobs by intelligence testing; the pattern of Intelligence Quotients is Normal, with mean 100. Note that while the Normal distribution extends infinitely, the real-life data has only a limited spread. This is only another illustration of mathematical modelling. The Normal pattern is a model, an idealized simplification, which allows us to do our calculations. However, it is by no means a perfect representation, nor need it be one, at least for measurements outside our range of interest.

(2) Where we are working with automatic machines set to produce a definite size of product (e.g. package filling machines or automatic lathes) there may well be problems that can be modelled with the Normal distribution. I have used it in TV receiver production, treating the entire factory as a single machine, for predicting the performance of mass-produced receivers on the basis of measurements made on a dozen trial models. The idea was to calculate, before full production began, the proportion of sets that would prove to be outside tolerance, and hence decide the number of repair staff to be trained. It worked.

(3) Whenever we take samples and work with their means the Normal pattern inevitably comes in. This topic is so important that Chapter IX is devoted to it.

(4) We have seen that the Binomial situation gives rise to intolerable calculations when the sample size is large. Where the p of the formula is near $\frac{1}{2}$ the

Binomial pattern is fairly symmetrical, and is exactly so for $p = 0.5$ precisely. Apart from gaps between the integer values the shape looks quite like the Normal one. So long as the sample size N is large enough to give trouble with the Binomial itself, the Normal is a good approximation to the Binomial under either of the following conditions:

(a) p is about 0.5.

(b) p, if not about $\frac{1}{2}$, is nevertheless neither small nor large (i.e. it is more than about 0.1 and less than about 0.9), and also the mean of the Binomial, Np, is more than about 8.

If one of these conditions fits, then the Normal to use has $\mu = Np$ and $\sigma = \sqrt{Npq}$ where N, p and q are the Binomial data. Note that if conditions are the opposite of those in (b), the Poisson approximation is valid instead. Finding which approximation to use is summarized in Appendix B (page 251).

Where the Normal, a continuous distribution, is used to replace the Binomial which is discrete (only 0, 1, 2, etc.) there is a possible trap. In finding the chance of 'up to 3', for instance, we have to remember that with the Normal 3 must represent the range '$2\frac{1}{2}$ to $3\frac{1}{2}$', and so we must instead find the chance of 'up to $3\frac{1}{2}$' or we shall have too small an answer. As an example, suppose that a large firm employs twice as many men as women, but it is noticed one day that there are only 55 men among the 100 employees using the canteen. The welfare officer wonders whether the men dislike the canteen. What is the answer? With no bias against the canteen we would expect the 100 users to be split $2:1$, i.e. about 66 or 67 men and about 34 or 33 women. Our sample was split $55:45$ and we must find whether this shows bias. We have a Binomial situation with $N = 100$ and, if there is no bias, $p = \frac{1}{3}$. Thus

$$\Pr (55 \text{ men}) = {}^{100}C_{55} \left(\tfrac{2}{3}\right)^{55} \left(\tfrac{1}{3}\right)^{45}$$

which is a dreadful thing to calculate. However, the conditions for using the Normal approximation are satisfied; verify this for yourself. The Normal in question will have a mean μ of $66\frac{2}{3}$ and a σ of $\sqrt{Npq} = \sqrt{100 \times \tfrac{1}{3} \times \tfrac{2}{3}} = 4.71$. The chance of getting 55 men is the probability of getting between 54.5 and 55.5 with this Normal distribution; the distances from the mean (see Figure 8.13) are respectively

$$\frac{54.4 - 66.67}{4.71} \text{ and } \frac{55.5 - 66.67}{4.71},$$

i.e. 2.58 and 2.37 standard deviations below the mean. From our tables, the areas in the tail are:

2.37σ:	0.00889
2.58σ:	0.00494
difference	0.00395

Thus 0.004 or 0.4% of the distribution can be classified as 'exactly 55 men'

Figure 8.13

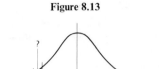

and this is the random chance of seeing just 55 men in 100 canteen users if men and women have similar views about it. With such a remote chance the welfare officer is almost surely right to wonder. Incidentally, the chance of 55 men *or less* is 0.00889 or 0.89%, still very tiny. We shall have to consider the problem in this light when discussing significance testing in Chapter 10.

The Lognormal distribution
The Normal distribution arises through random individual deviations adding to one another, but there are many cases where they do not, and it is dangerous to assume a Normal pattern just because large frequencies are involved. Another pattern which often arises is one where the logarithms of the frequencies have a Normal distribution pattern. It is as if the random deviations multiplied one another. The Lognormal has been found to apply to many personal income situations (a few very rich and very poor, with most people near the average and a minimum of zero), to the pattern of particle sizes in industrial grinding operations, to length-of-service data in personnel work, to stock utilization patterns and to many length-of-life situations such as the life of ball-bearing greases. The pattern is seen in Figure 8.14; there is only one infinitely long tail. Fortunately, by using logarithmic probability paper we are able to work exactly as with the Normal pattern. Figure 8.15 shows how the probability scale is set against a logarithmic one (available in 1, 2 or more cycles depending on the range of data involved). A straight line indicates the lognormality of the distribution being plotted, the mean being at 50% probability and the standard deviation being found from the $\pm\sigma = 68\%$ or $\pm 2\sigma = 95\%$ rules, as before.

Figure 8.14 The Lognormal distribution.

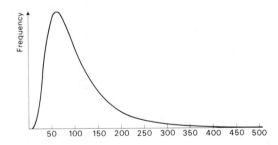

Figure 8.15 Logarithmic probability paper (3 cycles) showing the distribution of Figure 8.14.

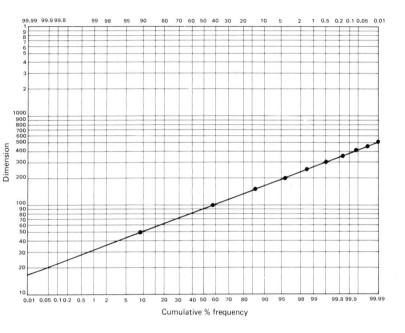

Truncated distributions

Theoretically the Normal and Lognormal curves and also the Poisson distribution extend infinitely far. However, our observations often cannot fit the ends of such patterns, e.g. people's heights must be positive numbers and cannot extend infinitely far. Nevertheless, they, like many other items of data that we meet, fit nicely to part of a theoretical pattern. We might see on probability paper a straight line of finite length. Commonsense tells us in such cases to regard the theoretical pattern as relevant where it works and to disregard the impossible parts. Thus Figure 8.5 contains a truncated lognormal curve for salaries in a firm.

There is no problem, either conceptually or in practice, in handling parts of patterns, which is all that truncated distributions are. We simply have to remember to exclude the impossible.

IX
SAMPLING, ITS USES AND RISKS

A middle manager complains that he spends $\frac{3}{4}$ of his time answering telephoned queries. Could he please have authorization for another telephone extension so that he can allocate a junior to filter off the many easy ones?

The answer to this question might depend ultimately on the relative costs of the manager's time and the junior-plus-telephone. The latter is fairly easy to ascertain but the manager's part involves testing the truth of his assertion. How much of his time really is spent on work that could be done at a lower and cheaper level? The only way to find out is to study his work, with his collaboration. Let us ask him, then, for an account of a typical day (or week, or other period) during which he will keep a clear record of time spent on junior's work. Almost certainly he will reply that there is no such thing as a typical period; every day (or week, etc.) is different from every other one, and unpredictably so. How does he know, then, that $\frac{3}{4}$ of his time is spent as he claims?

It is becoming clear that the problem is a statistical one, that of finding a sample that will fairly represent a population (in this case, the man's time) and then of drawing inferences from the sample that are valid for the entire population.

In some cases this problem is not difficult. For instance brewers buy quite large quantities of grain at prices set partly by the examination of small samples from the bulk. The point here is that the population, while being millions of individual grains in a batch, may be considered homogeneous if well mixed, so that a jugful or so does indeed represent the whole. Where a population is not homogeneous, as with the voting intentions of an electorate, the germination properties of seeds grown for sale, the lengths of life of lamp-bulbs in a batch or the work-pattern of a manager, both halves of the problem (choosing the sample and reaching valid conclusions from it) strike with full force. This leads us to ask whether sampling can be avoided. The answer is yes, if (but only if) the entire population is looked at. There are obvious objections to this, on the grounds of actual impossibility in many cases and of cost in others. Thus we are almost always forced back on to sampling.

Since the object of choosing a sample is to have it represent the population as fairly as possible, the *random* sample is usually preferred. This is one in which every member of the population has an equal chance of being chosen, and is often easier said than done. In a raffle all the tickets may readily be mixed so that it is purely chance that determines which ones come to hand. However, when selecting a sample of a workforce from a drawer full of their record cards in alphabetical order, is each card truly as likely as any other to be drawn? Would we not tend to go for the middle of the stack rather than the ends, thus reducing the chances of Miss Aarons or Mr Young in favour of Mr Evans or Mrs McIntyre? People simply cannot be trusted to draw random samples unless some mechanical aid, such as a rotating drum for the raffle tickets, imposes equality of opportunity. Unequal chances, for whatever reason, are known as *bias*; all work which relies on sampling, including market research, public opinion polling and quality control, is a continuous battle against suspected or unsuspected sources of bias.

A random sample is by definition unbiased. The problem is therefore to obtain one when, as with the personnel record cards, it is out of the question to use lucky dip methods. What we do instead is to use *random numbers*. There are many ways of obtaining a random digit or sequence of digits, for example by throwing dice (10-sided dice for digits 0 to 9), or spinning suitably calibrated roulette wheels, or by electronic means as ERNIE of the premium bond lottery scheme. A few thousands of such digits are no less random when preserved on paper for future reference than when newly generated. Appendix D (page 253) is a table of random numbers produced electronically by a computer. If the personnel records include staff numbers, say of 4 digits, one can pick a sample by treating the random number tables as groups of 4 digits (the existing grouping is merely for legibility) and taking sets of 4 from a random starting point. When a set corresponds with a member of staff he/she is selected, otherwise it is ignored. We then proceed to the next group of 4 until the desired sample size is complete. The random starting point may be picked out with closed eyes and a pin, or alternatively this (only partly random) method may be used for just 2 or 3 digits, so that if the pin lands at the 3 of 80183 70760, the digits 37 might mean starting at the 7th row of column 3 of the table. Of course the table may be read forwards or backwards, as determined by the toss of a coin, or any other way that may be devised.

If there are no employee numbers but (for example) 687 cards, we can use the table in groups of 3 digits, with 001 meaning the first card, 349 the 349th and so on. In effect, then, a table of random numbers is a means of overcoming bias. If, as may happen, an individual chosen randomly is in some way 'unfortunate' as a member of the sample (for example, his complicated record would need a lot of work to use), this is no reason for rejecting him. Indeed, such action could introduce bias. On the other hand, there are cases of physical impossibility in the use of properly selected samples. In a market survey, what if the randomly chosen person absolutely refuses to collaborate? Or how does one pick a truly random half-metre of copper wire for tests of its enamelling if it comes in batches of 5 kg reels, each of enormous length? All one can afford to do is pick a few reels at random and test their exposed ends, hoping that there is no source of bias in their manufacture that would put all bad parts inside the reels and leave perfect end lengths.

All the sampling theory which follows assumes unbiased samples, which usually means random samples. Unfortunately, random selection cannot guarantee that the sample is fair in representing its population. After all, a sample of 30 people from a workforce of 600 males and 400 females could easily be, by chance, either all male or all female (the Normal approximation to the Binomial will give you the probabilities) and in any case is very unlikely to be split *exactly* 18:12 like the workforce. If the sex pattern of the sample matters in our study (it might in looking at absenteeism, for example), it is almost bound to be unrepresentative.

For the sake of cost-effectiveness many ways have been developed of trying to force samples to be representative as well as unbiased. Among these is *stratified random* sampling, also known as *quota* sampling. Here, if it is known that the labour force has the 600:400 sex ratio, a sample of 30 will contain 18 men and 12 women who will be selected at random until their category has been filled. If, say, the 12 women are found in the first 25 people chosen, any further random choices will be rejected if they happen to be women. Similarly an age pattern, job status distribution or any other classification may be used to subdivide the sex classes if it is felt that they might affect the matter being studied. Fairness is thus imposed, to give the most effective sample for the money available, but only if one has the necessary background knowledge about the population, and also at the price of randomness. True, each individual selected has been chosen at random, but many others may have been rejected after being so chosen. Redefining randomness to include having a definite chance of being chosen (rather than the same chance as everyone else) saves some consciences, but it does not quite conform to a statistical theory based on true randomness. However, sampling is already so full of problems that this one more is usually ignored.

We see our dilemma clearly. To take samples is often bad, but to try to avoid them is either too costly or impossible. Their contents depend on chance, which is variable by definition. But statistics is the science of variability and is designed to deal above all with the variability that comes with sampling. We shall now look at how it helps when we take a sample in order to estimate: the mean of a population; the standard deviation or the median of a population; in the Binomial case, the proportion or percentage of each category in the population.

Estimating means from samples

As part of a study of labour relations, a personnel department found that 50 employees chosen at random had between them 181.4 years service, i.e. an average of 3.628 years per individual. Is this a good estimate of the average for the entire payroll of several thousands?

To begin with, 3.628 years looks extremely precise, and if it were quoted by someone of authority the figure might well be taken as correct, i.e. as if the speaker knew what he was saying. The figure is exact for the chosen sample of 50, of course, but an equally precise yet quite different figure could result from each of the thousands of alternative samples of 50 that only chance prevented us from choosing instead. What is the true mean length of service, then? By definition it is the average of the entire population (the payroll), but if we think in terms of samples of 50, it could also be found by averaging the means of all the many samples of 50 that we could choose, including the 3.628 that was actually found. No-one would dream of going about finding the average in this way, but visualizing the concept, surprisingly, leads us to the real answer. In effect we consider the real sample as a single representative from the population of samples that we might have chosen, and its mean is our single representative of the *population of means* of all those samples. While we shall see none of this population but the mean we have, (i.e. 3.628), let us consider the overall pattern that must be there.

A piece of statistical theory so fundamental that it is called the *central limit* theorem tells us that:

1. If many samples, all of a given size N, are drawn from a Normal population, then the distribution of the means from these samples is also Normal.
2. Even if the population from which our samples of size N are drawn is not Normal, the pattern of sample means is approximately Normal.

These two taken together allow us to go straight to the Normal pattern whenever we are using the mean of a sample, without even needing to think about the shape of the parent population. Thus we are able to say that 3.628, our mean of a sample of size 50, is a member of a certain Normal pattern. But which one? The central limit theorem goes on to say

3. The mean of this Normal (or approximately Normal) pattern is the same as the mean of the parent population from which the samples were drawn.

This agrees with our statement above, that the true average is the mean of all the thousands of sample averages. From now on we shall ignore the approximation; for practical purposes the Normal will suffice for us.

4. The standard deviation of this Normal pattern is $\sqrt{N}$ times smaller than the standard deviation of the parent population.

In other words, if the standard deviation of the parent population is σ, then the standard deviation of the Normal pattern that includes our mean is $\sigma/\sqrt{N}$; for our example it is $\sigma/\sqrt{50}$ or $\sigma/7.07$ as the size of our sample is 50. So when trying to find the mean μ of a population via a sample drawn from it, we must become involved in the Normal distribution and also the standard deviation σ of the population being studied. It will be very unusual for us to know σ when we do not know μ, and we shall see in a moment how to estimate σ also.

You may wish to try (or consider) a small experiment to show what this is all about. Take a pack of playing cards and regard the values from ace to king as being numbers 1 to 13. If cards are picked one at a time and immediately replaced, we can build up a list of 200 or so cards, in order of being drawn. Considering a sample as comprising any number of cards desired, you can then construct a series of averages for samples of size 5, for example, by taking sequences of 5. Thus in a few minutes you can find the means of 40 or so samples of 5 cards. These could well be 40 different numbers, of course, but theory says that they will mostly be clustered near the mean of the pack of cards, which is 7. Work out the cumulative percentages and plot them on Normal probability paper. This should give a straight line showing reasonable fit to a Normal pattern. The mean, 7, should be around the 50% mark. The standard deviation (a quarter of the distance between the $2\frac{1}{2}$% and $97\frac{1}{2}$% levels) should in theory be about $3.749/\sqrt{5}$, i.e. 1.680, because σ for a pack of cards work out at 3.749. You could repeat this for samples of other sizes and try again. Figure 9.1 shows the implications as a diagram; the rectangular distribution of the parent population gives rise to Normal distributions for means of samples and these become narrower as the sample size rises. The triumph of the central limit theorem is that it quantifies them; they become $\sqrt{N}$ times narrower.

Figure 9.1

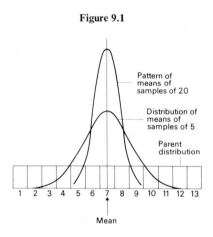

This experiment is just to help understanding, of course. In real life we have only one sample and no knowledge of the parent population; it is to gain this knowledge that we take the sample from it. However, still pretending for the moment that we know (or can find) σ, the standard deviation of the parent population, we can see how the theorem explains the consequences of our length-of-service sample with mean 3.628. This value belongs to a Normal distribution (see Figure 9.2), of which the mean is the unknown true mean length of service, μ, and the standard deviation is $\sigma/\sqrt{50}$, i.e. about a seventh of the standard deviation of all individual lengths of service. But where does 3.628 lie within this pattern to which it belongs? Since in effect the pattern is six standard deviations wide, the lowest value it is likely to have (only 1 in 1000 being lower) is 3 standard deviations below the unknown mean, and similarly its highest likely value is 3 standard deviations above this mean. Since our sample mean of 3.628 is trying to estimate the true mean, these standard deviations are measures of the error involved, so $\sigma/\sqrt{50}$ (or $\sigma/\sqrt{N}$ with a sample of size N) is called the *standard error of the mean* of our sample.

Clearly the true mean will almost always lie between 3 standard errors above the sample mean of 3.628 (if 3.628 happened to be the lowest likely value) and

Figure 9.2

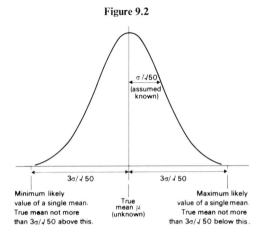

3 standard errors below it (if the other extreme arose). In more mathematical terms, there is a 99.8 % chance that the true mean which we are trying to estimate lies within the range $3.628 \pm 3\dfrac{\sigma}{\sqrt{50}}$. Similarly, there is a 95 % chance that it is within $3.628 \pm 2\dfrac{\sigma}{\sqrt{50}}$.

In general terms, if a sample of size N has a mean $\bar{X}$, we can assert that the mean of the population from which the sample came lies within

$$X \pm 3\frac{\sigma}{\sqrt{N}} \text{ with 99.8 \% confidence in our assertion}$$

or $$X \pm 2\frac{\sigma}{\sqrt{N}} \text{ with 95 \% confidence in our assertion}$$

or $$X \pm \frac{\sigma}{\sqrt{N}} \text{ with 68 \% confidence in our assertion}$$

Any other *confidence interval* can be given from the tables of the Normal distribution, the appropriate number of standard errors being used. (Check, for example, that the 80 % confidence limits are about $\pm 1.28\,\dfrac{\sigma}{\sqrt{N}}$.)

For greater confidence in establishing the truth, we must quote a wider range within which it should lie. Indeed, for absolute certainty the band should extend from negative to positive infinity. However, for practical decision-making we need a reasonably narrow range. To say, for instance, that the average length of service of our employees is between 1.2 and 19.8 years (with only 1 chance in a million that it is outside these limits) is hardly the basis for decisions on a new personnel policy. We therefore have to compromise between a suitably narrow interval and a sensible chance of error attached to it. Incidentally, the practical error may be only half the theoretical risk in cases where only one direction of error matters, since half the risk of error applies to the truth being above and half to it being below the stated confidence interval. As a rule of thumb, the 95% confidence interval is widely seen as a useful working compromise, giving a reasonably small interval with only a $2\frac{1}{2}\%$ chance of error at each end, i.e. single-ended odds of 39 to 1 in our favour.

Finding the standard deviation

The normal model of the sampling situation has helped us to estimate a mean, but leaves us with the problem of finding σ, the standard deviation of the parent population. However, we have our sample to help us in this too.

If the sample is smallish we cannot reasonably expect (unless luck has played an unusual part) that it shows the same spread as the population it comes from. The spread of relatively few individuals is almost sure to be less than the total spread. On the other hand, it is unlikely that all of the (random) sample will come from a very limited part of the population, so the sample's spread need not be much less than that of the parent. With large samples it is much more reasonable to expect the sample to give a moderately fair representation of the spread of the parent.

The mathematician Bessel studied the relationship between the standard deviation of a sample (call it s) and the best estimate it can give us of the standard deviation of its parent population (called $\hat{\sigma}$ or sigma-hat to show that it is only an estimate and not the true value σ). He found the relationship, for a sample of size N,

$$\hat{\sigma} = s \sqrt{\frac{N}{N-1}}$$

s can always be calculated from the data of the sample. $\hat{\sigma}$ is a bit larger than s; $\sqrt{\frac{2}{1}}$ or 1.414 times larger if N is 2, $\sqrt{\frac{3}{2}}$ or 1.225 times larger with a sample of 3, and so on. By the time we reach samples of 30, $\sqrt{\frac{N}{N-1}}$ (which is called *Bessel's correction*) is $\sqrt{\frac{30}{29}}$ or $\sqrt{1.0345}$ or 1.015, so near to 1 that for samples of 30 or more we may take the calculated standard deviation of the sample to be the same as $\hat{\sigma}$, the best estimate of $\hat{\sigma}$ that we can get.

With large samples then, where Bessel's correction may be taken as 1, our confidence intervals for the mean are easily found. In our example, if the standard deviation of the sample lengths-of-service is 0.85 years, we can say that the true mean length of service probably lies within

$$3.628 \pm R \frac{0.85}{\sqrt{50}}$$

where R is chosen from the Normal tables according to the degree of confidence we seek, e.g. $R = 1.96$ (say 2) for 95% confidence.

With small samples (i.e. under 30) the problem is more difficult, for two reasons:

1. We have to include Bessel's correction $\sqrt{\dfrac{N}{N-1}}$ in finding $\hat{\sigma}$.

2. While the Normal is correct if, exceptionally, we happen to know σ, it unfortunately does not apply with small samples when we use the same sample to estimate both the mean and the standard deviation.

We must instead use a pattern called t-distribution, which looks like the Normal but is rather wider. In fact its width depends on the sample size, smaller samples demanding a wider t-pattern to allow for the greater uncertainty they bring in. Thus there is a whole family of t-distributions and, because they appear in other circumstances (e.g. in Chapter X), they are calibrated not in sample sizes but in what are called degrees of freedom, which can apply also in the other cases. In this case of estimating means, the number of degrees of freedom is $N-1$.

A table of this family of patterns is given in Appendix E (page 254). It resembles the Normal table (with less detail), in that it relates areas (probabilities) to numbers of standard deviations from the mean, but it is laid out the other way, with the standard deviations in the body of the table and round probabilities at the top. For example, the row for 10 degrees of freedom shows 10% of the area for 1.812 standard deviations, 5% for 2.228 standard deviations and 1% for 3.169 standard deviations from the mean. The areas shown here are 2-tailed, for instance the 5% figure tells us that 95% of the area lies within ± 2.228 standard errors of the mean and hence gives us a 95% confidence figure if we use it. Note also that for more than 30 degrees of freedom the percentages are those of the Normal (2-tailed) which is why we are able to use the Normal tables with large samples.

The table of t is easy enough to use. To estimate a mean from a small sample we must proceed as follows:

1. Find the sample's mean $\bar{X}$ and standard deviation s (e.g. a sample of size 10 has a mean $\bar{X}$ of 2.8 years and a standard deviation s of 0.84 years).

2. Estimate the standard deviation of the parent population with Bessel's correction, then find the standard error of the mean (e.g. $\hat{\sigma} = 0.84 \times \sqrt{\dfrac{10}{9}}$, hence $\dfrac{\hat{\sigma}}{\sqrt{N}} = 0.84 \times \sqrt{\dfrac{10}{9}} \times \dfrac{1}{\sqrt{10}} = \dfrac{0.84}{3} = 0.28$).

3. Decide the required confidence level (e.g. 90%).

4. The number of degrees of freedom is $N-1$ (i.e. 9).

5. Find the number of standard errors corresponding to the allowed chance of error (e.g. this is 100% less our desired 90% confidence, i.e. 10% chance of error. Entering the table of t with 9 degrees of freedom, we find under 10% probability the value 1.833).

6. Hence, if the value in the table is called t, μ is in the interval $\bar{X} \pm t \dfrac{\hat{\sigma}}{\sqrt{N}}$. In

our example, we can say with 90% confidence that μ is in the interval $2.8 \pm 1.833 \times 0.28$, i.e. 2.8 ± 0.513, or between 2.287 and 3.313.

We have looked hard at this problem of estimating the mean because it is central to so much work in management; samples *are* used in personnel records to find average lengths of service, as in production to find an average dimension (i.e. the size to which a machine is set), and so on. The usual procedure is to hope that the sample is representative and that its average may therefore be taken as the overall average. As we have now seen, it is possible both to recognize that this is wrong and to put practical limits to the error. The desire to be more certain leads to meaninglessly wide limits, the desire for usefully narrow limits leads to uncertainty, and a useful compromise is often 95% certainty.

Accuracy of the standard deviation and median

We need less often to find an interval within which the true standard deviation of a population will lie, but similar reasoning may also be used for this. The *standard error of the standard deviation* is $\dfrac{\sigma}{\sqrt{2N}}$, and using the Normal tables for large samples or the *t*-distribution for small samples allows us to quote any desired confidence intervals. For example, if the standard deviation of a sample of size 50 is 0.85, we may say with 95% confidence that

$$\sigma \text{ lies in the range } 0.85 \pm 2\,\frac{0.85}{\sqrt{100}}$$

i.e. within 0.85 ± 0.17, or between 0.68 and 1.02.

The use of the median is growing, for example in studies of salaries and wages, where the median, as we have seen, is often a fairer measure of location than the mean. The *standard error of the median* is $\dfrac{1.43\sigma}{\sqrt{N}}$ and the confidence intervals will therefore be found exactly as for the mean, but will be 1.43 times wider.

Accuracy of a percentage

Before a by-election, a poll of 1000 voters showed 480 in favour of party A and 520 for B with no 'don't knows'. Is it clear that B will win?

Newspapers supporting B would certainly proclaim that party 4 points ahead, but we now know enough about margins of error to be more cautious. A sample of a given size with counted (not measured) contents of two kinds gives a Binomial situation. Even if there are more than two kinds of contents it is easy still to use the Binomial since, considering each kind in turn, the sample contains a certain percentage of this kind and the balance of the other kinds, thus reducing the picture to two kinds again. Incidentally, in elections as in market research or in the work study technique called activity sampling, the sample mix is usually described in percentages of its ingredients rather than as actual numbers.

The mean of the Binomial is Np, the expected number of the ingredient whose proportion in the population is p. The standard deviation is $\sqrt{Npq}$. As before we do not know p, but are trying to estimate it from the sample, with the Normal distribution of sample means coming to our aid. If we wish to work in percentages, we may say that the mean of this distribution is the true percentage of the ingredient we are examining. Using capital letters P and Q for percentages where p and q were proportions, we have P from our sample as an estimate of the true percentage, and seek an interval $P \pm L$ within which the truth will probably lie. Again we need the standard error of the mean of our Normal distribution and the $\sqrt{Npq}$, since it comes from a sampling distribution, is itself the standard error of the mean. It converts, when working in percentages, to $\sqrt{\dfrac{PQ}{N}}$. Two of these on either side of the sample's P give us an interval associated with 95% confidence. In other words, the true percentage is 95% probably within the interval $P \pm 2\sqrt{\dfrac{PQ}{N}}$, while other confidence intervals are found in a similar way.

It has become conventional, at least in work study, to label this 2-standard-errors as L, to dispense with Q for $(100-P)$ and to work with 95% confidence, so that the activity sampling formula is

$$L^2 = \frac{4P(100 - P)}{N}$$

In our illustration party B has $P = 52$ with $N = 100$

whence
$$L^2 = \frac{4 \times 52 \times 48}{1000} = 9.984$$

and
$$L = \pm 3.16$$

So B's true support is 95% probably in the interval $52 \pm 3.16\%$, i.e. between 48.84% and 55.16%. There is even a $2\frac{1}{2}\%$ chance that it will be below 48.84%. Since A's percentage of the sample is all the remaining 48%, its error is also 3.16% and its support in the whole electorate is 95% probably $48 \pm 3.16\%$, i.e. between 44.84 and 51.16% with a $2\frac{1}{2}\%$ chance of over 51.16%. So on this evidence A might win. Many a public opinion poll has seemed to go wrong because of these errors, due purely to the luck of the draw in choosing the sample. The headline B APPARENTLY 4 POINTS AHEAD BUT MIGHT BE 2.32 POINTS BEHIND seems to be out of favour with journalists.

If we want to be reasonably sure that the apparent result is the true one, the only answer is to take a bigger sample. With A 48% and B 52%, for instance, the error must not pass 2% so that B does not fall below A. Inverting the formula, $N = \dfrac{4P(100 - P)}{L^2}$ and with P at 52 (or 48) and L at 2, $N = \dfrac{4 \times 52 \times 48}{4} = 2496$. The 52/48 split calls for another 1496 people to be questioned and then, assuming that the replies still hold the same overall proportion, we may be $97\frac{1}{2}\%$ sure that B will win. If the split changes, the first version of the formula will give the new accuracy. Repeated use of the alternative formula will tell us when we have sampled enough.

With 'don't know's' and other political parties intervening, the same procedures are used to look at each party's support versus all the rest. The activity sampling problem at the start of this chapter may be tackled by taking, for example, 100 observations of the man at pre-determined random moments. What percentage of these observations is spent on the telephone as he claims? What are the consequent 95% confidence limits? Is this conclusive enough? If not, we use the inverted formula to find the number of observations needed, and repeat until a conclusion can be reached.

The size of error depends on the percentage present in the sample; try out the formula with $N = 1000$ and a party with 2% or 98% instead of the 52 or 48 we used above. This will show that quite small samples are enough to convince us that an event is either very rare or very common, though much larger samples are needed to pinpoint the size moderately accurately.

Summary

Above all we note from the standard error formulae $\dfrac{\sigma}{\sqrt{N}}$ (of the mean), $\dfrac{\sigma}{\sqrt{2N}}$ (of the standard deviation) or $\dfrac{1.43\sigma}{\sqrt{N}}$ (of the median) that

> The accuracy given by any sample is proportional to the square root of the sample size.

Thus it takes 4 times the size of sample (at perhaps 4 times the cost) to halve the error, no matter whether we are trying to estimate a mean, a median, a percentage or whatever. This is the fundamental and unavoidable problem in sampling. Note that we make no mention here of the size of the population. The reason is illustrated in the thought that, for example, an electorate 44% in favour of party A offers the same chances of A or not-A specimens when choosing from it, no matter whether the electorate is of 1000 or a million. It is still the 44%, and only that, which counts. Of course, we have to assume that our sample is tiny compared with its population, so that the chances are not really altered as each sample member is selected. In all other respects the population size does not matter.

The aim of this chapter has been to eliminate the idea that a statistic (e.g. a mean) found in a sample may be taken baldly as the right figure for the population concerned. We have replaced this happy but false assurance with two levels of uncertainty; an interval within which the truth may lie, though we cannot say exactly where in it, and then a chance that the truth may not even lie in the stated interval.

This may seem at first to be clambering out of the marshes of error only to fall into the quicksands of ignorance, but in practice we have the basis of better decisions. It may be easier to reach a firm conclusion from a fixed premise, but surely ease is not the only factor in decision-making: there is also the matter of errors. The costs of making a mistake may frequently be clear, but the likelihood of having to pay these costs are often not, especially using the simple approach. Now we are equipped to measure the risk of having to pay for a wrong decision. It is surely better to know that on the available information there is a 5%, or 15% or 80% risk of being wrong. A little calculation is a small premium to pay for the assurance of knowing both sides of a management problem.

X
SIGNIFICANCE TESTING

A firm has two factories. A sample of 10 people was chosen from each to check the response to a new pension scheme. Six of the 10 from A had joined but only 3 from sample B had done so. Thus it seems that plant A is more favourably disposed to the scheme than is B. Is this true?

Chapter IX dealt with one aspect of sampling, in which we sought to estimate population statistics, such as the mean, from sample statistics. We saw that samples may be unrepresentative and may therefore lead to estimates that are too high or too low. The same problem of unrepresentative samples may also arise if they are taken to make comparisons rather than for measurements. Tests of significance are concerned with the accuracy of comparisons.

The example above illustrates the point. There are two samples, one from each population. A appears to like the new scheme more than B does (or at least has a higher proportion of joiners), but this results from the evidence of samples of only 10. A test of significance has to take the sample size into account when looking at the apparent difference, and seeks to test whether the difference is likely to be genuine (i.e. significant) or could easily be accounted for just by the luck of the draw in choosing the samples.

An apparent difference may also arise where a single sample is being compared with a known standard, as when trying out new drugs in medicine or in testing new manufacturing processes.

A certain type of integrated circuit is made on an automatic machine on which a reject rate of 50% of the finished circuits is normal. A new process, laboriously tried out in prototype form, produces 20 of the circuits of which 16 work perfectly. Should an expensive machine be built to use the new process?

In this example the reject rate appears to have dropped from 50% to 20%, but we need to be very sure of ourselves before spending a large amount on the new machine. The question normally asked in these circumstances is 'How likely is it that a 20% reject rate will be maintained?' However, this is really unanswerable, at least in measured terms. We can rephrase the question in more statistical language: 'How likely is it that a machine no better than the present one could make 16 good products in a sample of 20?' This helps us in two ways. We have a standard (that of the present machine) against which to judge the new process, and we can use this standard in probability calculations to reach a decision.

The null hypothesis
When checking the chance of an apparent difference being genuine (which is significance testing), the null hypothesis is the standard from which we measure

that chance. In our second example we guess that the new process is no better than the old one, and then (as we shall see) force the new one to prove itself better if it can. This cautious approach at least prevents us from spending money on dubious novelties, even if it sometimes hinders us from acting quickly and thereby benefiting. It has proved safest in the long run. In our first example there is no existing standard of comparison between A and B so we have to produce one. We might, for example, take either of the samples as the standard for its population, then see whether the other sample is significantly different, but the cautious way is to say that there is no difference between A's and B's view of the pension scheme and that the apparent difference is due entirely to sampling. Then we check whether our invented assertion is realistic.

The method of significance testing

Both our examples adopt the standard of 'no difference', which accounts for the rather Victorian name of the null hypothesis. What we are doing is accusing the sample(s) of being unrepresentative, of seeming to show a difference where none exists in the parent populations. Then, on the assumption of no difference, we somehow calculate the chance of selecting the kind of samples that have turned up. If there is a reasonably high chance of eliciting the samples we actually chose, this would mean that the observed differences are not very surprising, even with no true differences in the populations. On the other hand, if the chance of the difference we found is very small, we are forced to doubt our basic assumption of no difference in the populations. The best way of seeing what this means is to work through our two examples. If the new process really has a 50% reject rate, what is the chance of getting only 4 rejects in a sample of 20? This is a Binomial situation with $N = 20$ and $p = 0.5$, so

$$Pr(4) = {}^{20}C_4 \left(\tfrac{1}{2}\right)^4 \left(\tfrac{1}{2}\right)^{16}$$
$$= {}^{20}C_4 \left(\tfrac{1}{2}\right)^{20} = \frac{4845}{1048576} = 0.004621$$

giving a 0.46% chance of getting 4 rejects out of 20 on the assumption of a 50% overall reject rate. This is not a very likely event, yet we have seen it happen. It follows that our assumption of the 50% reject rate was very probably wrong. Indeed, we may have 99.54% confidence (i.e. 100–0.46%) that the new process is better than the old one. Do we then invest in the new machine at once? Here we must leave statistics and talk management. What does the new machine cost? What is the continuing cost of our present 50% reject rate? What will be the life of the new machine? When all these and other questions have been answered, what is the chance that our decision to go ahead may be wrong, making us waste our money?

The answer to this last question seems to be 0.46%, as far as our one sample of 20 can tell us. However, management is always ultra-cautious about making changes that cost money, and may insist that the new process prove itself more thoroughly even than this. To this end we might have asked what are the chances, if the new process has a true reject rate of 50%, of getting a sample at least as extreme as the one we have? In statistical terms this means finding the probability of 4 *or less* rejects in our sample of 20:

$$\text{Pr (4 rejects)} = 4845/1048576$$

$$\text{Pr (3 rejects)} = 1140/1048576$$

$$\text{Pr (2 rejects)} = 190/1048576$$

$$\text{Pr (1 reject)} = 20/1048576$$

$$\text{Pr (0 rejects)} = 1/1048576$$

hence $$\text{Pr (4 rejects or less)} = (4845 + 1140 + 190 + 20 + 1)/1048576$$

$$= 6196/1048576 = 0.0059 \text{ or } 0.59\%$$

This approach of looking for the difference *or worse* increases the calculated chances and makes the new process fight that much harder to try to establish its superiority. Seen in this light, the risk of being wrong if we accept the new procedure is just over $\frac{1}{2}\%$, and the manager may make his decision on the basis of this knowledge. If he considers the $\frac{1}{2}\%$ a small risk he will go ahead; otherwise he will stick to his present method or perhaps order further trials so that the larger sample may be even more conclusive.

The pension scheme example gave A 6 out of 10 members and B only 3 out of 10. We wish to start from the proposition (the null hypothesis) that there is no difference between the populations A and B. (Note: this does not mean no difference between the samples, which are visibly different.) The fairest method is to pool the samples, which gives an overall proportion of 9 out of 20, or 45%. This, we say, is the proportion in the identical populations from which both samples come. We again have a Binomial situation, with $p = 0.45$, so that we expect $4\frac{1}{2}$ members in each sample of 10. We must now calculate the chance of getting 6 in one and 3 in the other, or something even more extreme. In other words we need, with $p = 0.45$,

Pr (6 or more *and* 3 or less), which is

Pr (6 or more out of 10) $\times$ Pr (3 or less out of 10)

Without showing the calculations,

Pr (6 or 7 or 8 or 9 or 10) $= 0.261562$

and   Pr (0 or 1 or 2 or 3) $= 0.266038$

So the probability we seek is 0.069585, i.e. 6.96% or say 7%. In words, if the population indicated by the combined samples is the true one and both A and B belong to it, then the chance of getting two random samples at least as different as those we had is 7%. The odds are against it but dare we conclude that these samples would not arise in our assumed circumstances? On the other hand, dare we say definitely that the observed differences were due only to luck in picking the samples? (The first of these conclusions says that our assumption of no difference is wrong, the second that it is right.) Once again we must leave statistics and think management. By quantifying the risks of wrong decisions we now see that, on the evidence we have, there is a 7% chance that A and B feel alike about the scheme, and there is a 93% chance that they feel differently about it. We have not considered the kind of decision needed, but whatever it is these figures give the chances of being wrong. My opinion is that there is not enough certainty either way for any safe conclusion to be reached. In other words the verdict is 'Not Proven' and more evidence from larger samples is needed before we may be sufficiently sure.

We can now review what tests of significance are about.

1. A sample appears to give a result different from an accepted standard or from another sample.

2. Before we can accept the apparent difference at its face value, we have to check whether it might have come from unrepresentative sampling. Since recognizing that a difference is true may well mean that we have to make changes and spend money, we insist at first that the alleged difference does not reflect reality, i.e. we say that there are no differences between the populations concerned.

3. On the basis of this assertion we work out the chance of choosing samples at least as extreme as those we have. The calculations invariably take the sample sizes into account.

4. If the samples we selected could easily occur by chance, then the apparent difference might well be consistent with no underlying difference. However, if our samples were unlikely or very unlikely, it is correspondingly probable that they are not consistent with our theory of no underlying difference. Since the samples are real enough it is the theory that might then have to be abandoned.

5. The probability that we calculated at 3 above gives the chance of being wrong if we assert that there is no true difference. The levels of probability at which we are prepared to make or deny this assertion depend on the cost of being wrong, and are outside the realm of statistics. However, as a rule of thumb in most cases, a probability of below 5% is usually enough to let us admit that the apparent difference is probably genuine; below 1% and we usually have no hesitation that there is a real difference. If my life were at risk I would like more assurance even than this, but most management risks do not involve such extreme penalties for wrong decisions and lesser assurance levels will do.

6. Come what may, the test can never prove absolutely that the null hypothesis is or is not true. Since it started with only a sample, the test can end only with a probability. We insist on a low risk of error before we reject a null hypothesis and accept the genuineness of an apparent difference. We are therefore biased in favour of the null hypothesis and resist the need for change until it is proved beyond reasonable doubt. Unless we can come down overwhelmingly against the 'no difference' hypothesis, our verdict upon it is Not Proven.

There are many kinds of difference that may arise; does an average seem to change, or a spread, or an overall fit, or a proportion, etc. There is a correspondingly wealth of different tests of significance, and the art of using them consists mainly of recognizing the situation in order to pick the simplest test that will meet it. We have so far carried out tests from first principles, having spotted that the situations were Binomial and using this distribution to calculate the probability of the samples being consistent with the null hypothesis. However most formal tests do not call for first principles, but only on special distribution patterns that have been proved by eminent statisticians to lead quickly to the required probability at stage 3 above. The tests are easy enough to use once we have learned how, but it is impossible while using them to see just what we are doing. My suggestion is therefore that, until long practice has made matters clear, continual reference is made to the 6 points above, particularly numbers 4 and 5, once the test has been carried out and the right conclusion is sought from the results. All too many students learn to carry through the calculations expertly and then fail to see the conclusion that is required.

We shall now look at a few formal tests of significance.

The variance ratio test or F-test

This test compares the standard deviations (or rather their squares the variances) of two samples, to see whether their parent populations might have the same variance. We commence with it because it is simple to carry out, and it is a necessary preliminary to the t-test which is discussed next.

The procedure is as follows:

1. There are two samples, of which the sizes are N_1 and N_2.

2. We calculate their variances; they are respectively V_1 and V_2.

3. If the variances are equal we have no evidence whatever against the underlying population variances being identical. Normally V_1 and V_2 are different. Divide the bigger one by the smaller; thus if $V_1 > V_2$ calculate V_1/V_2.

4. The numbers of degrees of freedom (DoF) are respectively $(N_1 - 1)$ and $(N_2 - 1)$.

5. We now enter the table in Appendix F (page 255). The column to use has $(N_1 - 1)$ degrees of freedom; the row to use has $(N_2 - 1)$ degrees of freedom. This assumes $V_1 > V_2$; if it is the other way round we switch the row and column. If the exact number of degrees of freedom is not in the table, we must interpolate as necessary (i.e. split the difference in the proportion called for).

6. The row and column meet at a set of four numbers. Reading downwards these correspond to 10%, 5%, 1% and 0.1% probability. Where does the calculated ratio V_1/V_2 fit among them? From its position we judge the probability %.

7. The probability found from the table is the chance of random samples giving a V_1/V_2 ratio at least as remote from 1 as it is, if the underlying

variances are equal. On it we base our decision to accept that the population variances are, or are not, genuinely different from one another.

This test is far easier to do than to describe. For instance:

The numbers of breakdowns per week of a machine were recorded before and after a major overhaul. Can the overhaul be said to have made it run more reliably?

Week	1	2	3	4	5	6	Overhaul	1	2	3	4	5
Breakdowns	4	5	8	8	6	6		3	5	6	6	3

The question is not whether the average has genuinely improved (we shall look at this next), but whether the pattern is less variable, i.e. whether the standard deviation is genuinely lower.

Calculating the variances, $V_{before} = 2.1389$

$$V_{after} = 1.84$$

On the face of it, there seems to be some improvement. $V_b/V_a = 2.1389/1.84 = 1.1624$, on 5 and 4 degrees of freedom. Entering Appendix F in column 5 DoF and row 4 DoF, we have the figures:

10%	4.05
5%	6.26
1%	15.52
0.1%	51.71

and we see that our ratio of 1.1624 is less than the smallest number in this group. Since the percentages fall as the numbers rise (because it is less likely that large differences will arise just through sampling), we realize that our probability must be well above 10%.

So it is very easy to choose samples in which the variances differ at least as much as ours have done, even if the overhaul has not affected the variability of the breakdowns. It would thus be most unwise to rule out 'no change in variability'. The verdict is Not Proven, but we cannot reject 'no change' and accept that the population variances before and after may be the same. Of course we may be wrong in doing so. The difference may be genuine but the evidence for this is not strong enough. The null hypothesis of No Genuine Difference cannot be condemned unless found Guilty through being sufficiently unlikely (i.e. a low probability figure). Not Proven does not mean Innocent, but neither is it strong enough to mean Guilty.

The *t*-test

This test compares the means of two samples to see whether the underlying populations might have the same mean. The idea is to find the difference between the means of the two samples, then to see how many of its own standard errors this difference includes. Looking up this number of standard errors in the tables will tell us the proportion of the distribution that is further out even than that. This is the probability we seek, that of getting sample means at least as divergent as those we have, on the assumption that the underlying means are the same.

Thus
$$t = \frac{\text{difference between means}}{\text{standard error of that difference}}$$

Where the two samples are of the same size N, this comes down to

$$t = \frac{\bar{X} - \bar{Y}}{\sigma/\sqrt{N}}$$

In the most unlikely event that we know σ, the true standard deviation of the difference, the calculated t will have a Normal distribution. There is a more complicated formula, again involving σ, if the samples are of different sizes. Such knowledge of σ is so rare that we may forget about it. In the usual cases;

1. We do not know whether both samples have the same standard deviation or variance; unless they do we are in trouble trying to find the standard error of the difference.

2. Even if they do, we do not know what it is and must estimate it from the samples themselves, with Bessel's correction and the t-distribution of Appendix E instead of the Normal distribution.

To answer point 1, we must always precede a t-test with an F-test, for if the variances of the two populations are significantly different the t-test will not work. However, if an F-test shows that the two samples might come from populations with the same variance we may use this fact and, for the t-test, pool the samples to get the best possible estimate of that variance. To save working through from the beginning each time, there are two formulae which do all this and give t directly from the sample data:

(a) *With equal-sized samples*

The size of each sample is N, the data items are $X_1, X_2 \ldots X_N$ and $Y_1, Y_2 \ldots Y_N$ for the two samples, and the means are X and Y.

$$t = \frac{\bar{X} - \bar{Y}}{\sqrt{\dfrac{\sigma_X^2 + \sigma_Y^2}{N - 1}}} \qquad \text{on } (2N - 2) \text{ degrees of freedom.}$$

The numerator may be positive or negative but it is the size of the difference, regardless of sign, that matters.

(b) *With samples of different sizes*

The samples sizes are N_X and N_Y, the other labels being as before.

$$t = \frac{\bar{X} - \bar{Y}}{\sqrt{\left(\dfrac{N_X \sigma_X^2 + N_Y \sigma_Y^2}{N_X + N_Y - 2}\right)\left(\dfrac{N_X + N_Y}{N_X N_Y}\right)}} \qquad \begin{array}{l}\text{on } (N_X + N_Y - 2) \\ \text{degrees of freedom.}\end{array}$$

Again it is the size, not the sign, that matters.

Fearsome as these formulae may look, they involve nothing harder than squaring and adding. Let us try the machine overhaul problem, above, to see whether the average weekly number of breakdowns has changed. The F-test has already shown that we may assume a common variance. The means of $6\frac{1}{6}$ and $4\frac{3}{5}$ certainly look different.

Working with the second and more complicated formula for t, we have:

X	Y	X^2	Y^2
4	3	16	9
5	5	25	25
8	6	64	36
8	6	64	36
6	3	36	9
6		36	
37	23	241	115

$$N_X = 6 \qquad N_Y = 5 \qquad \uparrow \qquad \uparrow$$
$$\bar{X} = 6.1667 \qquad \bar{Y} = 4.6 \qquad \sum X^2 \qquad \sum Y^2$$
$$\sigma_X^2 = 2.1389 \qquad \sigma_Y^2 = 1.84$$

$$t = \frac{\bar{X} - \bar{Y}}{\sqrt{\left(\dfrac{N_X \sigma_X^2 + N_Y \sigma_Y^2}{N_X + N_Y - 2}\right)\left(\dfrac{N_X + N_Y}{N_X N_Y}\right)}}$$

$$= \frac{6.1667 - 4.6}{\sqrt{\left(\dfrac{(6 \times 2.1389) + (5 \times 1.84)}{6 + 5 - 2}\right)\left(\dfrac{6 + 5}{6 \times 5}\right)}}$$

$$= \frac{1.5667}{\sqrt{\dfrac{22.033}{9} \times \dfrac{11}{30}}} = \frac{1.5667}{\sqrt{0.8977}} = \frac{1.5667}{0.9475} = 1.6535$$

on $(6 + 5 - 2) = 9$ degrees of freedom.

Entering the table of the t-distribution at Appendix E under 9 degrees of freedom, we find 1.100 at 30% and 1.833 at 10%. Clearly 1.6535 corresponds to about 20% so that, even if the overhaul had made no difference to the average weekly number of breakdowns (which is our null hypothesis), 6 and 5 experimental weeks have a substantial chance of producing differences at least as large as the one we found. Obviously we dare not attach any importance to the apparent improvement; it could so easily be due to chance.

While our decision must be 'no change', we could be wrong. There is a possibility that the underlying pattern of breakdowns is genuinely different, but so far we have too little evidence. Our knowledge even of the pre-overhaul pattern is gleaned from only 6 weeks' observations and when working with such tiny samples it should not be surprising if a good test of significance refuses to give a clear indication unless the samples show a really large apparent difference.

Let us try another example.

Random samples of 20 men and 20 women from the same workforce had the numbers of days absent from work during the past year shown in Table 10.1. It appears that the average for women may be higher than that for men. Is this true?

Table 10.1

Men	7	8	7	3	4	6½	2	8	0	5	3	2	
Women	6	13	11	5	20	8	3	11	9	11	12	13	

Men	6	18	1	0	3	5	7	2	4.875	Average
Women	7	11	13	6	8	10	10	7	9.700	Average

First comes the F-test.

$$\frac{\text{Variance}}{\text{Men}} = \frac{\sum X^2}{N} - \left(\frac{\sum X^2}{N}\right) = \frac{783.25}{20} - 4.875^2 = 15.397$$

$$\frac{\text{Variance}}{\text{Women}} = \frac{\sum Y^2}{N} - \left(\frac{\sum Y}{N}\right)^2 = \frac{2148}{20} - 9.7^2 = 13.31$$

So the pattern for men looks slightly more erratic. But can we be sure that it is so?

$$\frac{V_M}{V_W} = \frac{15.397}{13.31} = 1.157 \text{ on 19 and 19 degrees of freedom}$$

Our table in Appendix F gives:

		16 DoF	20 DoF
	10%	1.93	1.89
16	5%	2.33	2.28
DoF	1%	3.37	3.25
	0.1%	5.19	4.99
	10%	1.83	1.79
20	5%	2.18	2.12
DoF	1%	3.05	2.94
	0.1%	4.70	4.29

Interpolating for 19 and 19 degrees of freedom obviously shows a probability well above 10%. With such a high chance of getting this difference between samples if the populations have identical variances, we may safely assume that the underlying variances are the same and proceed to the t-test.

Note that the t-test uses much of the same calculated data as the F-test which preceded it.

$$t = \frac{\bar{X} - \bar{Y}}{\sqrt{\dfrac{\sigma_X^2 + \sigma_Y^2}{N-1}}} = \frac{4.875 - 9.7}{\sqrt{\dfrac{15.397 + 13.31}{20}}} = \frac{-4.825}{\sqrt{1.435}}$$

$$= \frac{-4.825}{1.198} = -4.027 \text{ on 38 degrees of freedom}$$

The negative sign does not matter. Entering the t-table for 38 degrees of freedom, i.e. using 30 and infinite DoF and interpolating, we find

DoF	1%	0.1%
30	2.750	3.646
∞	2.576	3.291

Our t of 4.027 clearly leads to a probability of less than 0.1%; at this level precision is not important. We may say we have a 0.1% chance of our samples showing a difference at least as great as the one we found, even if men and women truly have the same average absence levels. Correspondingly, there is a 99.9% chance of having a smaller difference; ours is more impressive than 99.9% of those that would appear by chance. Thus if we wish to declare that one sex is absent more than the other, there is (on the available evidence) a 99.9% chance that we shall be right and a 0.1% chance (the same figure that the table gave us) of being wrong. Should we make this declaration? After all, the samples were only 20 of each sex.

The odds are certainly with us if we do. However, we must still ask whether they are strongly enough in our favour. As always, the answer is non-statistical, being concerned with the cost of a wrong decision. If as a result of the declaration we decide to employ one sex and not the other the implications are many and important. If we are wrong the cost could be enormous. On the other hand, if we decide that the evidence is not strong enough to show that there is a real difference between the sexes, we carry on as before and the cost of being wrong in this case is merely something we are already accustomed to paying. This is why the verdict Not Proven is so prevalent and why it takes strong evidence to make us accept that a difference in samples reflects a true underlying difference.

One tail or two?

In our example the absence rate for women was about double that for men. A layman might say that such a difference is clearly overwhelming evidence, at least that women are absent more than men if not that the difference is a factor of 2.

For many purposes we do not know before a test whether the difference might be one way or the other. For instance, many an overhaul has been known to make a machine or car run worse rather than better. Our table of the t-distribution takes this into account by being two-tailed. The 0.1% probability we found represents 0.05% of the distribution in each tail and allows for samples to show men absent more than women, as well as women absent more than men, to the extent we found. If we have reason to believe that the change, if any, can be only in one direction, we are interested in only one tail of the distribution. If we rule out the possibility of men's absence rate overall being higher than women's, we shall no longer ask whether there is a difference between the sexes, which could be either way, but whether women are absent more than men, which is one-way and concerns only one tail of the distribution. The probability of being wrong if we answer in the affirmative is 0.05% (or even less in this case).

Again, the arguments for and against declaring a difference are non-statistical, as above. At 0.05% we are almost sure to accept a difference as genuine; the layman's view is amply confirmed. Nevertheless, the statistical answer should not be enough for the manager. All it does is tell him the exact chance of being wrong, whichever decision he takes. It is for him then to weigh chances and costs together when deciding.

The t-test is also used to check the validity of a correlation coefficient. This is described in Chapter 11.

The x^2-test

χ is a Greek letter often anglicized as chi. The closest English approximation to its correct pronounciation is kye, and so we have the kye-squared test.

This is a test of the overall fit of one set of data with another. The null hypothesis is that there is no difference between the two populations from which the data came, i.e. that the fit ought to be perfect apart from sampling errors in collecting the data. If the observed differences between the sets can be accounted for by sampling errors the probability at the end will be reasonably high, while a low probability points to the likelihood of a genuinely poor fit.

Each item of one set of data may or may not coincide with the corresponding item in the other set. The difference, squared to get rid of any negative signs, contributes to an overall total difference formula, but since a difference of 2 when the size should be about 3 is in a very different class of fit from a difference of 2 when the size should be about 300, we standardize by dividing the squared difference by the expected size at that point. Then all these standardized differences are totalled to get a measure of the overall divergences.

We are almost always comparing an observed set of data with an expected set. Abbreviating these to O and E respectively, we calculate χ^2 from the formula

$$\chi^2 = \sum \frac{(O - E)^2}{E}$$

which matches the wording of the previous paragraph. Then we look up the value of χ^2 in the body of the tables at Appendix G (page 258) to get the probability figure for the test. This χ^2 distribution is another involving degrees of freedom; the relevant number of DoF to use is one less than the number of pairs contributing to the total χ^2. However, when population parameters such as the mean are also to be estimated from the same data, one more DoF is lost for each parameter estimated. We shall soon have an example of this.

The most frequent applications of the χ^2-test are:

1. When fitting the best line or curve to some data, as a check to see how good the fit is,
2. Where data comes as a table with several components, to see whether the different components are consistent with one another.

The fit of a line to data

In Chapter VIII we used Normal probability paper in Figure 8.12 to see whether certain salary data fitted the Normal pattern, and concluded by eye that the straight line was a poor fit. Let us now check this with the χ^2-test to illustrate how it works.

In Table 10.2 the actual data is, of course, observed and the Normal distribution that we try to fit, shown in the straight line in Figure 8.12 (page 92), provides the theoretical expected set of data read off the probability paper.

Table 10.2

Salary up to £	15	20	25	30	35	40
Observed people	148	204	233	287	327	500
Observed %	4.44	6.12	6.98	8.60	9.80	14.98
Expected %	1.42	2.90	5.50	9.50	15.20	24

Salary up to £	45	50	60	70	80	100
Observed people	698	921	1403	2384	2990	3337
Observed %	20.92	27.60	42.04	71.44	89.60	100
Expected %	33.20	44.50	67.50	85.20	94.90	99.70

$$\chi^2 = \sum \frac{(O - E)^2}{E}$$

$$= \frac{(4.44 - 1.42)^2}{1.42} + \frac{(6.12 - 2.9)^2}{2.9} + \frac{(6.98 - 5.5)^2}{5.5} + \frac{(8.60 - 9.5)^2}{9.5}$$

$$+ \frac{(9.80 - 15.2)^2}{15.2} + \frac{(14.98 - 24)^2}{24} + \frac{(20.92 - 33.2)^2}{33.2} + \frac{(17.60 - 44.5)^2}{44.5}$$

$$+ \frac{(42.04 - 67.5)^2}{67.5} + \frac{(71.44 - 85.2)^2}{85.2} + \frac{(89.60 - 94.9)^2}{94.9} + \frac{(100 - 99.7)^2}{99.7}$$

$$= 6.42 + 3.58 + 0.40 + 0.09 + 1.92 + 3.39 + 4.54 + 6.42 + 9.60$$
$$+ 2.22 + 0.30 + 0.00$$

$$= 38.88 \text{ on } (12 - 1) = 9 \text{ degrees of freedom}$$

There are 9 degrees of freedom because there are 12 pairs contributing to the χ^2 calculation; then 2 degrees are lost beeause the data was used twice to estimate the mean and standard deviation of the proposed Normal.

Under 9 degrees of freedom our table shows 21.67 for 1% and 27.88 for 0.1% probability. Our calculated 38.88 must be less than 0.1% likely to arise by chance so we are almost certain that there really is a difference between our population and the Normal pattern we tried to impose on it. In short, the fit is terrible and there is hardly any chance of our being wrong if we say so. What is more, the cost of being wrong may well be low in this case, so statistician and manager may readily agree. Unfortunately, few real problems are as clear-cut as this one.

Very often one tries to fit a line or curve to a set of pairs of data, e.g. for forecasting. The closeness of fit of this curve to the data may be tested with χ^2 as shown in Chapter XII, which discusses the line-fitting techniques and looks at ways of verifying a really close fit.

The self-consistency of a table of data

A chief inspector suspected that his people were not working to the same standards. He asked two of them to classify work from the same batch, but this was needed so urgently that they could not both inspect the same items. Table 10.3 shows the results of the test. Were the standards different?

Table 10.3

	Good	Acceptable	Poor
Inspector A	140	100	15
Inspector B	140	50	20

This sort of problem is frequently encountered and such tables, with counts of classifications, are often called *contingency tables*. The question is whether the proportions among the various classifications, which appear to be different, could come from the same population, i.e. are consistent with one another subject to sampling errors. In this case the particular question is whether the proportions of good: acceptable: poor for A are compatible with those for B. Could they have been drawn from the same population?

We cannot ask directly how well 140:100:15 fits with 140:50:20 since the totals are not the same. We need a similarly sized table of expected values with which to compare the entire table, but we have no theoretical basis on which to construct it. There is no theoretical frequency distribution or anything else of the kind: we have only the data itself. To be as fair as possible we make the assumption that both A and B might have used the same proportions when dividing their totals of 255 and 210 items. In this way we use the whole of the data in constructing the table of expected values. The totals in the Observed table must be retained, of course, as in Table 10.4. Thus the 280 good items, the

Table 10.4

	Good	Acceptable	Poor	Totals
A	140	100	15	255
B	140	50	20	210
Totals	280	150	35	465

150 acceptable and the 35 poor should each have been divided among A and B in the proportion 255:210, i.e. A should have $\frac{255}{465}$ of each classification while B should have the remaining $\frac{210}{465}$ of each group. This gives an Expected table as Table 10.5 which leads on to Table 10.6, with the totals as before.

Table 10.5

	Good	Acceptable	Poor
A	$\dfrac{255}{465} \times 280$	$\dfrac{255}{465} \times 150$	$\dfrac{255}{465} \times 35$
B	$\dfrac{210}{465} \times 280$	$\dfrac{210}{465} \times 150$	$\dfrac{210}{465} \times 35$

Table 10.6

	Good	Acceptable	Poor	Totals
A	153.55	82.26	19.19	255
B	126.45	67.74	15.81	210
Totals	280	150	35	465

Some students will prefer to argue through from the first principles each time, as we have done. Others will prefer a formula to tell them how to find the expected values. They will notice that each position is filled by

$$\frac{\text{row total} \times \text{column total}}{\text{grand total}}$$

Our hypothesis, then, is that the difference between the observed and expected figures is due purely to the luck of the draw in providing A and B with the items they received for inspection, their standards being identical. χ^2 is calculated item by item for all 6:

$$\chi^2 = \sum \frac{(O - E)^2}{E}$$

$$= \frac{13.55^2}{153.55} + \frac{17.74^2}{82.26} + \frac{4.19^2}{19.19} + \frac{13.55^2}{126.45} + \frac{17.74^2}{67.64} + \frac{4.19^2}{15.81}$$

$$= 1.196 + 3.826 + 0.915 + 1.452 + 4.653 + 1.110 = 13.152$$

With a table ($M \times N$) in size, the number of degrees of freedom is $(M - 1) \times (N - 1)$. Our table is 2×3 or 3×2, so we have 1×2 or 2 degrees of freedom. Entering our χ^2 table we find a probability of about 1%. As always, this is the chance of being wrong if we reject the null hypothesis and declare that the observed difference is due not to chance but to a real difference in A's and B's standards.

This 1% looks like a very small chance of being wrong, but before we accept the risk let us leave the statistics and look at the cost of being wrong if we were to do so. Conceivably the action taken in such a situation would involve some training or re-training of the inspectors. Since this never does any harm and the cost is only that of the time, the risk might well be accepted and the standards declared different. If instead the action meant firing some inspectors, this would be a different matter and further examination should be made. Common-sense must come first and the statistics afterwards.

This example has brought out all but one of the principles used in tackling contingency tables with the χ^2 test. The main points to remember so far are:

1. Each entry in the Expected table is

$$\frac{\text{row total} \times \text{column total}}{\text{grand total}}$$

2. The number of degrees of freedom is $(M - 1) \times (N - 1)$ for a table of size $M \times N$. Of course it does not matter which of M or N is the number of rows and which is the number of columns.

The principle not yet used arises when dealing with a 2 × 2 table. If the numbers involved are small, the percentage jump in the calculated χ^2 would be considerable if a mere single item were in the other classification instead of its own. This is something that could easily happen when sampling. The χ^2 distribution is a continuous one and jumps like these can give widely different answers. To smooth things out and avoid some of this source of potential error we use what is called *Yates's correction for continuity*. In conditions where a contingency table is 2 × 2 and any cell is smaller than 10 in size, we reduce by 0.5 each observed frequency that is greater than the corresponding expected one and increase by 0.5 each observed frequency that is less than its expected one. Thus each $(O - E)$ difference is reduced by 0.5 and the calculated χ^2 is smaller than it would otherwise have been. Here is an example.

Forty-four workpeople were asked their opinion of the works canteen. The results were:

	Men	Women	Totals
Like	21	10	31
Dislike	4	9	13
Totals	25	19	44

Are the men really more favourably disposed to it than are the women? The Expected table is

$\dfrac{31 \times 25}{44}$	$\dfrac{31 \times 19}{44}$
$\dfrac{13 \times 25}{44}$	$\dfrac{13 \times 19}{44}$

or

17.61	13.39
7.39	5.61

Modifying the Observed table with Yates's correction gives us, with unchanged totals:

20.5	10.5
4.5	8.5

Then

$$\chi^2 = \frac{(20.5 - 17.61)^2}{17.61} + \frac{(10.5 - 13.39)^2}{13.39} + \frac{(4.5 - 7.39)^2}{7.39} + \frac{(8.5 - 5.61)^2}{5.61}$$

$$= 0.47 + 0.62 + 1.13 + 1.49$$

$$= 3.71$$

On 1 DoF this gives a probability of between 5% and 10%, perhaps about 6%. This is probably not conclusive, although the odds are that the apparent effect really is there. A larger sample is needed before anything should be done.

Other tests of significance

Significance tests are often considered in two classes. The *parametric* tests are based on the assumption that the statistic being tested has some named underlying pattern like the Normal or *F*- or *t*-distributions. The *non-parametric* tests, which include χ^2, are those where no such assumption is made. We have looked at the underlying reasoning for the parametric tests we mentioned, but it is far beyond the scope of this book to explain the non-parametrics. Nevertheless, they are extremely easy to carry out; a few manipulations and a glance at a special table gives us the required probability. Many of these tests are very powerful, too, bringing in clear and correct decisions where other tests give an unsatisfying Not Proven. It is not surprising that the number and use of non-parametric tests increase almost daily.

One major test that must be mentioned is the *analysis of variance*. All the tests we have so far tried compared two things at a time, but when a mass experiment is going on involving, for example, several machines each making a range of products or several people each doing a variety of jobs, the number of possible pair-comparisons may be enormous. If all these pairs were tested one at a time, each test would end with a probability and there might well be several of 5% or 1% or even less, that might be deemed conclusive. However, for every hundred such tests we would expect five probabilities of 5% and one of 1% to arise on average, just by chance. Their presence thus cannot be taken as something unlikely, leading to probably valid decisions. Instead a single overall test is needed, covering the whole area at once. This is what analysis of variance does in looking for significantly different means.

Taking the machines/products example, any differences between machines could be eliminated by using, instead of individual results, the average over all machines in part of the calculation, regarding each product as made on the average machine. Differences between products could similarly be eliminated by using the average over all products and so on. Then a routine of adding squares is followed which in effect lets us break down the overall variance of all results into parts, one caused by differences between products, another caused by differences between machines, and so forth. Finally there is a part which cannot be accounted for by any of the factors already considered. This is the residual, the unexplained part of the overall variance. *F*-tests check whether any particular explained part of the total is significantly greater than the residual. If so then the variation among the means in that part may be significantly large. Suppose that the variance due to the machines is significantly greater than the residual, then the differences between machine means may be significant.

This is the briefest of simplified outlines of this method. The calculations involved become extremely tedious without a computer, but the point to remember is that an overall test is needed because ordinary t-tests are inadequate when large numbers of them are called for in the same problem.

The computer in significance testing

There are probably hundreds of different tests of significance, of which some dozens are so widely used that they may be considered standard tests. Every worthwhile computer, including very small ones, has statistical packages which include many of these tests. Usually they proceed straight to the answer, performing the analysis of variance or giving the calculated value of F, t, χ^2, etc., the number of degrees of freedom and, with larger machines, the probability. Sometimes only the probability emerges, all intermediate stages being suppressed. The tests are very rapidly performed, which means that, particularly where a multi-access computer terminal is available, there is no excuse for taking numerical impressions at their face value, especially if they are based on samples.

XI
CORRELATION

In dealing with data we have seen that the mean and the standard deviation together summarize the behaviour of the variable being studied. For example, in researching the cosmetics market we might find the age pattern of women who buy cosmetics, with the mean and standard deviation of their ages. At the same time we might find separately the pattern, mean and standard deviation of the women's annual expenditures on cosmetics. But it is surely much more useful to look for a relationship between a woman's age and her yearly spending on cosmetics than to treat the two variables separately. If some association can be found then one might reach management decisions, for example, to concentrate advertising on the age-group which already spends heavily, or to do the opposite and try to build a poor market into a better one.

Alternatively, we might consider absenteeism as a factor in lost production. If we could somehow specify a relationship to something else which is predictable, we might be able to predict the absenteeism before it occurs and hence plan our production more realistically. There may be many factors which affect absenteeism. A seasonal or other cyclic effect, for example, relates absenteeism to the date and may give a first approximation to its expected level. The weather may also signify weather has obvious connections with the date, but in Britain it may be good or bad almost regardless of the date. At all events, weather is difficult to measure as one single number but there might be some aspect of it, such as the temperature, which is predominant. Thus we might try and look for an association between absenteeism and temperature.

Table 11.1 gives a certain firm's absenteeism figures for 1971, together with the maximum daily temperature. The separate means and standard deviations are:

	Mean	Standard deviation
Temperature	$\bar{T} = 14.72$	$\sigma_t = 5.96$
Absenteeism	$\bar{A} = 3.72$	$\sigma_a = 1.31$

These figures may be interesting but do not offer us much assistance. We could obtain a better view of the situation by preserving the links between the absenteeism/temperature pairs and plotting each pair as a point on a graph called a *scatter diagram*, which displays one variable against the other. Figure 11.1 is one such scatter diagram and shows that higher absenteeism tends to

Table 11.1

		TEMP °C	ABS %			TEMP °C	ABS %			TEMP °C	ABS %			TEMP °C	ABS %
JANUARY				**MARCH**				**JUNE**				**OCTOBER**			
	1	4.3	5.8	MON	29	11.8	5.1	MON	28	18.6	4.0	MON	11	19.3	4.0
				TUE	30	14.3	3.8	TUE	29	18.0	3.1	TUE	12	19.1	3.2
				WED	31	10.4	3.0	WED	30	21.2	2.6	WED	13	10.2	3.9
MON	4	1.7	3.6	**APRIL**				**JULY**				THUR	14	12.0	3.0
TUE	5	0.5	4.9	THUR	1	7.8	2.2	THUR	1	23.0	2.1	FRI	15	12.0	4.1
WED	6	6.0	3.1	FRI	2	11.9	2.9	FRI	2	24.9	3.1				
THUR	7	11.0	2.8									MON	18	18.7	5.0
FRI	8	12.0	3.0	MON	5	9.0	5.0	MON	5	22.7	6.0	TUE	19	17.3	3.9
				TUE	6	9.9	3.9	TUE	6	23.7	4.1	WED	20	14.6	3.2
MON	11	6.5	7.0	WED	7	10.2	2.6	WED	7	24.2	3.6	THUR	21	18.1	2.8
TUE	12	10.1	5.5	THUR	8	9.8	3.8	THUR	8	28.6	2.6	FRI	22	21.1	3.0
WED	13	9.2	5.6	FRI	9	(HOLIDAY)		FRI	9	28.8	4.2				
THUR	14	6.4	3.0									MON	25	15.1	5.3
FRI	15	8.7	4.2	MON	12	(HOLIDAY)		MON	12	23.6	6.1	TUE	26	13.8	4.1
				TUE	13	10.0	5.1	TUE	13	22.6	6.1	WED	27	15.7	3.1
MON	18	7.8	6.9	WED	14	8.2	3.7	WED	14	25.2	3.3	THUR	28	14.5	2.5
TUE	19	10.1	5.2	THUR	15	16.7	1.5	THUR	15	27.7	2.8	FRI	29	15.1	3.2
WED	20	9.6	4.4	FRI	16	13.2	2.5	FRI	16	21.2	3.4				
THUR	21	9.8	3.0									**NOVEMBER**			
FRI	22	8.2	4.3	MON	19	15.3	4.6	MON	19	22.0	4.6	MON	1	17.6	5.4
				TUE	20	18.7	3.2	TUE	20	22.0	3.6	TUE	2	17.9	3.6
MON	25	9.4	6.8	WED	21	17.3	2.9	WED	21	21.4	2.6	WED	3	16.8	3.4
TUE	26	9.8	5.8	THUR	22	21.4	1.9	THUR	22	24.6	1.6	THUR	4	15.8	2.3
WED	27	10.5	4.1	FRI	23	14.6	3.7	FRI	23	22.2	3.3	FRI	5	14.6	3.8
THUR	28	10.3	2.9							(2 WEEKS' CLOSURE)					
FRI	29	9.6	4.0	MON	26	5.6	5.6	**AUGUST**				MON	8	11.2	5.6
				TUE	27	11.0	4.2	MON	9	22.5	6.1	TUE	9	8.3	5.0
FEBRUARY				WED	28	14.0	3.4	TUE	10	19.1	2.0	WED	10	8.1	4.1
MON	1	4.4	7.1	THUR	29	13.9	2.1	WED	11	20.0	2.8	THUR	11	9.5	2.8
TUE	2	6.5	6.5	FRI	30	11.2	3.8	THUR	12	17.2	1.4	FRI	12	11.0	3.8
WED	3	12.0	3.2	**MAY**				FRI	13	21.0	2.2				
THUR	4	11.0	2.6	MON	3	16.6	4.9					MON	15	10.2	5.6
FRI	5	8.7	4.1	TUE	4	19.0	3.2	MON	16	22.1	4.0	TUE	16	14.3	4.6
				WED	5	18.8	2.1	TUE	17	20.4	2.9	WED	17	10.8	4.0
MON	8	8.9	5.9	THUR	6	22.0	1.9	WED	18	23.8	2.4	THUR	18	15.0	2.1
TUE	9	8.2	5.0	FRI	7	16.1	3.5	THUR	19	27.2	2.0	FRI	19	5.1	5.1
WED	10	10.0	3.3					FRI	20	17.3	2.4				
THUR	11	8.3	2.8	MON	10	22.0	5.3					MON	22	5.5	6.2
FRI	12	11.6	3.6	TUE	11	24.1	4.1	MON	23	23.0	3.9	TUE	23	4.5	5.5
				WED	12	23.0	3.6	TUE	24	23.3	2.6	WED	24	7.1	5.4
				THUR	13	20.1	2.2	WED	25	22.3	2.3	THUR	25	11.0	2.2
				FRI	14	19.9	3.2	THUR	26	21.4	2.2	FRI	26	13.0	2.9
								FRI	27	21.2	3.8				

MARCH / JUNE

Day	Date	TEMP °C	ABS %
MON	15	7.3	5.8
TUE	16	5.2	5.1
WED	17	8.3	3.8
THUR	18	10.0	2.6
FRI	19	12.1	3.2
MON	22	12.8	5.3
TUE	23	12.8	3.9
WED	24	13.8	2.8
THUR	25	11.3	2.5
FRI	26	10.0	3.0
MON	1	7.2	6.2
TUE	2	9.1	5.3
WED	3	7.6	4.8
THUR	4	3.6	3.0
FRI	5	3.3	5.2
MON	8	8.1	7.0
TUE	9	12.8	5.0
WED	10	9.9	4.5
THUR	11	11.9	2.3
FRI	12	12.4	3.6
MON	15	9.2	5.7
TUE	16	10.2	4.7
WED	17	12.3	3.5
THUR	18	10.6	2.3
FRI	19	8.3	3.9
MON	22	10.3	5.3
TUE	23	12.5	4.0
WED	24	13.7	3.0
THUR	25	12.1	2.8
FRI	26	12.1	2.8

JUNE

TEMP °C	ABS %
16.3	4.7
20.0	3.5
20.4	2.8
20.0	1.6
18.0	2.9
19.2	4.3
11.0	3.0
15.0	3.4
13.5	2.4
16.9	3.2
(HOLIDAY)	
21.3	4.2
21.0	2.1
23.8	3.3
16.8	3.3
17.0	4.1
16.1	3.2
16.0	2.2
13.0	2.2
14.7	3.4
12.7	5.0
15.0	3.1
17.3	1.8
16.7	2.8
14.8	2.8
17.6	4.1
20.8	3.8
20.2	2.6
24.4	2.2
19.7	2.9

SEPTEMBER / OCTOBER

Date	TEMP °C	ABS %
30	(HOLIDAY)	
31	19.6	5.2
1	23.1	1.9
2	22.7	1.1
3	20.0	2.5
6	21.8	5.0
7	22.4	2.1
8	23.1	3.0
9	21.6	2.0
10	20.0	2.8
13	18.0	4.8
14	18.9	2.9
15	17.5	2.4
16	20.2	1.9
17	19.3	2.3
20	22.1	4.6
21	21.9	2.8
22	22.7	2.1
23	21.8	1.9
24	18.7	2.4
27	16.1	4.6
28	16.3	4.0
29	20.2	2.9
30	21.7	2.1
1	21.7	2.6
4	17.9	3.8
5	17.1	3.0
6	18.7	2.2
7	20.2	1.8
8	17.3	2.4

DECEMBER

Date	TEMP °C	ABS %
29	7.0	5.8
30	6.7	5.1
1	7.0	4.2
2	8.0	2.5
3	6.0	3.7
6	9.9	5.6
7	8.5	5.0
8	8.9	4.1
9	10.9	2.4
10	11.4	3.4
13	12.9	5.3
14	12.2	4.4
15	14.1	3.4
16	13.0	2.3
17	19.3	4.0
20	14.8	5.2
21	15.4	4.8
22	13.0	4.1
23	9.9	4.7
24	(HOLIDAY)	
27	(HOLIDAY)	6.8
28	7.1	6.9
29	2.9	6.2
30	3.3	8.1
31	5.5	

Figure 11.1   Scatter diagram of temperature/absenteeism: data of Table 11.1.

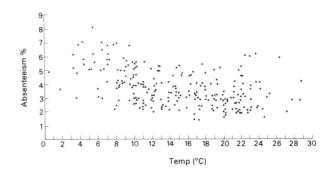

Temp (°C)

accompany lower temperatures, but clearly the association, if there is one, is less than perfect. After all, in dealing with such variables as human beings one can hardly expect to find laws of behaviour which are precise and invariable.

Almost instinctively, we draw from the scatter diagram the idea that the association between the variables may be considered a strong one if the points fit a straight line fairly closely, while a weak association would have a more random scatter pattern. This idea is brought out in Figures 11.2 (perfect association), 11.3 (perfect scatter) and 11.4 or 11.5 (in between). But the perfect circle of points of Figure 11.6 also do not fit a straight line yet they must have some association. There is evidently room for some higher-powered thinking. For the moment we shall look only at the linear type of association and see whether we can find some way of measuring its strength.

The correlation coefficient

Remembering that the standard deviation measures the scatter about the mean in one dimension, could we develop a two-dimensional equivalent? If so it might take into account the deviation of every point from the 'average point', $(\bar{X}, \bar{Y})$, or in the present case $(\bar{T}, \bar{A})$. The horizontal and vertical deviations of four selected points of our scatter diagram are shown in Figure 11.7; multiplying them gives an area of deviation, so to speak, which is a 2-dimensional deviation from the 2-dimensional average point. Some deviations are positive and others negative; being to the right of the average point for T, or above it for A, is called positive. Thus the areas for points to the north-east ($+$ times $+$) and south-west ($-$ times $-$) of the average point are positive and those to the north-west and south-east ($+$ times $-$) are negative. Totalling the areas over all points will give a positive figure if the points tend to fit a line rising from lower left to upper right with the two variables tending to rise or fall together, or a negative figure for a line descending from left to right where one variable tends to rise as the other falls, like absenteeism and temperature in our example.

Perfectly random scatter, or special curves like the circle, give positive and negative areas which cancel one another completely when totalled, giving zero.

Figure 11.2 Perfect association.   **Figure 11.3** Perfect scatter.

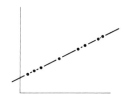 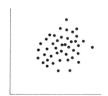

Figure 11.4 Some association (negative). **Figure 11.5** Some association (positive).

 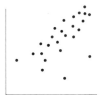

Figure 11.6 A non-linear association.

On the other hand, perfect fit to a straight line gives areas which all have the same sign; thus totalling, with no cancelling possible at all, gives a maximum value, positive or negative as the case may be. Both these situations are rare; there will nearly always be some cancelling to leave a positive or negative total, the size of which will depend of course on the number of pairs of data. Dividing the total by this number, N, gives an average area of deviation which (ignoring the sign) will be fairly large if there is reasonable fit to a straight line and fairly small if the fit is poor. It is therefore a measure of linear association between the pairs of data.

Looked at algebraically, the deviations of any point from the average point will be $(T - \bar{T})$ and $(A - \bar{A})$. Its area of deviation is therefore $(T - \bar{T})(A - \bar{A})$ and the average of all such areas is

$$\frac{\sum(T - \bar{T})(A - \bar{A})}{N}$$

Figure 11.7

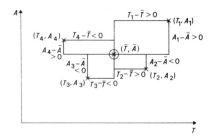

By analogy with the variances like $\dfrac{\sum(T-T)^2}{N}$, this quantity is called the *covariance of* T *with* A. While it is a measure of fit to a straight line, the meaning of the covariance is not clear. We do not know which line the fit refers to, and this will have to await Chapter XII. The units in which covariance is measured may be strange; in our example $(T - \bar{T})$ is in degrees of temperature while $(A - \bar{A})$ is a percentage, so the covariance is in degrees $- \%$ absenteeism, a concept rather difficult to grasp. If we were comparing women's ages with their expenditure on cosmetics the units would be year $-$ pounds. For clear understanding we need to be rid of these awkward units. Further, we do not know how our average area compares with the maximum possible value (the one for perfect straight-line fit), as we do not know the size of the maximum. Thus we have no yardstick for judging the worth of our covariance as a measure of linear association.

Dividing the covariance by both standard deviations σ_T and σ_A solves both problems at once. It gets rid of the units because the standard deviations are expressed in these same units; division of degrees by degrees and % by % or whatever, leaves a pure number. It happens also to ensure that the size of the result is always between -1 and $+1$. The covariance standardized in this way is thus an ideal measure of linear association. It is called the correlation coefficient and usually has the symbol r or ρ (rho, the Greek r). Thus in the general case:

$$r = \frac{\sum(X - \bar{X})(Y - \bar{Y})}{N\sigma_X\,\sigma_Y}$$

More properly, r is the *product moment correlation coefficient*, but this inordinate length is usually cut to the last two words only. A value of zero for r indicates perfect scatter as in Figure 11.3, or alternatively a perfect circle or some other curve which differs totally from a straight line. A size of 1 means an exact straight line relationship with $+1$ if the variables rise and fall together and -1 if they change in opposite directions. Between zero and 1 or -1 the linear association is better than nothing but less than perfect, improving as the size increases. Positive correlation is shown in Figure 11.5, negative in Figure 11.4.

As happened with the standard deviation formula, the version which displays the meaning of what is happening is difficult to calculate with, for it requires each item to be subtracted from the overall mean. Fortunately, it is quite easy to convert the formula into another which is much easier to use, though meaning no longer shows through. The calculation version is:

$$r = \frac{\sum xy - N\bar{X}\bar{Y}}{N\sigma_x \sigma_y}$$

As an example of the use of the correlation coefficient let us take a sample of, say, 12 random pairs from the absenteeism/temperature data of Table 11.1. As always with a statistical formula, the procedure is best carried out in tabular form with the headings dictated by the formula itself. In this case we need as column headings T, A, TA, and, for the standard deviations, also T^2 and A^2. The calculation then proceeds as follows:

T	A	$T \times A$	T^2	A^2
9.1	5.3	48.23	82.81	28.09
20.0	2.5	50.00	400.00	6.25
20.1	2.2	44.22	404.01	4.84
15.0	3.1	46.50	225.00	9.61
16.1	4.6	74.06	259.21	21.16
7.1	5.4	38.34	50.41	29.16
13.2	2.5	33.00	174.24	6.25
18.6	4.0	74.40	345.96	16.00
17.3	2.4	41.52	299.29	5.76
13.9	2.1	29.19	193.21	4.41
10.0	2.6	26.00	100.00	6.76
22.7	2.1	47.67	515.29	4.41
183.1	38.8	553.13	3049.43	142.70

$$\sigma_T = \sqrt{\frac{\sum T^2}{N} - \left(\frac{\sum T}{N}\right)^2} = \sqrt{\frac{3049.43}{12} - \left(\frac{183.1}{12}\right)^2} = \sqrt{21.25} = 4.61$$

$$\sigma_A = \sqrt{\frac{\sum A^2}{N} - \left(\frac{\sum A}{N}\right)^2} = \sqrt{\frac{142.7}{12} - \left(\frac{38.8}{12}\right)^2} = \sqrt{1.44} = 1.20$$

$$r = \frac{\sum TA - N\bar{T}\bar{A}}{N\sigma_T \sigma_A} = \frac{553.13 - (183.1 \times 38.3/12)}{12 \times 4.61 \times 1.20}$$

$$= -0.586$$

While simple in principle like almost all statistical calculations, the work can be very tedious and the computer is the obvious aid. With it the correlation coefficient for the entire 245 pairs of data has been found to be $r = -0.482$, which seems reasonably near to our sample figure.

Significance of the correlation coefficient

What is the meaning of a correlation coefficient of -0.482, and what would an r of 0.995 or -0.013 or any other value really mean? In measuring the strength of a straight-line association we must remember that any two pairs of data, as two points, are always on a straight line and by themselves must give a correlation coefficient of 1 or -1. Similarly, any three points are almost bound to give a high value. The more points there are, the lower the correlation will be unless there is a genuine linear association to keep the value high. Looking at it the other way, an r of say 0.624 will represent a much stronger association if it comes from 30 pairs of data than from only 5.

Clearly we need to assess the validity of r, or rather of the linear association it sets out to measure, with a significance test that takes the amount of data into account. This is quite simple to do in practice. One approach is to go ahead and find the best straight line to fit the data (we shall do this as the regression procedure in Chapter XII) and then measure its goodness of fit with a χ^2-test. The other, quicker approach compares the r we have found with the correlation coefficients that might arise from the same number of pairs of data if all such data was random. In this way we find the probability of finding, just by chance, a correlation at least as large as the one we have. Studies have shown that the t-distribution applies. All we need do is calculate t from the formula:

$$t = \frac{r\sqrt{N-2}}{\sqrt{1-r^2}}$$

and then look up the table of t on $(N-2)$ degrees of freedom to find the probability of getting at least such a high r from N random pairs. If this probability is quite high, then our r does not necessarily indicate a true association as it could easily arise from *any* N pairs of data. The probability must be low for our correlation coefficient to be significant, i.e. significantly different from zero, to verify a genuine linear relationship. As always in significance tests, the probability coming from the t-test is our chance of being wrong if we assert categorically that there is this linear association.

The significance test of course ignores the sign of r, which is reasonable as the sign refers only to the direction of the relationship line and not to the strength of the association itself.

In our example with 12 pairs of data r was -0.586 so

$$t = \frac{r\sqrt{N-2}}{\sqrt{1-r^2}} = \frac{-0.586 \times \sqrt{10}}{\sqrt{1-0.586^2}} = -2.287$$

on 10 degrees of freedom. The probability from the t-table is thus just under 5%. Since this is small it is unlikely that we should obtain such a value of r just by chance, so there is probably an association between T and A.

For the full data and using the computer, the r of -0.482 gives $t = -8.569$ on 243 degrees of freedom. The probability is therefore far below 0.1%, making it virtually certain that there really is a negative association between temperature and absenteeism.

So we see that much the same correlation coefficient can produce entirely different results when tested for being significantly different from zero. −0.586 from 12 pairs just about makes the grade whereas −0.482, apparently smaller, is overwhelmingly valid if derived from 245 pairs. This illustrates clearly the extent to which the correlation coefficient is a *relative* measurement. It means quite different things, depending on the amount of data from which it comes.

The meaning of the correlation coefficient

We have demonstrated a clear association between temperature and absenteeism, but must now ask what the existence of this association proves. It obviously does not prove that low absenteeism *causes* high temperatures. The assertion that low temperatures *cause* high absenteeism cannot be dismissed quite as readily, but it is important to remember that demonstrating an association does not prove cause and effect. There may be some third factor (rain, little day-light, influenza) which happens to coincide with low temperature and causes absenteeism, thereby giving an incidental though significant correlation. To take a different case, A's age measured at January 1st in each year correlates perfectly with B's age measured on April 1st three years earlier. There is no relationship between cause and effect here, just the common factor of time which increases both ages at the same rate. Here are two other well-known examples of such *spurious correlations*.

1. The human birth-rate in Sweden in the first 50 years of this century correlated positively and very highly significantly with the population of nesting storks there over the same period.

2. In Britain in the 1930s there was a very high and significant positive correlation between the annual numbers of wireless licences and the numbers of mental defectives.

Some statisticians and economists get much pleasure from seeking obviously spurious correlations like these, but managers have other things to do. For them it is important to find causes for observed phenomena and they will not be interested in correlation analysis unless it is of direct use to them. Yet we must admit that, speaking with rigid logic, correlation cannot prove causation. What it does instead is to point to likely associations that are worth investigating for causes. Thus it was correlation analysis that demonstrated an association between smoking and lung cancer, leading medical workers to look for carcinogenic substances in tobacco. Only when these had been found with biochemical techniques could one speak of smoking causing the disease in some people.

Using correlations

Now that we have discovered an association between temperature and absenteeism, what can we do? Unless we are part of the organization that provided the data, the answer is very little. The results apply only to the data used and unless it is found that the same association holds everywhere, no general statement may be made, though other firms may choose to test whether it is true also for them.

Where the association is found to hold, we may proceed even without looking for causes. We can recognize that if we can predict temperatures we can also predict absenteeism, so long as we can specify the relationship. This we shall do in the next chapter by fitting the best line to the data. So with reasonable weather forecasts we should be able to predict the labour force available and thus plan output nearer to what will be feasible. Limited though this may be, it will surely be welcomed by works managers and production controllers.

Correlation calculations are so routine that every computer has a correlation package available at quite low cost. Many of these packages allow a widespread investigation of correlations to take place by accepting data not just in pairs but with twenty or thirty different measurements for each individual. Thus the absenteeism on a given day may be fed into the computer together with that day's temperature, atmospheric pressure, humidity, rainfall, date, hours of sunshine, factory output of the previous day, number of local football matches on the day, and so on.

Anything that can be measured and that might conceivably be relevant may be fed in; the computer will calculate and print out all the correlation coefficients for every pairing of the variables it is given, and as often as not carry out the significance tests at the same time. Then, when desired, it will go to on fit the best straight lines (the regression procedure to be discussed in the next chapter). However, this is only worth doing where it is justified by the correlation coefficients being significant.

Some packages go further still and allow transformations of the variables before correlation, so that absenteeism might be compared with a weather comfort index comprising, for example, index = temperature + (humidity $\times 1\frac{1}{2}$) + (sunshine hours $\times \frac{1}{4}$), or any other combination that the investigator considers relevant. The processing speed is almost instantaneous for these packages and further runs with new transformations are very easy and cheap to perform. Thus correlation analysis, which is the obvious weapon for investigating the results of market research surveys, is readily available in an extremely versatile and powerful form. Twenty or more characteristics of women could be measured in a survey and compared with say, their expenditure on cosmetics; in this way the correlation can point to some interesting and perhaps surprising ideas for sales promotion without the need to prove cause and effect. Incidentally, if there are more than just a few items of data the amount of calculation called for in correlation analysis is almost impossible without a computer. A desk calculator would need at least 4 memories to keep track of all the totals required and few such machines exist.

Rank correlation
As discussed so far, correlation techniques involve measurements of the variables concerned. Sometimes exact measurements are not available, but instead the individuals being studied are placed in some order of rank. Thus the survey on cosmetics might ask the women to list a number of items in order of preference and these preferences, as a ranked list, might be compared with income or age or whatever.

To perform the correlation one must work with two ranked lists, so the measured variable must be converted merely to give each woman's position in the table, then paired with her position in the preference table of the item being studied. The difference in the two rank positions is then called D in the formula

$$R = 1 - \frac{6\sum D^2}{N^3 - N}$$

with N, of course as the number of pairs of ranked data, i.e. the number of women in this case.

R is a coefficient comparable entirely with the product moment correlation coefficient that we have been discussing. Its size is between -1 and 1. A positive value indicates that the two ranked lists run in the same general order whereas a negative value arises from lists running in opposite ways; zero means no linear relationship whatever between them. While generally labelled with a roman R, this rank correlation coefficient, named after its discoverer Spearman, is usually called Spearman's Rho. Since a ranked list may not have uniformly-spaced gaps between adjacent ranks, Spearman's Rho is less accurate than the ordinary correlation coefficient. Despite the extra arithmetic, we therefore prefer to avoid ranking techniques when we can.

Spearman's Rho may be tested for significance in exactly the same way as r, the ordinary correlation coefficient. However, it is not possible to fit a straight line to ranked data and preserve a sensible meaning, so the significance test usually concludes the work in this case, without proceeding to regression.

Non-linear correlation

A curved line may well fit the relationship between two variables better than a straight line does. We have, for example, justified a straight-line fit to the temperature/absenteeism data of Table 11.1 and Figure 11.1, but is there not some tendency for absenteeism to increase with very high temperatures as well as very low ones? If so, perhaps a curve like the one in Figure 11.8 might give an even better fit?

There are non-linear correlation procedures for this and a host of other types of curve. The formulae become very complicated indeed, but with the help of a computer it is easy enough to carry out the calculations painlessly. There is no need for us to look at the formulae here.

A common reason for measuring correlation, linear or otherwise, is to see whether it is justifiable to fit the line or curve to the data. If this can be justified

Figure 11.8

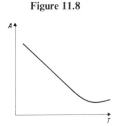

by a sufficiently large (and significant) correlation coefficient, then the line or curve is used for making predictions. For this reason the non-linear correlation procedure is often bypassed. Instead the best desired curve is fitted with the aid of the computer, then a χ^2 or similar test checks the closeness of fit. As we shall see, this procedure is suspect in many ways, but its simplicity overcomes all objections and it is widely followed. The matter is discussed again in the chapters on Regression (XII) and Forecasting (XV).

Multiple correlation

Just as correlation, as we have discussed it, measures an association between two variables, so one can look for a relationship between 3 or more variables at one time. For instance, absenteeism may depend on some combination of temperature and humidity, for example, and by gathering appropriate data one may find a multiple correlation coefficient which measures the 3-way association, if any. Bringing in barometric pressure, the degree of cloudiness, wind velocity, etc. also may allow 4-variable or more multiple correlation coefficients to be found using formulae which become increasingly complicated. Of course the computer can rapidly produce the answers, but more to the point is our ability to draw meaning from the figures which emerge. We can readily understand the implications of a straight-line or curvilinear relationship between two variables, but what happens when we have three? The association may be represented in 3 dimensions by a plane or a regular curved surface which is just about comprehensible, but the forecasting implications using such a surface are not too easy. With 4 or more variables no geometrical analogy is possible at all and the whole thing, while feasible in numbers, becomes impenetrable to managers and therefore of little practical use. As industry and commerce become even more demanding of management scientists, the use of the so-called multivariate techniques is growing and the mathematical background is being developed. A statistician, if one is employed, should be able to produce practical results from multi-variable data if this is really necessary, but it is probably still best in practice for the manager to treat his variables only two at a time.

XII
REGRESSION

Linear regression means fitting the best straight line to a set of paired data such as that of Figure 11.1. In Figure 12.1 we see a straight line superimposed on this. The fit appears to be reasonably good, but if we insist on having the best fit we must name the criteria that this demands. A good fit must obviously involve having small total distances from all the points to the line. However, distances will be positive or negative in the usual way, so to avoid all the ambiguities that signs bring in we continue our usual practice and square the distances. We may then define the best line on the *principle of least squares* as the line for which the total of squared deviations from all the points is a minimum.

Figure 12.1

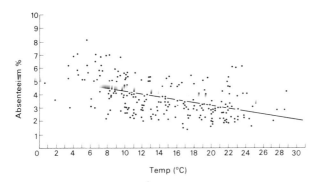

We have still not quite finished, since we need to define deviation. It may seem obvious that this should be the perpendicular kind, as in Figure 12.2; it is after all the shortest distance between point and line. However, the regression situation is rather special. In fitting a line we are implying that it represents the true relationship underlying the observed data. It follows that any points not sitting squarely on the line are somehow in error, perhaps due to the waywardness of the people or the awkwardness of the things being observed, or at least because of other factors that are not currently being taken explicitly into account. Thus if we are using a line to predict absenteeism from temperature as in Figure 12.1, the points off the line may be considered as in error for reasons beyond our control. The error is not one of temperature (the independent variable) about which nothing could be done; it must be in the absenteeism (the dependent variable which is at least in part a response to

Figure 12.2   The deviations of a point from a line.

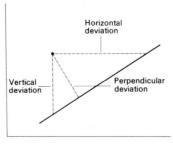

temperature), which is either too high or too low. In short, it makes sense to use the vertical deviations from the line rather than the perpendicular shortest distances.

In cases where no element of causation can be imagined, for example, when correlating absenteeism in one department with that in another where neither variable can depend on the other, the scatter diagram can be drawn with either variable horizontal and it may be convenient to consider the horizontal deviations, rather than the vertical ones, as being in error. Thus there are two entirely different sets of deviations, vertical or horizontal, which could be squared and totalled. Two different best lines may therefore emerge. The one using vertical deviations is called the *regression of* y *on* x and is used to predict y from x. The one using horizontal deviations is used to predict x from y and is the *regression of* x *on* y.

Both best lines pass through the average point ($\bar{X}$, $\bar{Y}$), but their slopes may differ somewhat. If there is doubt about which line to use either may be chosen, usually with only small divergences being involved unless one extrapolates some distance beyond the data. Mostly however, an independent variable will be clearly identifiable if there is one, and the regression of the dependent on the independent variable is the one to choose. Since independent variables usually occupy the x axis, the regression line of y on x is more commonly used and we shall consider it first.

Regression of Y on X

Since the best line is going to be a straight line, it must have the equation $y = mx + c$, with m being the slope and c the height at which it crosses the vertical axis. Our problem is to find the values of m and c which meet our least squares criterion.

Let us look at the vertical deviation for a typical point (X, Y) as shown in Figure 12.3. Directly below our point is a point on the line $y = mx + c$ for which the horizontal coordinate is also X. The vertical coordinate of this point, since it is on the line, is therefore $mX + c$. The vertical deviation is the difference between the two vertical coordinates Y and $(mX + c)$, i.e. $(Y - mX - c)$. Squaring this and totalling similar squares for all the points gives $\sum(Y - mX - c)^2$. This has to be minimized by finding the right values of m and c for the purpose. Here the differential calculus helps; only a few lines of

Figure 12.3

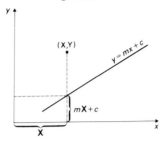

working are needed. The answers may be expressed in three different ways which give the same regression line equation; the choice depends as much on taste as anything else.

1. With the equation of the regression line being $y = mx + c$, m and c are found by solving the simultaneous equations

$$\left.\begin{array}{l} Nc + m\sum x = \sum y \\ c\sum x + m\sum x^2 = \sum xy \end{array}\right\}$$

A table with headings x, y, xy and x^2 will allow us to find the necessary four totals to put into these equations which are then solved by any of the usual methods. For example, to fit the regression line to our dozen pairs of points selected from Table 11.1 and used in Chapter XI, we use the totals (worked out on page 131)

$$\sum T = 183.1, \ \sum A = 38.8. \ \sum TA = 553.13, \ \sum T^2 = 3049.43$$

whence

$$12c + 183.1m \qquad = 38.8 \qquad\qquad (12.1)$$

$$183.1c + 3049.43m = 553.13 \qquad\qquad (12.2)$$

Multiplying (*12.1*) by 183.1 and (*12.2*) by 12,

$$2197.2c + 33525.61m = 7104.28 \qquad\qquad (12.3)$$

$$2197.2c + 36593.16m = 6637.56 \qquad\qquad (12.4)$$

Subtracting (*12.3*) from (*12.4*)

$$3067.55m = -466.72$$

so

$$\boxed{m = -0.15}$$

Substituting in (*12.1*),

$$12c - 27.858 = 38.8$$

$$\therefore 12c = 38.8 + 27.858 = 66.658$$

so

$$c = 5.55$$

and the regression line of A on T is

$$A = -0.15T + 5.55$$

2. Many people are unwilling to tackle simultaneous equations. Algebraic methods allow equations to be solved once and for all with formulae as the results. In this case

$$m = \frac{N\sum xy - (\sum x)(\sum y)}{N\sum x^2 - (\sum x)^2}$$

and

$$c = \frac{(\sum x)(\sum xy) - (\sum y)(\sum x^2)}{(\sum x)^2 - N\sum x^2}$$

These call for the same four totals as method 1 above, namely $\sum x$, $\sum y$, $\sum xy$ and $\sum x^2$. Taking the same example,

$$m = \frac{(12 \times 553.13) - (183.1 \times 38.8)}{(12 \times 3049.43) - 183.1^2} = -0.15$$

$$c = \frac{(183.1 \times 553.13) - (38.8 \times 3049.43)}{183.1^2 - (12 \times 3049.43)} = 5.55$$

so the regression line of A on T is again

$$A = -0.15T + 5.55$$

3. The equation of the line of regression of y on x is

$$(y - \bar{y}) = \frac{r\sigma_y}{\sigma_x}(x - \bar{x})$$

In this, $\bar{x}$ and $\bar{y}$ are the means and σ_x and σ_y the standard deviations of the variables separately. r is the correlation coefficient. All these are numbers calculated from the data so, appearing with just x and y in the equation, they do represent a straight line. Of course the correlation coefficient and the means and the standard deviations have to be worked out before this equation can be used. However, finding r already involves finding $\bar{x}$, $\bar{y}$, σ_x and σ_y so the regression equation can be written down directly from the correlation work. Taking the same example, we had $r = -0.586$, $\bar{T} = 15.26$, $\bar{A} = 3.23$, $\sigma_T = 4.61$ and $\sigma_A = 1.20$, so the regression equation is

$$A - 3.23 = \frac{-0.586 \times 1.20}{4.61}(T - 15.26)$$

$$= -0.15(T - 15.26)$$

so
$$A = -0.15T + (0.15 \times 15.26) + 3.23$$
$$= -0.15T + 5.55 \text{ as before.}$$

Incidentally, a computer worked out the regression equation for the entire 245 pairs of data as

$$A = -0.107T + 5.314$$

which is quite close to the line we have found for the sample dozen pairs.

Note that, since m is the slope of the line $y = mx + c$, its calculated value shows the change in y for a change of 1 unit in x. For our 245 pairs of data, $m = -0.107$ so that, on average, a rise of 1°C in temperature brings on a fall of 0.107% in absenteeism.

Three methods have been discussed, of which methods 1 and 2 go straight to the regression equation; method 3 uses correlation to reach it. All give the same answer and all are widely used. However, to help us see whether any of the three is in any way superior, let us consider a little example:

x	1	2	3	4	5
y	1	2	3	4	0

Figure 12.4

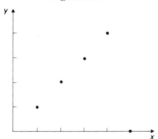

The scatter diagram is shown in Figure 12.4. For all methods we are going to need the calculations:

x	y	xy	x^2
1	1	1	1
2	2	4	4
3	3	9	9
4	4	16	16
5	0	0	25
15	10	30	55

so $\sum x = 15$, $\bar{x} = 3$, $y = 10$, $\bar{y} = 2$, $\sum xy = 30$, $\sum x^2 = 55$ with $N = 5$.

Method 1

$$\left. \begin{array}{l} Nc + m\sum x = \sum y \\ c\sum x + m\sum \times 2 = \sum xy \end{array} \right\}$$

hence
$$5c + 15m = 10 \tag{12.5}$$

$$15c + 55m = 30 \tag{12.6}$$

Multiplying the first by 3,
$$15c + 45m = 30 \tag{12.7}$$

and still
$$15c + 55m = 30 \tag{12.8}$$

Subtracting $\qquad\qquad\qquad 10m = 0 \quad$ so $m = 0$

Substituting in the first equation, $5c + 0 = 10$

so $c = 2$ and the line is $\boxed{y = 2}$

Method 2

$$m = \frac{(5 \times 30) - (15 \times 10)}{(5 \times 55) - 15^2} = 0$$

and $\qquad c = \dfrac{(15 \times 30) - (10 \times 55)}{15^2 - (5 \times 55)} = \dfrac{450 - 550}{225 - 275} = \dfrac{-100}{-50} = 2$

and the line is $\boxed{y = 2}$

Method 3

We also need $\qquad \sum y^2 = 1 + 4 + 9 + 16 + 0 = 30$

Hence $\qquad\qquad \sigma_x = \sqrt{\dfrac{55}{5} - 3^2} = \sqrt{2}$

and $\qquad\qquad \sigma_y = \sqrt{\dfrac{30}{5} - 2^2} = \sqrt{2}$

so $\qquad\qquad r = \dfrac{\sum xy - N\bar{x}\bar{y}}{N\sigma_x \sigma_y} = \dfrac{30 - (5 \times 3 \times 2)}{5 \times \sqrt{2} \times \sqrt{2}} = 0$

With a correlation coefficient of zero, i.e. with no linear relationship whatever, what can possibly be the justification for fitting a best straight line? Even the best must be useless. This method is the only one of the three to apply the test first, and possibly avoid unnecessary later work. However, the method continues:

$$(y - \bar{y}) = \frac{r\sigma_y}{\sigma_x} (X - \bar{X})$$

so $\qquad\qquad y - 2 = \dfrac{0 \times \sqrt{2}}{\sqrt{2}} (x - 3) = 0$

and again $y = 2$ is the best line, though we now know that it is worthless.

Validity of a regression line

A χ^2-test comparing the observed data with expected values given by a regression line (i.e. by the $y = mx + c$ formula) will give a low probability if there is enough evidence of a really bad fit. However, like all significance tests, it offers a much wider area of no conclusion than of poor fit; it does not test for very good fit if used in the way we have adopted so far. Let us try it on our little zero-correlation example, with $y = 2$ as the regression equation:

Observed y	1	2	3	4	0
Expected y	2	2	2	2	2

$$\chi^2 = \frac{(1-2)^2}{2} + \frac{(2-2)^2}{2} + \frac{(3-2)^2}{2} + \frac{(4-2)^2}{2} + \frac{(0-2)^2}{2}$$

$$= \tfrac{1}{2} + 0 + \tfrac{1}{2} + 2 + 2$$

$$= 5 \text{ on 4 degrees of freedom.}$$

From the table, $\chi^2 = 7.779$ corresponds to 10% and 9.488 to 5%. Our χ^2 of 5 thus represents more than 10%, perhaps 15% or 20%, which is far too high to let us assert that the fit is poor. In the ordinary way we would have to say that on the meagre evidence provided by only 5 points we have no reason to doubt the closeness of the fit. Nevertheless we are definitely in the Not Proven area; there is certainly no firm evidence of a good fit either.

As we know, a correlation of zero means no straight-line relationship at all, i.e. no real fit, and our χ^2 test has obviously let us down. However, where correlation coefficients are not merely significant but also high (for example, 0.9 or so, indicating real closeness to a linear relationship) the regression line will of course pass very near to most of the points, and a χ^2-test will give a very high probability. For this reason χ^2-test tables often (as in Appendix G, page 258) include probabilities upwards of 90%. A χ^2-test with, for example, a 99% probability at the end does more than say Not Proven; it is strong evidence of a very good fit indeed. Where such results are forthcoming they do verify the validity of a regression line fitted to data without reference to correlation, and at the same time confirm a high correlation coefficient without measuring it.

It remains true, however, that a significant correlation coefficient is the one straightforward test of how justified is a regression line. In my view, therefore, method 3 is the best means of fitting the line, since it uses the correlation coefficient on the way.

Computer packages, of course, go for the easiest computation and tend to use variations of method 2. For those who are conscientious enough to wonder whether the computed regression line is justified, some packages then go on to give a percentage validity for the line. This is found by comparing the sum of squared deviations which is accounted for by the regression equation with the total sum of squared deviations. This is one of many possible mathematical tests. The manager, however, is recommended to concentrate on correlation as the test.

The accuracy of using regression

Regression equations are used mostly for forecasting. Thus our temperature/absenteeism regression line is

$$A = -0.107T + 5.314$$

If the weather forecast is for a maximum day temperature of $-2°C$ (or $28.4°F$), the forecast level of absenteeism is

$$A = (-0.107 \times -2) + 5.314$$

$$0.214 + 5.314 = 5.528\%$$

It is as simple as that. Of course, looking at the regression line among the original data (and Figure 12.1 shows this best line), we realize at once that this ultra-precise forecast is subject to considerable error. A regression line is a sort of running mean level through the data, and as with any statistic based on a sample, there is a standard error (SE) which helps us set confidence limits within which we would expect the truth probably to lie. The standard error of the estimate of y based on regression is a certain proportion of the standard deviation of the ys in the original data. The proportion is $\sqrt{1 - r^2}$, where r is the correlation coefficient. $\sqrt{1 - r^2}$ is never more than 1, and is 0 for perfect correlation. After all, a correlation of 1 means a true straight-line law, so there are no errors in forecasting with it. On the other hand, zero correlation means no linear relationship, so the spread of possible forecasts is the same as the vertical spread of the original data.

So we have $SE_y = \sigma_y\sqrt{1 - r^2}$. In our example, $\sigma_A = 1.31$ and $r = -0.482$ for the entire sample of 245 pairs, and

$$SE_A = \sigma_A\sqrt{1 - r^2}$$

$$= 1.31 \times \sqrt{1 - 0.482^2} = 1.31 \times \sqrt{0.768}$$

$$= 1.31 \times 0.876 \qquad = 1.148$$

As usual, 95% of all predictions will lie within ±2 of these standard errors, so we may say with 95% confidence that our estimate of absenteeism at a temperature of $-2°$ lies within $5.476 \pm 2.296\%$, i.e. between 3.180% and 7.772%.

We had earlier met the expression $\sqrt{1 - r^2}$ in the construction of t for the correlation coefficient: $t = \dfrac{r\sqrt{N - 2}}{\sqrt{1 - r^2}}$. Just as r is a measure of the strength of a linear association, so $\sqrt{1 - r^2}$ is a measure of how strong it is not. It is sometimes known as the coefficient of alienation. Its square, $(1 - r^2)$, is sometimes called the coefficient of nondetermination, and r^2, the square of the correlation coefficient, is called the coefficient of determination. These names are met in the statistics used by psychologists and personnel workers, and are used to test the accuracy of regression estimates, along the lines we have mentioned.

Regression of X on Y

The formulae are symmetrical with those of the y on x regressions, x and y being interchanged everywhere. Thus:

1. This line is $x = my + c$, with m and c being found by solving

$$Nc + m\sum y = \sum x$$
$$c\sum y + m\sum y^2 = \sum xy$$

2. Without needing to solve simultaneous equations,

$$m = \frac{N\sum xy - (\sum x)(\sum y)}{N\sum y^2 - (\sum y)^2}$$

and

$$c = \frac{(\sum y)(\sum xy) - (\sum x)(\sum y^2)}{(\sum y)^2 - N\sum y^2}$$

3. The equation of the line is

$$(x - \bar{x}) = \frac{r\sigma_x}{\sigma_y}(y - \bar{y})$$

Try finding the regression line of x on y for the 12-pair example we used earlier, plotting the two lines with the data and seeing the difference.

4. The standard error of an estimate from the regression equation of x on y is

$$SE_x = \sigma_x\sqrt{1 - r^2}$$

The regression of y on x is used for predicting y for a given value of x. Similarly, to predict x for a given y we use the regression of x on y.

Limitations of regression analysis

The main reason for fitting a line to data is to extend the line beyond the limits of the current data, i.e. to forecast. This is especially so if time is the independent variable; what manager would not like a glimpse into the future?

However, we must be cautious. A regression line is calculated using all the available data. As another period passes and another pair of data items becomes available, a new regression line may be calculated. Unless the new point happens to sit precisely on the old regression line, the new line, based on old and new data, will be different. If the new data is fairly far from the old line, which is more probable than a direct hit on it, the new line may be considerably different. True, the gap between old and new lines may not be wide for the next period or two, since both are calculated from data which is mostly identical, but any divergence will only increase as we look further and further ahead. Accuracy beyond one or two periods ahead is therefore most highly suspect. This is partly why estimates of the UK's population in the year 2000 are subject to frequent drastic revisions. Business organizations cannot run well on this basis.

Non-linear regression

The least squares principle may be used as readily to fit the best curve as the best straight line, but the kind of curve has to be decided first. Just as we started with the straight-line equation $y = mx + c$ for linear regression, so we must state the general equation of the curve we wish to fit before the deviations can be expressed, squared and minimized in non-linear work.

The calculations become so laborious that the computer is *de rigueur* in curve fitting. Standard packages allow for a wide variety of the types of curve used in marketing, share portfolio analysis and so on. They calculate the constants in the equations that fit a particular curve to the data, and usually go on to state the % validity or something similar. The multi-access terminal is the ideal instrument for this work, although the input of large amounts of data may call for some higher-speed device originally. When working, the amounts of supplementary input and output are quite small and suited to the terminal. A manager may then swiftly try out a range of fits for his data, and produce his calculated predictions. The new art/science of market modelling is based on this approach.

Multiple regression, the fitting of surfaces and hyper-surfaces for 3 or more variables, is also essentially a computer-based task these days. As with multiple correlation, the meanings may be lost in the detail; multiple regression is therefore a topic that most managers will not consider.

XIII
INDEX NUMBERS

We saw in Chapter VI how necessary it is to summarize a mass of data in order to assimilate and understand something about it. Measures like means, modes, ranges and standard deviations look at different facets of the data in order to perform their task of summarization, but they all have one thing in common; the variation that they handle belongs to one single variable. Correlation and regression, we later saw, were attempts to look at two or more variables together, but at only one joint aspect, the relationship, if any, between them.

As a rule, life offers much more complicated fare than this, but demands, at least for descriptive purposes, something much less complex than multiple regression. Index numbers are descriptive tools to meet this need. We are accustomed to hearing of the cost-of-living or retail price index, the *Financial Times* Share Index, the index of production and so on; economists use dozens of them.

An index number is a condensation of a multi-variable situation into a single number, rather like an average. It is a feature of the index that it follows the overall changes that time brings, being measured on a scale which compares its size now with its size at a certain starting date. Usually the scale is adjusted so that the starting size is called 100. An index number 25% higher than the starting one would then be called 125.

To see how it works, let us construct a simplified form of retail price index. Everyone's cost of living is the cost of the goods and services he buys in the course of living. One individual's cost is usually different from another's, but over society as a whole certain buying patterns become clear and by means of an ongoing survey of the ways in which several hundred typical families spend their money—the Family Expenditure Survey—the government continuously monitors what is being bought, in what quantities and at what prices. Apart from the prices, it becomes possible at any moment to conceive of a typical shopping basket of goods and services consumed by a family in a week. For our simplified example, let us suppose that this consists of the items and quantities in Table 13.1. The assumption is that the shopping basket remains the same but as the list of prices varies, not necessarily to the same extent for each item, we shall be able to watch for changes in total cost and make the desired comparisons. Every few years the Family Expenditure Survey may show that the standard basket is out of date; a new one can be specified and the monitoring of prices may re-commence on this new basis.

Table 13.1 shows our initial prices and quantities, and multiplying price-per-unit by quantity we calculate the costs shown, with a weekly total of £12.26 for

Table 13.1

Item	Quantity	Price	£ Unit price	£ Cost
Beef	3 lb	30p/lb	0.30	0.90
Potatoes	8 lb	2p/lb	0.02	0.16
Fish	3 lb	25p/lb	0.25	0.75
Cigarettes	150	30p/20	0.015	2.25
Petrol	3 gal	40p/gal	0.40	1.20
Accommodation	1	£4.50/week	4.50	4.50
Heat and light	1	£2.50/week	2.50	2.50
				£12.26

the basket. To construct the index this sum is to be called 100. The arithmetic of the transformation is, of course, to divide by the 12.26 and multiply by 100, a procedure to be used on all future total prices in the life of this index.

At a later date, still assuming that the contents and quantities in the basket are the same, prices might be those of Table 13.2. The total cost is now £16.31$\frac{1}{2}$. Applying the transformation, we find

$$\frac{16.315}{12.26} \times 100 = 133.08$$

so the new retail price index is 133.08. This is just an alternative way of saying that there has been a rise of 33.08% since this particular index began. If, still later, the total cost reaches £17.48, the index would be 142.58. This is 42.58% above the original cost, and is called $(142.58 - 133.08) = 9.5$ points above the second index figure. It is not 9.5% above it, however; as compared with the second figure, the third one is only $\frac{142.58}{133.08} \times 100 = 107.14$, i.e. 7.14% higher.

It is only a matter of percentages calculated on different bases, which some people find confusing. The index shows the percentage change on the original figure as base. It is simple and consistent. Regrettably, political discussions about the cost of living tend to revolve around percentages more favourable

Table 13.2

Item	Quantity	Price	£ Unit price	£ Cost
Beef	3 lb	70p/lb	0.70	2.10
Potatoes	8 lb	3p/lb	0.03	0.24
Fish	3 lb	50p/lb	0.50	1.50
Cigarettes	150	35p/20	0.0175	2.62$\frac{1}{2}$
Petrol	3 gal	55p/gal	0.55	1.65
Accommodation	1	£5.00	5.00	5.00
Heat and light	1	£3.20	3.20	3.20
				£16.31$\frac{1}{2}$

to the speaker; after all, a 7.14% rise sounds less than a 9.5 point rise though as we have seen they may mean precisely the same.

Seen as a formula, the index we have looked at is

$$\frac{\sum(\text{new unit price} \times \text{quantity})}{\sum(\text{original unit price} \times \text{quantity})} \times 100$$

or, in short,

$$\frac{\sum p_0 q}{\sum p_1 q} \times 100$$

q, the quantity, is taken at the original level, assumed unchanged, and to complete the logic in the formula, which is named after the economist Laspeyres,

$$\text{Laspeyres index} = \frac{\sum p_0 q_0}{\sum p_1 q_0} \times 100$$

Thus a Laspeyres index shows how the present cost of the original basket compares with its original cost. If the current purchasing pattern differs to an important extent from the original one, it may be advisable to change the basket. However, it is unwise to change the basis of an index too often, otherwise it cannot allow for the straightforward comparisons which are its primary purpose.

Where there are fairly frequent changes of quantities which would make a standard basket impracticable, an alternative approach is to use both current and original prices with current quantities. An index built this way shows how the present cost of the present basket compares with the original cost of the present basket. This approach is named after one Paasche:

$$\text{Paasche index} = \frac{\sum p_1 q_1}{\sum p_1 q_1} \times 100$$

The old Board of Trade and its successors publish a Paasche index for price in reporting Britain's external trade.

By keeping the price fixed at either the original (for Laspeyres) or current (for Paasche) level and using old and new quantities, we can construct volume indices instead of the price indices we have discussed. The Index of Industrial Production is an example of a volume index of the Laspeyres type.

The *Financial Times* Industrial Ordinary Share Index is quite different. It is the geometric mean of the prices of 30 selected shares, related in the usual way to the geometric mean at the start date of 1st July 1935. In other words,

$$FT \text{ Index} = \frac{\sqrt[30]{(p_1)_0 \times (p_2)_0 \times (p_3)_0 \times \ldots (p_{30})_0}}{\sqrt[30]{(p_1)_1 \times (p_2)_1 \times (p_3)_1 \times \ldots (p_{30})_1}} \times 100$$

The calculation of a 30th root after multiplying thirty numbers is a trivial enough task for a computer, but why is this method used rather than the much simpler arithmetic mean? A small example will illustrate the reason. Consider just five shares used to construct an index. On the base date, let us say, their prices were respectively 100, 200, 300, 400 and 500. The shares are all of equal status so there is no need to multiply each by some number. The total price for one each of the 5 shares was 1500, so to construct a Laspeyres index we simply divide a current total price by 1500 and multiply by 100, i.e. divide by 15. The base index is, of course, 100. The geometric mean is

$$\sqrt[5]{100 \times 200 \times 300 \times 400 \times 500}$$

$$= 100 \times \sqrt[5]{120}$$

$$= 260.52$$

so to make this a base index of 100 we divide it, and all later geometric means, by 2.6052.

If all shares double in price after a certain time, we have prices of 200, 400, 600, 800 and 1000. The total is 3000 so the Laspeyres index is 200, as it should be. The geometric mean is

$$\sqrt[5]{200 \times 400 \times 600 \times 800 \times 10000}$$

$$= 200 \times \sqrt[5]{120}$$

$$= 521.04$$

so the index is again 200, correctly. Thus if all shares change uniformly there is no difference in the effects of the arithmetic and geometric methods.

However, what if one share changes differently from the others? As an extreme case, suppose one doubles while the rest are static. From the stock market's point of view, one share doubling its price has exactly the same importance as any comparable share doubling its price, whether the starting price was 10 or 100 or 1000. In short, the market works on proportions and not on actual levels. What happens to the two indexes, though, if (a) the cheapest share doubles, or alternatively (b) the dearest one doubles?

(a) We have prices of 200, 200, 300, 400, 500 making a total of 1600 and a Laspeyres index of 106.67. The geometric mean is
$\sqrt[5]{200 \times 200 \times 300 \times 400 \times 500} = 100 \times \sqrt[5]{240} = 299.26$, so the *FT* index is 114.87.

(b) With prices of 100, 200, 300, 400 and 1000 the total is 2000 and the Laspeyres index is 133.33, much larger than before. The geometric mean is $\sqrt[5]{100 \times 200 \times 300 \times 400 \times 1000} = 100 \times \sqrt[5]{240} = 299.26$. The *FT* index is exactly the same at 114.87.

So only the geometric mean reflects the needs of the stock market, for which the index is intended. It treats every share on an equal footing, looking at its percentage change in price and not (as the arithmetic means or totals do) at the actual size of a price change.

The 30 share prices used are not a random sample, of course. They are carefully chosen stable, sizeable companies whose prices tended to go along with the market as a whole and from whom nothing spectacularly different, good or bad, was to be expected. The choice should therefore have been proof against the major disadvantage of the geometric mean method, that if any figure falls to zero then the multiplication gives zero and the index must be zero. Thus in 1971, when Rolls-Royce Ltd. was in difficulties, the *Financial Times* removed them from the select 30, replacing them with a similar (but untroubled) share. The announcement of this change some months before the collapse of Rolls-Royce should have been a clear warning to anyone understanding how the index works, but as relatively few shareholders seem to have responded to it one may perhaps wonder.

All the index numbers we have so far considered are used mainly by specialists. Management use of them is almost incidental and mostly limited to pay levels, though some countries officially base pay scales of major groups of workers on the national retail price index, and threshold payments have appeared in Britain. However, as a rough-and-ready guide to overall average levels in a complex situation, the index-number idea can be of real value to managers, who can readily construct their own index to suit their purpose. The only trick to remember is that, if desired, each item used may have a weighting attached to its measured level. (If not, as with shares, the weights are in effect all 1). In the retail price index, for example, the weightings are the separate quantities bought, while the measurement is the unit price.

A manager may wish to incorporate the outputs of two plants in an output index. In a particular period plant M may produce 1276 units, while N produces 752. However, if N's products are considered twice as important (or complex, or anything else) as those of M, the calculation might proceed

	Units	Weighting	Contribution to index
M	1276	1	1276
N	752	2	1504
			2780

and this weighted total of 2780 is compared with the original one to make the current index number. Laspeyres or Paasche indexes could be arranged respectively by always using the original weights or always using the current ones.

But the manager's own index does not have to be a Laspeyres, or a Paasche or a geometric mean; any arrangement which is both consistent and meaningful for the purpose can be used. I have been involved in using a more complex index for quality control purposes. The product was a piece of electronic equipment made and used in large numbers, and the idea was to construct an index showing the quality of current production. Quality is one of the most complicated aspects to describe, yet we were able to devise a workable system. After consultation between the producers and the inspectors it was agreed that overall quality would be assessed by re-checking equipment which had been through all the factory procedures including final testing and adjustment, and which was already packed for delivery. Note would be taken of all the faults found in a random sample of 10 sets of equipment unpacked and re-inspected.

Weighting was attached to each fault by classifying it as major, medium and minor according to clearly-defined standards; major faults were weighted with 10 penalty points, medium with 7 and minor with 3 points each. Every sample of 10 sets of equipments started with a score of 100, and the total number of penalty points from the ten was deducted from this 100. Thus perfect quality was rated 100 on the index scale and the lower the final number the poorer the current quality. Relatively few major faults or a large number of minor ones could yield the same quality index.

Naturally the variations from sample to sample were considerable, and were reflected in widely fluctuating quality numbers. To smooth out these sampling variations, the moving average idea was used: the average of the scores from the last 10 samples (corresponding to 100 equipments re-tested) was quoted as the quality number so that one freak sample did not distort the index excessively. It was found that, by publishing the current quality number to the workers concerned in an appropriate way, a real interest in quality was generated and the overall quality of the product improved to the good of the firm's reputation. No less important, publication to the middle managers normally concerned only with output aroused their interest in quality also. As with so many managerial innovations, the idea gradually lost effect and was dropped after some years, but it proved genuinely useful while it lasted. The cost of running the index was tiny compared to the results obtained. I feel that the success was largely because the quoted index number was one which conveyed information clearly and succinctly, with no need for calculations to be introduced.

PART IV OPERATIONAL RESEARCH
XIV
WHAT OPERATIONAL RESEARCH IS ABOUT

No fully satisfactory definition of operational research (alternatively called operations research, or OR) has yet been put forward. This is the confession of most, if not all, who have so far attempted to define it. We shall look at several attempts here and shall hope to grasp what OR is about despite its problems of definition.

OR is about solving management problems. This definition merely raises other questions such as 'Which problems?' Suppose a manager says that he desperately needs a sum of money, a common enough problem: can OR help? In the sense that it cannot produce money, the answer is obviously, no. A source of funds such as a bank would begin by asking the manager general questions (How much? For what purpose? For how long?) and would then try to establish whether an advance would be secure and whether interest could be afforded. OR would ask more fundamental questions, tending to establish whether lack of cash was the central problem or only symptomatic of a deeper fault, and if the latter, to find out what the true problem was. It would then seek a solution to the newly-formulated problem. In the long term this could be of the greatest benefit to that firm and its manager, but it does take a little time. Often the firm cannot wait because the symptom can kill even though the disease is curable: if the immediate cash shortage is because the wage bill must be paid tomorrow or else the firm closes, it is no use looking first at the basic inefficiencies which led to the crisis. By next Monday there would be nothing left at which to look.

This leads us to our next definition. *OR is about solving long-term or non-immediate management problems.* Despite what has just been said, this is false. Many applications of OR are carried through so quickly that immediate problems can be solved. In many other cases, of course, the problem is of a long-term nature (for example, planning) and the urgency is not called for. Even then, OR provides the speediest possible answers.

As we have already seen, OR is concerned with making a fundamental analysis of a situation. The types of problem suited to this sort of analysis tend to be complex, and the types of solution tend to be theoretical. Let us take a trivially easy (and quickly solved) example to illustrate this idea.

A small firm makes one product, which it sells for £10 per unit. Materials and labour cost £5 per unit. It also costs £100 per week to keep the little factory in existence, however few or many products it turns out. In what conditions could the firm be profitable?

Most people can produce the answer after a few moments' mental arithmetic. However, let us explain to ourselves the methodical reasoning that leads to this particular arithmetic. One approach is to formulate the relationships:

$$\text{Profit} = \text{Revenue} - \text{Costs}$$
$$\text{Revenue} = (\text{Number of units sold}) \times (\text{Unit price})$$
$$\text{Costs} = \text{Fixed costs} + \text{Variable costs}$$
$$\text{Variable costs} = (\text{Number of units sold}) \times (\text{Unit cost})$$

whence

$$\text{Profit} = (\text{Number of units sold}) \times (\text{Unit price} - \text{Unit cost}) - \text{Fixed costs}$$

We have as given data

$$\left. \begin{array}{l} \text{Unit price} = £10 \\ \text{Unit cost} = £5 \end{array} \right\} \quad \text{hence (Unit price} - \text{Unit cost)} = £5$$
$$\text{Fixed costs} = £100 \text{ per week}$$

so

$$\text{Profit} = [(\text{Number of units sold}) \times £5] - £100 \text{ per week}$$

Since the problem postulates profitability, Profit > 0, hence

$$\text{Number of units sold} \times £5 > £100$$

and

$$\text{Number of units sold} > £100/£5 \text{ or } 20$$

So the firm will be profitable if it sells more than 20 units per week and will exactly break even at sales of 20.

An alternative approach is to create a graph from the relationships:

$$\text{Contribution per unit} = \text{Unit price} - \text{Unit cost}$$
$$= £10 - £5 = £5$$

and   Fixed costs $= £100$ per week

These points are plotted, related to the number of units sold per week as the independent variable. The contribution straight line passes through (no sales, no money) and (30 sales, £150). The fixed line is at the £100 level. Figure 14.1 shows that contribution is below fixed costs for all sales of less than 20 units, the two are equal at 20 and the contribution is greater if more than 20 units are sold in a week. This last is the condition for profitability, and the problem is solved.

We have laboured this simple example because it makes a number of important and basic points about OR:

1. The problem was a general one, of relevance both this week and in the future.
2. The solution was also a general one, in the sense that it answers the question for all time (i.e. until the background information changes). It does not, however, tell the manager of the firm how to ensure that he makes at least 20 sales per week. We are able merely to state dispassionately that in the weeks when he sells fewer than/exactly/more than 20 units, he will lose/break even/make a profit, respectively. We could go on to say how much the firm will make or lose in a week, depending on how many units it sells. In other words, both the problem and its solution are quantified.
3. The methods of tackling the problem, one algebraic and one graphical, were alike in essence. Both consisted of replacing the verbal description of the situation with some other representation of it (see Chapter I), respectively an inequality and a graph. The solution was then found by operating on these representations with their relevant rules. These alternative representations are models of the real-life situation.

Figure 14.1 A breakeven chart.

Units sold per week

We can now put forward another definition. *OR is about solving management problems by using models.* Bearing in mind our reservations about the types of problem concerned, there is much to be said for this definition. Our small firm manager could have solved his problem by going ahead with his business and each week noting how many units he sold and how much money he made or lost. After some time he might be able to notice the solution, if necessary after introducing some experimental sales variation, at least downwards by refusing orders. However, if sales were consistently either well above 20 or below it, he could not deduce the breakeven point from mere observation, and in the latter case he might go bankrupt before he felt his studies were completed.

The modelling approach offers the primary advantages of:

1. *Safety.* It is much less likely that the firm will collapse while we work with the model than if we experiment with the actual sales figures.
2. *Speed.* A model will invariably operate far more quickly than the situation it represents. This is why OR is often of immediate application to urgent problems.

3. *Cost*. In part this is related to the safety feature as already mentioned, in part it derives from the speed. In part, too, it may be inherent; for example, graph paper is much cheaper than an experimental selling effort.

4. *Versatility*. We can often treat a model in several different ways, to see the consequences and then pick the most favourable one. A range of trials is not usually possible in real life, even given unlimited time and money, for one single treatment will often change the situation permanently and prevent any other approach from being tried.

OR was a wartime development. The name operations research derives from research into military operations and it is perhaps a pity that the name has continued into business life where the words do not have this immediate meaning. OR originally tackled problems like increasing the accuracy of bomb-aiming or finding the best size and speed for a shipping convoy. When scientists of various disciplines were brought in to look at military problems it was natural for them to apply scientific methods. These included challenging the nature of the problem itself so as to find root causes, challenging the problem-posers so as to find their real objectives, and examining the collection of data which was often totally lacking. The approach was continued in peacetime when it was realized that many problems of business were of a similar nature to military ones, and success was immediate.

There is a well-known (post-war) story of the firm in which the employees complained continually about the slowness of the staff lifts, replacement of which would have cost a huge sum. A manager, trained in OR during the war, noticed that complaints were loudest in the ground-floor corridor, where everyone had to wait at some time, whatever their destination. When he collected data on the actual timings and compared them with other lifts elsewhere he found little or no difference. He therefore concluded that the problem was not one of slow lifts but of people thinking they were slow. His solution was a psychological one; he had large mirrors put on the corridor walls next to the ground floor lift gates and the grumbling stopped at once. Given something interesting to do (and what is more interesting than looking at oneself?) the people's sense of time changed. This example also illustrates that, even though OR solutions are theoretical, they are intended to be implemented successfully.

OR modelling does not have to be mathematical, then. In the above case, the model was a psychological but quantified conception of how people measure time while waiting. In most cases, however, mathematical or statistical techniques do come in and OR is considered to be in the quantitative area. All the maths and statistics included in this book have direct applications in business or in quality control. Having seen why things are so we shall now see how to use them: most people find this much the more interesting part.

We proceed to our next statement. *OR is about finding optimal solutions to problems*. Most management problems are difficult to define precisely, because they arise from the interaction of unclear forces and constraints. At school we looked at the water level in a tank filled by taps and emptied through pipes and holes, all involving fixed rates of flow. Management mathematics, being more realistic, has to operate with ill-defined rates; for example, sales could be not more than 1000 units, production not less than 1600 or we close down, raw material shortages mean that a maximum of 56 units of product A can be made, if we drill a hole there is an estimated 0.2 chance of striking oil, and so forth.

Mathematical models in such cases are rarely equations; more usually they are inequalities or interactions between frequency distributions. But there is usually a wide range of solutions that are feasible. Many of these can be reached by trial and error, politely called experience, so that business can continue to run. The nagging worry to the manager has always been to find better ways, i.e. those increasing profit, or cutting costs, or reducing idle time of men and machines. The difficulty is, how does the manager know whether there is a better solution and also, if one exists, in which direction to change things to achieve it? Then, what is the best solution, if there is one? It is here that the mathematics can help. Let us look at another, more realistic example.

A firm uses a material all the time, the total annual consumption being known. In what way should it place its orders for this material to achieve minimum total cost?

Where a firm does not wish to place a bulk order, but prefers to buy in quantities as needed, the total cost of the material may be considered as composed of three elements:

1. The price of the material.

2. The cost of the procedures to make the purchases.

3. The cost of holding material in stock.

The total cost, which we seek to minimize, is the sum of these three.

The data will have to be collected, but we could expect the purchasing procedure to cost the same for each order placed. The annual cost of this element for our material is thus

Number of orders × cost of placing an order

Placing fewer orders will reduce this cost. Similarly, the cost of holding stock is likely to be the same for each unit held, the annual cost being

Average number of units in stock × annual cost of holding a unit

Placing fewer orders must involve larger quantities per order and hence higher stock levels. Fewer orders will therefore increase this cost element, working against the ordering cost. The cost of the material may be subject to quantity discounts and may vary as time passes, but apart from such matters the number of orders will not affect the total annual cost of the material.

We are approaching a picture (a model) of the situation, and to take the first steps towards finalizing the model, to make a solution possible, let us simplify or even oversimplify the picture, hoping to bring back the complexities later if we can. For now let us assume the following.

1. The orders are all of the same size.

2. The rate of consumption is uniform, so that the orders will be placed at regular intervals throughout the year. Moreover, deliveries arrive just as stocks run out.

3. The price per unit of product is the same, regardless of the number or size of orders.

The price of the products will not now affect the issue, for we shall have to pay the total price of all our units however we order them. We seek only to minimize

Cost of placing orders + cost of holding stock

We can do so by choice of the size of an order, and hence of the number of orders placed annually.
Let us call

Annual consumption	$= D$	units of product
Cost of placing an order	$= C$	units of money
Cost of holding 1 unit of stock for 1 year	$= H$	units of money
Size of an order	$= S$	units of product

$$\text{The numbers of orders needed in a year} = \frac{\text{annual consumption}}{\text{size of order}} = \frac{D}{S}$$

$$\text{The total annual cost of placing these } \frac{D}{S} \text{ orders} = C \times \frac{D}{S}$$

The average amount of material held in stock is half the size of an order, since consumption is uniform. Thus

$$\text{The average amount held in stock} = \tfrac{1}{2}S$$

$$\text{The annual cost of holding it} = \tfrac{1}{2}SH$$

These two elements of total cost, $\dfrac{CD}{S}$ and $\dfrac{SH}{2}$, are both shown in Figure 14.2 which relates the annual costs concerned to the number of orders placed. The curves of the two cost elements may be added graphically by measuring the two curve heights at each given number of orders and plotting the sums of these two. This gives the total cost involved, which has a minimum, the guidance we seek. This coincides with where the two original curves cross, as can be proved.

The graphical model can be used in any real situation by putting figures to C D and H and plotting accurately; varying values of S will lead to the minimum. The alternative algebraic model is

$$\text{Total cost} = T = \frac{CD}{S} + \frac{SH}{2}$$

Figure 14.2   Relation between annual costs and number of orders placed.

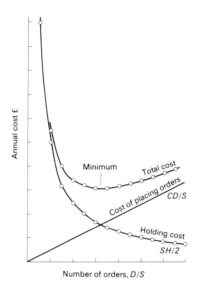

and we wish to minimize T by choice of S. The differential calculus, too large a topic for this book, speedily gives the answer; those unfamiliar with calculus should skip a few lines to the result.

$$\frac{dT}{dS} = -\frac{CD}{S^2} + \frac{H}{2} \quad 0$$

and

$$\frac{CD}{S^2} = \frac{H}{2}$$

and

$$S^2 = \frac{2CD}{H}$$

and

$$S = \sqrt{\frac{2CD}{H}}$$

This formula gives the order size which results in the minimum annual cost under our simplifying assumptions. It is often called the *economic order quantity* or EOQ. As an example, if it costs £2 per year to hold a unit in stock, if we use 0 000 units per year and it costs £5 to place an order, the EOQ is

$$EOQ = \sqrt{\frac{2 \times 5 \times 10\ 000}{2}} = \sqrt{50\ 000} = 223.6$$

which means that we should place 10 000/223.6 or 44.7 orders per year. Obviously we would use 45 orders of 222 or 223 units each to make up our

10 000, going slightly above minimum cost to be practical. However, even this may not work if the supplier accepts orders only in round figures. The analysis can therefore go on to show how much cost above the minimum will be incurred by departures from EOQ. (This can be read directly from the graphical model.) The algebraic method can also proceed to take quantity discounts into account, thus becoming much more realistic.

It must be admitted, however, that the EOQ concept is rarely, if ever, used. There are three main reasons:

1. Uniform consumption rates, steady prices and precisely synchronized deliveries are rarely met in the same product.

2. When a number of products have to be used together and their EOQs differ, with consequent different ordering schedules, the task of administering the purchasing becomes overwhelming.

3. If a supplier can be induced, by means of a bulk order, not only to give quantity discounts but also to allow the customer to call for delivery when and as he wants it, the supplier and not the customer has to carry the main stock. This is much to the latter's advantage, completely upsets the model used, and is a very common practice.

Nevertheless, this example has illustrated our final definition. *OR is about solving quantified management problems in quantified terms.* This is still a definition that leaves out more than it includes, but it will suffice in the present context of several chapters of illustrations. The fact that our two examples so far have been over-simplified out of usefulness does not matter; we shall now go on to examine some OR applications that have become standard management techniques. All have in common the OR approach, which we can now recognize as being as follows.

1. *Formulate the problem.* It is not necessarily what was first presented. Account should be taken of management objectives.

2. *Develop a model* of the situation which is susceptible to scientific (often mathematical) analysis.

3. *Find the scientific solution* of the model.

4. *Interpret this solution* in practical terms, not forgetting the management objectives.

5. *Implement the solution* with the managers concerned.

6. *Verify the results.* If the model was not quite accurate (for example, through over-simplification) some modifications may be needed.

XV
FORECASTING

Probably the most important single document in any firm is the sales forecast, for much vital information is worked out from it; the production levels that will be needed, with their consequent capital expenditure, material purchasing, recruitment and training implications; the revenue and cash flow forecasts; profit forecasts and so on. In short, all the firm's planning derives ultimately from the sales forecast. Clearly, the most accurate possible forecasting is needed and any techniques that work reliably will be viewed with the utmost interest by management. Forecasting models, or predictive models, therefore figure prominently in OR applications.

Looking into the future is very difficult and one needs all the help one can find when doing so. Help comes from two types of source:

1. Information on past performance.

2. Knowledge of outside influences.

Of these, the second must be supreme. For example, if we sell ice cream and our recent sales up to yesterday show a rising trend, it is no use predicting that the rise will continue if we know that a spell of unseasonable, very cold weather is about to hit us. Tomorrow's and the next few days' forecasts should be at a lower level. All the methods we shall consider then, will produce forecasts that must be subject to modification in the light of any outside information we can bring to bear on them.

As an example to illustrate our techniques, let us take the absenteeism figures of Table 11.1, a little of which is reproduced here as Table 15.1. Ignoring the calendar, we have re-labelled the days as periods numbered from 1 upwards, and we shall pretend to be starting at period zero with an unknown future that will steadily be revealed as time passes. Our task is to try to forecast that future as accurately as we can. We assume further that at the outset we have no idea of what our first result could be.

It is both convenient and clearest if we think of any forecasting problem in graphical terms. At the very beginning, then, we have a pair of axes, Figure 15.1, and no inkling of where to put our forecast for period 1. Unless we can get some information, for example, by market research in a sales situation, we can only make a guess and attach no great value to it, or at least be prepared to be wildly wrong. In Figure 15.2 however, period 1 is over and we have a result, shown as a black dot on the chart. Forecasting period 2's result is that much easier; we must decide whether to go up or down or stay at the same level. The optimists will predict a fall in absenteeism as at A (with sales figures, they and those who believe that efforts will result in growing figures will forecast a rise), though the

Table 15.1   Absenteeism figures from Table 11.1

Time period	1	2	3	4	5	6	7	8	9	10
Day	F	M	T	W	Th	F	M	T	W	Th
Absenteeism %	5.8	3.6	4.9	3.1	2.8	3.0	7.0	5.5	4.6	3.0

Time period	11	12	13	14	15	16	17	18	19	20
Day	F	M	T	W	Th	F	M	T	W	Th
Absenteeism %	4.2	6.9	5.2	4.4	3.0	4.3	6.8	5.4	4.1	2.9

Time period	21	22	23	24	25	26	27	28	29	30
Day	F	M	T	W	Th	F	M	T	W	Th
Absenteeism %	4.0	7.1	6.5	3.2	2.6	4.1	5.9	5.0	3.3	2.8

Time period	31	32	33	34
Day	F	M	T	W
Absenteeism %	3.6	5.8	5.1	3.8

Figure 15.1

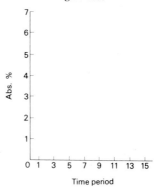

Figure 15.2

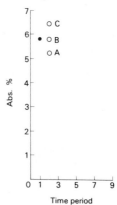

extent of it can only be guessed at unless there is outside information. Similarly C is a guess by the pessimists, and B is for those who see no reason to be either optimistic or pessimistic and argue that if one can only make a guess, it might as well be the same as the only piece of hard information available.

The result of period 2 turns out to be as in Figure 15.3. With two pieces of hard information available, forecasting the next result can be more scientific, and there are two main heads under which we can work:

1. Identifying and following trends from the past.

2. Using some sort of average of past data.

As always, outside information may override either, but we shall take this for granted from now on.

Figure 15.3

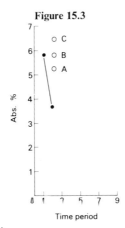

Time period

Forecasting by trend analysis

Regression

With only two points, as in Figure 15.4, there is only one possible straight line that can fit any trend exhibited by the data. The forecast will therefore be on

Figure 15.4

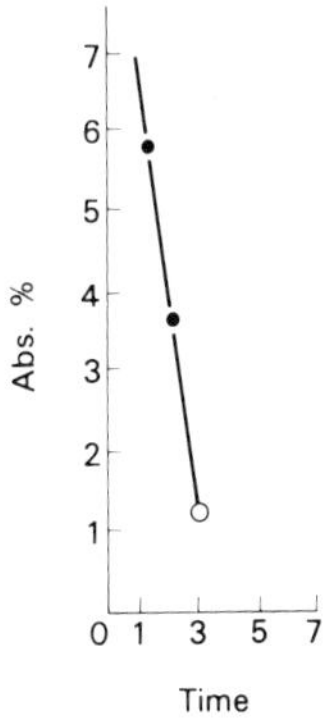

Time

this line. However, as time passes there is some choice of best line, and the regression line of data on time (in this case, absenteeism on time) is often used (see Figure 15.5). In this way we smooth out all the (assumed random) departures from the linear trend of our absenteeism, to arrive at as many forecasts as we wish to mark in on the line. Forecasting with the linear regression model is a widely used technique, the dangers of which have been discussed in Chapter XII. These dangers are least if we forecast only the shortest distance ahead, i.e.

Figure 15.5

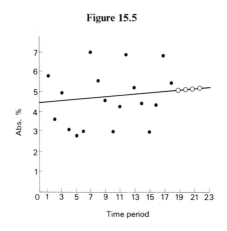

one period, and regression is popular for this as a quick, easy technique to apply. In particular, a computer can readily store all past data; calling it up with the regression program and adding just the one latest figure will produce an instant forecast based on the most up-to-date information. In Figure 15.6 the complete data of Table 15.1 has been graphed, every forecast being the linear regression projection of all previous data, i.e. we have forecast only one period

Figure 15.6

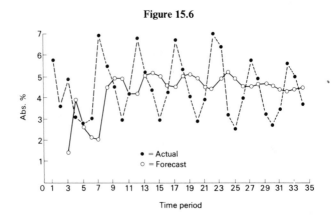

ahead in every case. This gives an idea of how this model worked with a particular set of actual data; it is a matter of trial and error to gauge whether it works well enough in whatever situation you may have in mind.

Curve fitting

As the calculations are more difficult, the computer is even more convenient for fitting curves than straight lines. If it is believed that some particular curve is a better model than the linear regression, the stored data can be used with the curve-fitting package to generate forecasts based on the desired curve.

With sales forecasting in particular, studies of many products have shown that they have a growth pattern in which sales tend to rise only slowly at first, then gather momentum as the product becomes known and wanted, finally tending to level out as the market saturates. Figure 15.7 shows such a curve. Several mathematical formulae have been proposed as models with this sort of shape, including the Gompertz (log $y = A - BC^t$) and Logistic ($1/y = A + BC^t$) curves familiar to marketing economists. The point in using such models is that, once the best such curve has been fitted to available sales data, quite long-term forecasting should become possible. This is how very large firms manage to look 10 years or so ahead. These curves are included in many curve-fitting computer packages.

Figure 15.7 A product growth pattern.

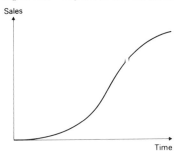

Time-series analysis

Very many situations include a seasonal or cyclic element as well as a general upward or downward trend. Ice-cream sales are an obvious example. The seasons of the year greatly affect short-term sales levels, but taking the figures a whole year at a time smooths out the seasonal effect and reveals whether sales are growing or declining overall. Our data of Table 11.1 probably contains a seasonal cycle as well as the obvious weekly one seen in Figure 15.6, both superimposed on any long-term trend that may be affecting absenteeism.

Time-series analysis is an economic statistician's tool designed to isolate and measure any trend and any cyclical effects in data coming from successive time periods. This involves smoothing out any random fluctuations. The analysis, by producing these components of variation for us, can assist in building OR models: let us then follow the economists' standard method.

Time-series analysis works by using the effect just described for ice-cream sales, namely that one complete cycle is much like another apart from trends, random fluctuations and outside influences. A graph quickly guides us towards finding the length of a cycle, but if we have no idea of it we can find it by adding up the data in pairs, then starting again in threes, then in fours, in fives, sixes, sevens and so on. When we hit the right periodicity there will be smooth changes from one total to the next, otherwise the totals will vary quite a lot. The additions in threes, say, will be done as follows:

$$1st + 2nd + 3rd$$
$$2nd + 3rd + 4th$$
$$3rd + 4th + 5th$$
$$4th + 5th + 6th \text{ and so on.}$$

Table 15.2   Finding the periodicity

Period	Abs. %	Totals in 2s	3s	4s	5s	6s	7s	8s	9s
1	5.8								
2	3.6	9.4							
3	4.9	8.5	14.3						
4	3.1	8.0	11.6	17.4					
5	2.8	5.9	10.8	14.4	20.2				
6	3.0	5.8	8.9	13.8	17.4	23.2			
7	7.0	10.0	12.8	15.9	20.8	24.4	30.2		
8	5.5	12.5	15.5	18.3	21.4	26.3	29.9	35.7	
9	4.6	10.1	17.1	20.1	22.9	26.0	30.9	34.5	40.3
10	3.0	7.6	13.1	20.1	23.1	25.9	29.0	33.9	37.5
11	4.2	7.2	11.8	17.3	24.3	27.3	30.1	33.2	38.1
12	6.9	11.1	14.1	18.7	24.2	31.2	34.2	37.0	40.1
13	5.2	12.1	16.3	19.3	23.9	29.4	36.4	39.4	42.2
14	4.4	9.6	16.5	20.7	23.7	28.3	33.8	40.8	43.8
15	3.0	7.4	12.6	19.5	23.7	26.7	31.3	36.8	43.8
16	4.3	7.3	11.7	16.9	23.8	28.0	31.0	35.6	41.1
17	6.8	11.1	14.1	18.5	23.7	30.6	34.8	37.8	42.4
18	5.4	12.2	16.5	19.5	23.9	29.1	36.0	40.2	43.2
19	4.1	9.5	16.3	20.6	23.6	28.0	33.2	40.1	44.3
20	2.9	7.0	12.4	19.2	23.5	26.5	30.9	36.1	43.0
21	4.0	6.9	11.0	16.4	23.2	27.5	30.5	34.9	40.1
22	7.1	11.1	14.0	18.1	23.5	30.3	34.6	37.6	42.0
23	6.5	13.6	17.6	20.5	24.6	30.0	36.8	41.1	44.1
24	3.2	9.7	16.8	20.8	23.7	27.8	33.2	40.0	44.3
25	2.6	5.8	12.3	19.4	23.4	26.3	30.4	35.8	42.6
26	4.1	6.7	9.9	16.4	23.5	27.5	30.4	34.5	39.9
27	5.9	10.0	12.6	15.8	22.3	29.4	33.4	36.3	40.4
28	5.0	10.9	15.0	17.6	20.8	27.3	34.4	38.4	41.3
29	3.3	8.3	14.2	18.3	20.9	24.1	30.6	37.7	41.7
30	2.8	6.1	11.1	17.0	21.1	23.7	26.9	33.4	40.5
31	3.6	6.4	9.7	14.7	20.6	24.7	27.3	30.5	37.0
32	5.8	9.4	12.2	15.5	20.5	26.4	30.5	33.1	36.3
33	5.1	10.9	14.5	17.3	20.6	26.5	31.5	35.6	38.2
34	3.8	8.9	14.7	18.3	21.1	24.4	29.4	35.3	39.4

In Table 15.2 this has been done on the data from Table 15.1. A periodicity of 5 is very clear (see Figure 15.6), showing that a week is a week whether counted from Monday to Friday, Wednesday to Tuesday or whatever. We find the trend and the cyclical effect by concentrating on the sums in fives as in Table 15.3. Column 1 contains the data. In column 2 it is added in fives, this being the length of a cycle. In column 3 the fives are added in pairs so that this column contains 10 days' total, thus:

$$1st + 2nd + 3rd + 4th + 5th$$
$$+ 2nd + 3rd + 4th + 5th + 6th$$

Table 15.3 Calculation of trend and cyclical effect

	Data (1)	Add in 5s (2)	Add Col. (2) in 2s (3)	Divide Col. (2) by 10 (4)	Col. (1) − Col (4) (5)
Fri.	5.8				
Mon.	3.6				
Tues.	4.9				
Wed.	3.1				
Thur.	2.8	20.2			
Fri.	3.0	17.4	37.6	3.76	−0.76
Mon.	7.0	20.8	38.2	3.82	3.18
Tues.	5.5	21.4	42.2	4.22	1.28
Wed.	4.6	22.9	44.3	4.43	0.17
Thur.	3.0	23.1	46.0	4.60	−1.60
Fri.	4.2	24.3	47.4	4.74	−0.54
Mon.	6.9	24.2	48.5	4.80	1.03
Tues.	5.2	23.9	48.1	4.81	0.39
Wed.	4.4	23.7	47.6	4.76	−0.36
Thur.	3.0	23.7	47.4	4.74	−1.74
Fri.	4.3	23.8	47.5	4.75	−0.45
Mon.	6.8	23.7	47.5	4.75	2.05
Tues.	5.4	23.9	47.6	4.76	0.64
Wed.	4.1	23.6	47.5	4.75	−0.65
Thur.	2.9	23.5	47.1	4.71	−1.81
Fri.	4.0	23.2	46.7	4.67	−0.67
Mon.	7.1	23.5	46.7	4.67	2.43
Tues.	6.5	24.6	48.1	4.81	1.69
Wed.	3.2	23.7	48.3	4.83	−1.63
Thur.	2.6	23.4	47.1	4.71	−2.11
Fri.	4.1	23.5	46.9	4.69	−0.59
Mon.	5.9	22.3	45.8	4.58	1.32
Tues.	5.0	20.8	43.1	4.31	0.69
Wed.	3.3	20.9	41.7	4.17	−0.87
Thur.	2.8	21.1	42.0	4.20	−1.40
Fri.	3.6	20.6	41.7	4.17	−0.57
Mon.	5.8	20.5	41.1	4.11	1.69
Tues.	5.1	20.6	41.1	4.11	0.99
Wed.	3.8	21.1	41.7	4.17	−0.37

'Seasonal adjustments' from Col. 5 figures

	Fri.	Mon.	Tues.	Wed.	Thur.
	−0.76	3.18	1.28	0.17	−1.60
	−0.54	2.05	0.39	−0.36	−1.74
	−0.45	2.05	0.64	−0.65	−1.81
	−0.67	2.43	1.69	−1.63	−2.11
	−0.59	1.32	0.69	−0.87	−1.40
	−0.57	1.69	0.99	−0.37	
Total	−3.58	12.72	5.68	−3.71	−8.66
Average	0.60	2.12	0.95	−0.62	−1.73

In column 4 the column 3 totals are divided by 10 to find the average daily figure in that overlapped double cycle. The changes in this column from one figure to the next come from

First figure	Second figure
$1 + 2 + 3 + 4 + 5$	$2 + 3 + 4 + 5 + 6$
$+ 2 + 3 + 4 + 5 + 6$	$+ 3 + 4 + 5 + 6 + 7$

and amount to: Add day 6 and day 7

Subtract day 1 and day 2

Hence column 4 contains the trend, which is shown plotted in Figure 15.8. All random fluctuations have been smoothed out by averaging.

Column 5 contains the trend subtracted from the data, i.e. column 4 subtracted from column 1. These figures are deviations from the trend and must therefore contain the cyclical element with the random fluctuations. These last

Figure 15.8

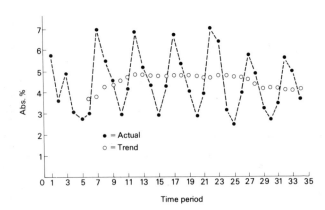

Time period

are averaged out, day by day, in the little table at the top of page 168. Groups of five figures from column 5 are written out in horizontal rows so that each day forms a column by itself. Totalling and averaging within each column gives the daily average deviations from the trend. Thus we have:

Mon.	Tues.	Wed.	Thur.	Fri.
+2.12	+0.95	−0.62	−1.73	−0.60

The total should be zero, so the rounding-off error (which amounts to 0.12) should be distributed among the deviations to bring them back to one decimal place again, like the original data:

Monday	2.1	above trend
Tuesday	0.9	above trend
Wednesday	0.6	below trend
Thursday	1.8	below trend
Friday	0.6	below trend

Economists go on to *seasonally adjust* their data by deducting these cyclic deviations from actual data. Thus, if a Monday gave an actual absenteeism of, say, 6.7%, the figure they would quote would be 6.7 − 2.1 or 4.6%, seasonally adjusted. This shows the current level without short-term fluctuation, i.e. the average expected for this week, which is the kind of result an economist needs for data such as exports or unemployment.

For our predictive model, however, it will work the other way round. If the general level predicted, no matter how, comes to 3.2%, then if it is a Monday a better prediction will be 3.2 + 2.1 or 5.3%. Again, the general level might be a weekly average.

We know from Chapter XI and Table 11.1 that there is a strong temperature element in the absenteeism figure, as well as a day-of-the-week element. So far we have treated each separately, and clearly we shall have a far better predictive model if it can include both components. This is discussed later in this chapter, under Market Modelling.

Forecasting by averages

Long-term averages

Figure 15.3 showed the results of two periods. If we argue that there is no reason to believe that the first and second results are anything other than typical, then the forecast for the third period (Figure 15.9) could well be their mean. If we have no outside information, this is a perfectly valid way to proceed. Continuing this argument as time passes, the next forecast will always be the average of all preceding actual figures. Figure 15.10 shows this happening with the data of Table 15.1. It is clear that the forecast is smoothing out the daily fluctuations of both random and cyclical origin.

However, if we continued with the entire year's data we should find ourselves fairly inaccurate. During the lower absenteeism of the summer our forecasts

Figure 15.9

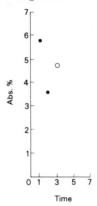

would still be burdened with old, high winter levels which would be no longer relevant. Then, next winter the summer levels would tend to weight the average against accuracy. In other words, this method is good at getting rid of random variations and unwanted short-term oscillations, but is poor at following changes of trend or long-term oscillations because it smooths these out at the same time.

Figure 15.10   Forecasting by long-term mean.

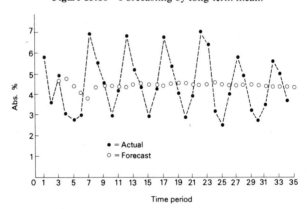

Moving averages

If we want our forecast to smooth out a short-term oscillation and yet follow a trend or long-term cycle, our average of past behaviour has to be taken over a period that bridges over the unwanted periodicity, but is short enough to ride up and down the longer-term changes. Table 15.2 showed this happening, with totals of fives ignoring the 5-day cycle and indicating the mean levels. Short-term averages generated in this way are called *moving averages*, or sometimes

Figure 15.11   5-day moving averages as forecasts.

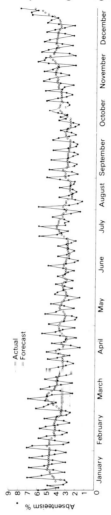

crawling averages. Figure 15.11 shows how a 5-day moving average follows the long-term (i.e. longer than cyclic) changes in the whole of the year's data, providing quite good forecasts in a smooth sequence. Its success as a model may be judged from the graph.

Exponential smoothing or exponentially weighted moving average
The moving average, of course, forecasts the next period as the average of the last few periods. It has smoothed out random variations along with the short-term cycles. If we are trying to predict the exact level for each period we need to use all the information we have, including the extent of random fluctuations.

But as we see, the moving average throws away information as fast as more arrives. Since in forecasting we rely on the past to guide us on the future, it would be wise to use the whole past in an appropriate way, if we can. The 'appropriate' way is in fact the vital part, for we do not want past irrelevancies to have undue influence. Exponential smoothing meets our need here. All we need say is

next forecast = last forecast + a certain fraction of the last error

The fraction used is always the same. As a formula, with the fraction called K,

$$F_{N+1} = F_N + K(A_N - F_N)$$

where F means forecast and A means actual.

To see how it works, let us take a value of 0.4 for the fraction and use the data in Table 15.1. Suppose we do not make a first forecast, but choose our prediction for period 2 as the actual of period 1, neither optimistic nor pessimistic. We have, once the actual for period 2 is known,

$$A_2 = \text{actual}_2 = 3.6$$
$$F_2 = \text{forecast}_2 = 5.8$$
$$A_2 - F_2 = \text{error}_2 = \underline{\underline{-2.2}}$$

so

$$\text{forecast}_3 = \text{forecast}_2 + (0.4 \times \text{error}_2)$$
$$= 5.8 - 0.88 = \underline{\underline{4.92}}$$

In due course it becomes known that actual_3 is 4.9, so error_3 is $4.9 - 4.92$ or -0.02, and

$$\text{forecast}_4 = \text{forecast}_3 + (0.4 \times \text{error}_3)$$
$$= 4.92 - 0.01 = \underline{\underline{4.91}}$$

Figure 15.12   Forecasting by exponential smoothing ($K = 0.4$).

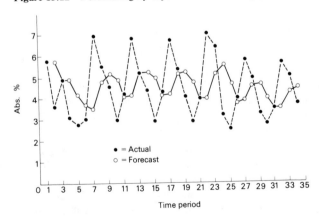

and so on. Figure 15.12 shows graphically what happens when this continues. We see that our forecast is always smoothing. This is because all past history is taken into account, including our own forecasting inaccuracy, so that a measure of self-correction is automatically present. Moreover, the recent past is taken more into consideration than the remoter past, i.e. it is used more prominently in the forecast. These statements may seem surprising at first with such a simple procedure, but their reasons are found when looking at the algebra:

$$F_{N+1} = F_N + K(A_N - F_N)$$
$$= KA_N + (1 - K)F_N$$

But $\quad\quad\quad\quad F_N$ was $KA_{N-1} + (1 - K)F_{N-1}$ in its turn,

so $\quad\quad\quad F_{N+1} = KA_N + (1 - K)[KA_{N-1} + (1 - K)F_{N-1}]$
$$= KA_N + K(1 - K)A_{N-1} + (1 - K)^2F_{N-1}$$

But $\quad\quad\quad\quad F_{N-1}$ was $KA_{N-2} + (1 - K)F_{N-2}$ in its turn,

so $\quad F_{N+1} = KA_N + K(1 - K)A_{N-1} + (1 - K)^2[KA_{N-2} + (1 - K)F_{N-2}]$
$$= KA_N + (K(1 - K)A_{N-1} + K(1 - K)^2A_{N-2} + (1 - K)^3F_{N-2}$$

and we can see the pattern of what is happening. Taking things right back to the start,

$$F_{N+1} = K[A_N + (1 - K)A_{N-1} + (1 - K)^2A_{N-2}$$
$$+ (1 - K)^3A_{N-3} + (1 - K)^4A_{N-4} + \cdots]$$

Now K is a fraction, i.e. less than 1, so $(1 - K)$ is also a fraction. This means that the powers $(1 - K)^2$, $(1 - K)^3$, $(1 - K)^4$, etc. get smaller as the index rises. The formula shows that a fraction K of the last actual A_N is included, with a smaller fraction $K(1 - K)$ of the previous actual A_{N-1}, a still smaller $K(1 - K)^2$ of A_{N-2}, and so on. All previous actuals are there, but they play an increasingly minor part as they drop further into the past. In index number language, their weightings decrease.

Still speaking of index numbers, the sum of the weightings has to be 1 if a true average and not an index number is to emerge. The sum of our weightings is:

$$K[1 + (1 - K) + (1 - K)^2 + (1 - K)^3 + (1 - K)^4 + \cdots]$$

Now formula 11 in our list of algebraic formulae of Chapter I, on page 19, makes it clear that

$$(1 - m)^{-1} = 1 + m + m^2 + m^3 + m^4 + \cdots$$

which looks like the contents of our square brackets, but with m instead of $1 - K$. Thus the square brackets may be replaced by $[1 - (1 - K)]^{-1}$ or K^{-1} or $1/K$. Our sum of weightings is therefore $K \times 1/K$ which is 1, and we have true average.

The reason for the phrase Exponentially Weighted Moving Average is now clear, but Exponential Smoothing is usually preferred for the sake of both brevity and pronounceability. The technique is very easy to use for short-term forecasting (it projects only one period ahead) and as we saw from Figure 15.12 it can provide a good forecasting model. Another advantage is that very little data needs to be stored to keep it going. However, its quality depends largely on the choice of K, the fraction of the error with which we correct our last forecast.

K is between 0 and 1. Looking at the extremes, if $K = 0$

$$F_{N+1} = F_N + 0(A_N - F_N)$$
$$= F_N$$

so that the next forecast is always the last forecast; it never changes. If $K = 1$,

$$F_{N+1} = F_N + 1(A_N - F_N)$$
$$= A_N$$

and the next forecast is the last actual. In this case our predictions would always be exact but one period too late. The nearer to 1 we choose K, the more sensitive to error the model becomes, i.e. the more closely we shall follow the fluctuations of the actuals (though a period late). The nearer to 0 we choose K, the more consistent the forecasts will be, though not necessarily very accurate.

There is no general rule for choosing the fraction K. The value that works best in a given situation is the one to use, and it is found by trial and error. Several values of K can be tried from the beginning, to see which gives results nearest to what happens. Where there is data from the past the trial can take place more quickly. Figure 15.13 shows what happens with $K = 0.1$ and 0.7 as well as our original 0.4, on the data of Table 15.1. This method of predicting the past will guide us to a suitable value quite easily if the trial ones are not seen as satisfactory. It can be tried from Figure 15.13.

Figure 15.13a

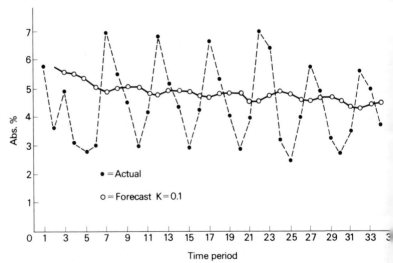

Figure 15.13b

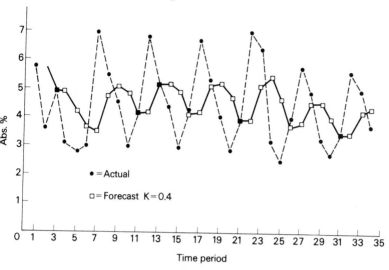

Figure 15.13c

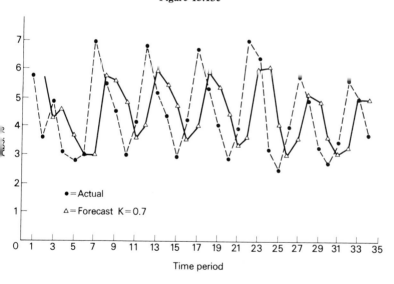

There are two circumstances in which exponential smoothing cannot predict accurately. These are after a high first forecast on a falling trend, and after a low first forecast on a rising trend. Figures 15.14 and 15.15 show these. The correction can never catch up with the trend. The obvious solution, once this situation

Figure 15.14

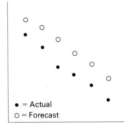

Figure 15.15

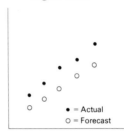

has been spotted, is to put the next forecast where we think it should go and not where the rule says. Other solutions involving more complicated formulae close the gap automatically, but at the price of more mathematics. It is beyond the scope of this book to discuss these techniques, reference to which may be made in books on inventory control.

Exponential growth and decay models

During World War II there was a major campaign against rats and mice as destroyers of food stocks. An advertisement of the time pictured two mice with several young and stated 'In three weeks, 2 can produce 50 more'. The implication was vivid; the next generations were multiplying at this rate every three weeks and the country would be overrun unless people did something about it. Today, only 30 years later, we are talking instead about a population explosion of humans.

The mathematics of these two situations are the same apart from the speed of growth. Each generation of two parents produces a certain number of offspring in a certain time. Inevitably, therefore, the breeding population will be double what it was after a definite number of days or years. Then start counting again, but with twice the initial population; after the same lapse of time there will be twice as many again. This describes a situation in which the rate of growth is proportional to the size of the population. Questions of rates involve the differential calculus:

$$\frac{dy}{dt} = My$$

from which we get the mathematical model of the population size y after a time of t:

$$y = A\,e^{kt}$$

where A and k are constants whose values fit the particular case being studied. A is the size of the population at time zero ($e^{k.0} = 1$ because anything to the power zero is 1), while k is the growth rate, faster in mice than in man. As Figure 15.16 shows, growth may be relatively slow at first, but there is rapid acceleration after a time, whatever the value of k.

Figure 15.16   Exponential growth curve $y = Ae^{kt}$.

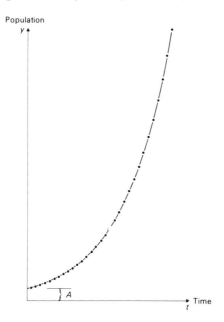

It will be clear that this curve is an easy model to use when the situation calls for it. All one has to do when fitting the curve (i.e. when finding the particular values of A and k to fit the situation) is to use two sets of data. Here is an example.

The population of a city was 100 000 in 1960 and 140 000 in 1970. Predict its future growth.

Assuming that growth is exponential, i.e. that its rate is proportional to the population, we use our exponential growth model and have

$$\text{Population} = Ae^{kt}$$

Thus for 1960, which is time zero,

$$100\ 000 = Ae^{k \cdot 0} = A$$

which fixes A, and using this for 1970 which is time 10,

$$140\ 000 = 100\ 000\ e^{10k}$$

so
$$e^{10k} = \frac{140\ 000}{100\ 000} = 1.4$$

But from tables of e^x, in Appendix I, $e^{0.34} = 1.4$

so
$$10k = 0.34$$

and
$$k = 0.034$$

Our model for this city is therefore

$$\text{Population} = 100\ 000\ e^{0.034t}$$

and the 1990 forecast, for instance, is

$$100\ 000\ e^{0.034 \times 30} = 100\ 000\ e^{1.02}$$
$$= 277\ 320$$

In practice this is probably too precise a forecast; it would be better to quote 275 000 or perhaps 280 000.

To find out how long it would take for this city to double in size, i.e. to reach 200 000, we proceed as follows:

$$200\ 000 = 100\ 000\ e^{0.034t}$$

so
$$e^{0.034t} = 2$$

But
$$e^{0.69} = 2, \text{ hence } 0.034t = 0.69$$

and
$$t = \frac{0.69}{0.034} = 20.29 \text{ years}$$

So it would take about 20 years for this population to double and we can forecast 200,000 in 1980, 400 000 in 2000, 800 000 in 2020, and so on. It is of course much quicker to fit this and similar curves by computer, pulling out forecasts as required.

This problem has been worded in terms of population growth, but it in fact applies wherever there is a steady percentage growth rate. Let us consider an example.

If inflation is running at 10% per year and an item costs £100 today, what will it cost in 20 years' time, other things being equal? Also, how long will it take for prices to double, i.e. for the value of money to be halved?

$$\text{Price} = £Ae^{0.1t}$$

since
$$10\% = 0.1 \text{ as a fraction}$$

Today
$$100 = Ae^0 \text{ and } A = 100$$

In 20 years	Price $= £100\,e^{0.1 \times 20} = £100\,e^2 = \underline{\underline{£738.91}}$
For the price to be £200	$200 = 100\,e^{0.1t}$
so	$e^{0.1t} = 2 = e^{0.69}$
and	$t = 6.9$ years

Another exponential growth situation arises where the law of diminishing returns is involved; the more a situation improves, the harder it becomes to make it better still. Where, as happens quite frequently, the rate of growth or improvement is inversely proportional to the situation (i.e. is proportional to the badness of the situation), the mathematical model becomes

$$y = A(1 - e^{-kt})$$

the graph of which is given in Figure 15.17. The level of y goes on rising, but less and less steeply as time passes, so that there is a limit beyond which the situation will not progress. The size of this maximum value is the A of the model, approached closely only for very large values of t but never reached.

Figure 15.17   Exponential growth curve $y = A(1_{-kt} - e^{-kt})$.

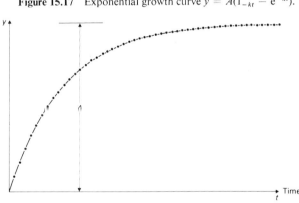

This model has an application in a learning situation, where it has been found that the rate of learning is proportional to the amount still to be learnt. Putting it another way, if a given percentage improvement follows from a certain amount of training or experience, that same percentage can occur again only after a multiple of that amount of further experience. For example, if a 10% improvement on a base standard takes a week of experience, a further 10% on the new level might take two weeks, the next 10% four weeks, and so on. Improvement is therefore rapid at the start where little is known, but the finer points take a long time to learn and the oldest hands admit cheerfully that they are still learning all the time. Let us look at an illustration.

An operator looking after a group of automatic machines can handle 40 routine stoppages per hour when fully experienced, but newly recruited people can manage only 20 per hour after one 5-day week of training. How long should we expect the new people to take to reach capabilities of 30, 35 and 40 per hour?

With the model $y = A(1 - e^{-kt})$, A will be the extreme limit of capability, approached only after years of experience. It must therefore be above 40, since fully-trained operators can be found with much less than a lifetime's experience. Let us guess that A is 50. Then, with $y = 20$ at $t = 5$,

$$20 = 50(1 - e^{-5k})$$

so
$$1 - e^{-5k} = 20/50 = 0.4$$

and
$$e^{-5k} = 0.6 \text{ which } = e^{-0.51} \text{ from tables}$$

so
$$5k = 0.51 \text{ and } k = 0.102$$

The specific model to fit the case is

$$y = 50(1 - e^{-0.102t})$$

With $y = 30$,
$$30 = 50(1 - e^{-0.102t})$$

so
$$1 - e^{-0.102t} = 0.6$$

and
$$e^{-0.102t} = 0.4 \text{ which } = e^{-0.92} \text{ from tables}$$

so
$$t = 0.92/0.102 = 9.019$$

i.e. it takes about 9 days to reach the 75% trained standard.

With $y = 35$,
$$35 = 50(1 - e^{-0.102t})$$

so
$$1 - e^{-0.102t} = 0.7 \text{ and } e^{-0.102t} = 0.3 = e^{-1.2}$$

Hence
$$t = 1.2/0.102 = 11.76$$

i.e. it takes about 12 days to become 7/8 trained.

Finally, for $y = 40$,
$$40 = 50(1 - e^{-0.102t})$$

so
$$1 - e^{-0.102t} = 0.8 \text{ and } e^{-0.102t} = 0.2 = e^{-1.61}$$

and
$$t = 1.61/0.102 = 15.78$$

Thus it takes about 16 days to reach full proficiency, only the first 5 days of which are needed to become semi-proficient.

All models are idealizations and this one is very obviously so. Some workers respond to training more quickly than others, and different final levels of achievement are the norm rather than the exception. Our guess of 50 for A may or may not be valid; we can judge only by comparing actual performance with those predicted by the model. A realistic way to find a value for A is via the average capability of all trained workers who have been in the factory long enough to stabilize their performance. A value a little above this average should be about right for the average trainee. Try some other value, for example $A = 45$, for yourself.

This practical approach to the use of the theory is typical of OR which is, after all, concerned with theory only because of its practical applications.

The above type of model can also be used for sales forecasting in a market approaching saturation. It is simpler than the Gompertz or Logistic curves which we shall refer to again under Market Modelling.

Decay models work much like growth models, a typical one being

$$y = Ae^{-kt}$$

to show the size of population left after a certain time t. Here the death rate is proportional to the population size. A perfect physical example of this is radioactive decay, where a fixed proportion of all atoms present will degenerate in a given period. As more decay there are fewer left from which the same proportion will be deducted in the next period. It is therefore quite sensible to talk of the half-life of a radioactive element, i.e. the time it takes for half of any lump of it to decay. The picture of this model is in Figure 15.18, with the extreme limit being zero. If for any reason the limit should be A, then

$$y = A(1 + e^{-kt})$$

can fit the situation. Where growth and decay take place at the same time, as in birth-and-death studies of a population, the models may be combined. This is done, for instance, when looking at market potential by way of population sizes.

Figure 15.18 Exponential decay curve $y = Ae^{-kt}$.

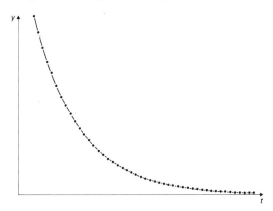

Market Modelling

Taking as our example the absenteeism figures in a factory we have seen that one measurement can be a consequence of many different factors interacting in complex ways. We found among other things that both temperature and the day of the week, as well as a random element, came into the picture, and all our attempts so far to predict absenteeism have been rather unsatisfactory, based as they are on only one cause at a time and treating all other causes as part of the random background.

The same picture emerges when forecasting sales. These may be affected by our own and our competitors' selling efforts (salesmen and/or advertising, etc.), our and their price levels, the economic climate and the weather, seasonal effects and the day of the week, and so on. Not all of these factors will apply in every case, and their relative importance may also vary from one product to another. Taking one particular product, its market model would be a formula that predicts its sales level if we specify how much of each factor is to come into play. Suppose, for instance, that our advertising expenditure is a factor in the model, and the sales director asks what would happen to sales if the expenditure on advertising were doubled. The model would take in the new value of this factor and produce the answer so that he could decide whether the extra expenditure would be justified or not. This sort of idea has been a pipe-dream of sales managers for many years. To try out advertising, or anything else, without risking thousands of pounds is to make the dream come true, and OR does just this through market modelling.

The market model itself is just an extension of the one-factor-at-a-time model, taking in as many factors as are thought relevant. Here is an outline of how to construct a market model.

1. Select the factors which can affect sales.

2. Find a suitable means of measuring them. For instance, is advertising to be counted as column-centimetres bought or as money spent?

3. Construct a reasonable formula which incorporates all the chosen factors. It is likely that different weights will be associated with them, but at this stage the relative weights may not be known.

4. Using past data, fit the model to the facts by calculating the values of the weightings that make the model work for the past, just as we did with the exponential growth models discussed above.

5. Repeat stages 3 and 4 if there are other reasonable formulae which might suit and choose as the model the one which seem most appropriate all round. The labour of calculation is likely to be considerable and a computer is not just useful but essential here. Indeed it is only the development of the computer, and in particular interactive access through the time-sharing terminal, that has made market modelling possible.

6. Test and use the model. Forecast with it, or try out changes in the variables under your own control (for example, the advertising) to find the best marketing tactics to adopt. Never fail to compare the actual results with the forecasts, so that the model is continually being monitored; refine it where it can be improved.

Market modelling is an art as much as a science, and the artistry is seen most at stage 3, the construction of the formula. There is a tendency for mathematically-minded people to go for powerful and/or elegant models involving lots of variables. Experience has shown, though, that such models are not helpful in the early stages; the best model to use is the simplest one that works. Another point arises when using the computer to fit the model. Invariably the curve-fitting routines, after announcing the constants for the curve of best fit, quote a % validity or some similar quantity. Mathematicians or (especially) statisticians may be tempted by their training to try different curve shapes and pick the one which the computer declares to be most valid. This is not necessarily the best model; it means that the fit is best to the data provided, on the least squares criterion. It is much more important to think in terms of a model being realistic than being the best possible fit to certain past data. It takes some experience to find the right balance.

In a simple way we can illustrate what happens in modelling by using our absenteeism figures again. There are only two factors we shall consider; temperature and day of the week. We might construct the following model:

1. Absenteeism $= A = KT + LF(\text{day}) + M$

where T is the temperature in degrees centigrade,

$F(\text{day})$ is a function of whatever day it is, for example, the cyclic corrections we found in time-series analysis,

K, L and M are constants which respectively multiply the temperature, multiply the daily correction and provide a base level.

Alternatively, with the same definitions we might have

2. $$A = K[\log T \times F(\text{day})] + M$$

or

3. $$A = Ke^{-LT} + F(\text{day}) + M$$

which at least has the higher temperatures causing less absenteeism. Another alternative is

4. $$A = K(1 + e^{-LTF(\text{day})})$$

which also drops absenteeism as temperature rises, and so on.

Thousands of models are possible. Let us begin with (1) as the simplest. Let us call the Monday to Friday corrections respectively, D_1, D_2, D_3, D_4 and D_5. For a Monday then,

$$A = KT + LD_1 + M$$

and so on. Our next job is to fit the model to the data, i.e. to find universal values for K, L and M which work; this will define our specific model. However, we also need values for D_1 to D_5 and here we note that if D_1 is to be fixed (which it is), then LD_1 is a constant, and so is LD_2, etc. But M is a constant also, hence $(LD_1 + M)$ and the others are all single constants, one for each day. Our Monday model thus reduces to

$$A = KT + C_1$$

with the daily constants now being called C_1 to C_5. We may expect K to be negative because absenteeism tends to fall with rising temperature.

These are straight-line formulae. In Chapter XII we found the one linear regression line which best fitted all days of the year; now we seek five such lines for better fit. The linear regression package fed with only the Mondays' figures will give the first of them, the Tuesdays' data will give the second, and so on. My computer runs gave the following results:

Monday	$A = 6.293 - 0.073T$	
Tuesday	$A = 6.021 - 0.125T$	
Wednesday	$A = 4.977 - 0.110T$	
Thursday	$A = 3.660 - 0.073T$	
Friday	$A = 4.985 - 0.103T$	

As with all forecasting techniques, it is advisable if possible to test the model by forecasting the past, using it to predict actuals that have already happened. Thus a Wednesday with a temperature of 6.5° is expected to have an absenteeism of 4.26%; we can check the data in Table 11.1 to see if this is reasonably accurate and should go on to try as many other examples as we can.

An alternative, equally simple model would have the daily correction as a multiplying factor of temperature, e.g. for Mondays

$$A = C_1 T + K$$

with K the same for all days. The Cs will probably be negative to allow absenteeism to fall as temperature rises; a simple model which produces the same effect with positive Cs is

$$A = \frac{C_1}{T} + K$$

It is a matter of trial and error to find the most satisfactory model in a given case. If you can use a computer, especially through a multi-access terminal, you might try fitting these two and testing their predictive abilities within Table 11.1.

Later refinements to the model might take into account the temperatures of the preceding day or days. For example, a cold snap which increases the prevalence of influenza or head colds might well provoke absences for recuperation. Monday's linear regression model might then develop into

$$A = KT_{\text{Monday}} + LT_{\text{Sunday}} + C_1$$

or perhaps into

$$(\text{change in } A) = K (\text{change in } T) + C_1$$

The previous absenteeism level may also be relevant and may have to be brought in separately.

These are enough examples to confirm that market modelling needs a lot of calculation and only the advent of the interactive computer terminal with instant response has made the idea feasible.

Market modelling is still in its early days. Some businesses, advanced in its use, have gone as far as developing models of their entire firms within their environments, to look at other implications of their activities. However, such firms are rare, mainly because these complex models require large amounts of stored data about both firm and environment, making a massive computer a prerequisite. It is interesting to note that some huge models (called database models because of the amount of stored data) have been abandoned as too complicated to be meaningful. It is worth repeating that the best model is the simplest one that works.

Those interested in following up these recent developments are referred to Clive Mann's little book *Market Models* (Mantec Publications) which is full of practical hints based on Mr Mann's experience as a consultant in this area with the Whitehead Consulting Group.

XVI
LINEAR PROGRAMMING IN ALLOCATION PROBLEMS

Here is a problem which is very common and quite simply stated.

Resources are limited and there are more than enough opportunities to use them. Of the many ways we could allocate our resources, which is the best?

Of course, we shall have to define what is meant by best. It is usually something like most profitable, least costly or involving least idle time for machines/men. The way to tackle the problem is as follows:

1. Formulate clear statements describing the limitations on each crucial resource. (Example: only 400 man-hours are available per week.)

2. Formulate a clear statement describing the test of the best solution. (Example: it maximizes the contribution to profit.)

3. Formulate clear statements defining each of the elements needed for the test. (Example: the contribution to profit of product A is £5.63 per unit.)

4. Put all these statements into the language of mathematical relationships. Finally, if it can be done,

5. Solve these mathematical relationships to find the answer defined as best.

This procedure is known as *mathematical programming* because it is a mathematical way to find the best programme of action, such as a production programme. As already implied, the maths can be carried through in only the simpler cases. We can consider here only the simplest of these, the ones where the mathematical statements about limitations on resources (the *constraints*) and the test of the best solution (the *objective function*) are linear. This means that the unknowns are in their simplest form, raised to no powers or roots and not multiplied by one another. Let us see what is involved by means of an example:

A firm of craftsmen makes reproduction furniture of high quality, and also undertakes the repair and refurbishing of genuine antiques. They are overwhelmed with orders in both areas, but due to the shortage of skilled men they have only 400 man-hours per week of productive labour. There is also a scarcity of the special timbers they use; in particular they can get only 1000 units per week of Timber A and 1500 units of Timber B.

The average repair uses 100 man-hours, 150 units of A and 50 units of B. The average new product uses 80 man-hours, 250 units of A and 400 units of B. The firm would like to earn the maximum contribution to profits from these limited resources. To stress to themselves the equal importance of both sides of their work, they feel that they must produce at least the equivalent of one average repair and one average product per week; their pricing is such that each brings in nearly the same contribution, £60 per repair and £70 per new product. At what proportions of products to repairs should they aim?

The statements of the constraints and the objective function are:

	A repair uses	A new product uses	Limit	
Man-hours	100	80	400	max
Timber A	150	250	1000	max
Timber B	50	400	1500	max
Repairs			1	min
Products			1	min

Objective function: $60 \times$ (number of repairs) $+ 70 \times$ (number of products) to be maximized.

The objective function in this case is a statement of the contribution that will be earned from whatever mix we decide to aim for.

The unknowns that we seek are two, the number of average repairs and the number of average products. Let us call them R and P respectively. The first constraint is on man-hours, and we see that each repair uses 100 of them. The R repairs to be done will have a total demand for $100\,R$ man-hours. The total man-hours to be used is thus $100\,R + 80\,P$. This may be less than, but may not exceed, the available maximum of 400 man-hours and the man-hours constraint reads, in mathematical form,

$$100\,R + 80\,P \leqslant 400$$

We note that the coefficients and the right-hand side could have been read straight from the statements above. By similar arguments, or directly from the statements, we may write out the full list of constraints as

Man-hours	$100\,R + 80\,P$	$\leqslant$	400
Timber A	$150\,R + 250\,P$	$\leqslant$	1000
Timber B	$50\,R + 400\,P$	$\leqslant$	1500
Repairs	R	$\geqslant$	1
Products	P	$\geqslant$	1

Note that maxima lead to $\leqslant$ and minima to $\geqslant$ in the constraints.

In school we were taught that N unknowns need N equations if solution is to be possible. Here we have 2 unknowns and 5 relationships, none of which is an equation. We are beyond the old school maths. However, it is quite easy to spot several solutions. For instance ($R = 2$, $P = 2$) works because it demands only 360 man-hours, 700 units of A and 900 units of B, all within limitations, while both R and P are more than 1. ($R = 3$, $P = 1$) also works, as does ($R = 1$, $P = 2$). Try them.

In fact there will be either an infinite number of solutions or no solution at all whenever the numbers of unknowns and relationships are out of balance. In this case, since we have already found some solutions, there must be an infinite number of them. Our problem is to find the one that is best for us, which is where the objective function comes into use. We seek the solution which maximizes contribution:

$$\text{Objective function} \qquad 60\,R + 70\,P$$

What of our 3 solutions so far?

$$\text{If } R = 2 \text{ and } P = 2, \qquad 60\,R + 70\,P = \text{£260}$$
$$\text{If } R = 3 \text{ and } P = 1, \qquad 60\,R + 70\,P = \text{£250}$$
$$\text{If } R = 1 \text{ and } P = 2, \qquad 60\,R + 70\,P = \text{£200}$$

Of these, then, the first is the best, yet can we be sure that it is the best answer of all?

A way of finding the optimal solution of a set of inequalities is known as the *simplex* method. With only two unknowns, as here, we may choose between graphical and algebraic versions of it, but with more than 2 unknowns graphs are impossible and only algebraic simplex works.

Graphical simplex

All we need do is plot the straight lines of the constraint relationships (which is why it is linear programming) to find the area where the solutions lie. Then we compare this area with the graph of the objective function to find our best solution.

Of course, we cannot draw the graph of an inequality. Instead we draw the line for the equality part of the constraint; the particular inequality will be represented by the total area lying to one side or other of the line and we check which it is. Let us consider our first constraint:

$$100\,R + 80\,P \leqslant 400$$

This involves a straight line (or a linear relationship) because R and P are present without powers or roots and without multiplying one another. To draw the straight line

$$100\,R + 80\,P = 400$$

is simple enough; we need only two points on it and these may most easily be found where it crosses the R and P axes. Putting $P = 0$ for the R axis, then,

$$100\,R + 0 = 400$$

So $R = 4$ and the point (4, 0) is on the line. Now putting $R = 0$ $0 + 80\,P = 400$. So $P = 5$ and the point (0, 5) is on the line. We draw the line through these two points (Figure 16.1).

For which side of the line is it true that $100\,R + 80\,P < 400$? If this is not obvious, we try any one point, the simplest being the origin (0, 0). The left-hand side is then zero, which is undoubtedly less than 400, so the area below this line

Figure 16.1

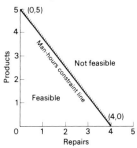

(i.e. the area including $(0, 0)$) is feasible as far as this constraint is concerned. For the next constraint we put $150 R + 250 P = 1000$. Then for $R = 0, P = 4$ giving the point $(0, 4)$ and for $P = 0, R = 6.667$ giving the point $(6\frac{2}{3}, 0)$. The feasible part is below the line through these two points. With the third constraint, $50 R + 400 P = 400$.

$$\text{For } R = 0, P = 3\tfrac{3}{4} \qquad \text{i.e. } (0, 3\tfrac{3}{4})$$
$$\text{For } P = 0, R = 30 \qquad \text{i.e. } (30, 0)$$

and the feasible part is again below the line.

Finally, $R \geqslant 1$ is to the right of a vertical line through $(1, 0)$ and $P \geqslant 1$ is above the horizontal line through $(0, 1)$.

Figure 16.2

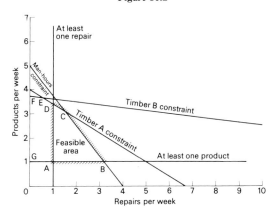

All five constraints are drawn in Figure 16.2, where it is seen that the area feasible when all constraints work together is inside the quadrilateral ABCD. As it happens, the Timber B constraint is excluded by the tightness of the others. (In real life things are often felt to be constraints until analysis shows otherwise.) Note that if we do not insist on at least one repair per week, the

Figure 16.3

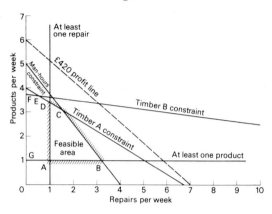

feasible area would be inside GBCEF and the B constraint would become involved.

Where a whole area is feasible, as here, the optimal answer, which is concerned with the most or the least of something, is bound to be at one of the corners, for these are the most extreme solutions and an extreme solution is called for. At this point we could therefore read from the graph the paired values of R and P at each corner, try them in the objective function and select the best, in this case the largest. However, this becomes laborious where there are many constraints and hence many corners, so let us go on to see the graphical relationship between the feasible area and the objective function.

The function $60\ R + 70\ P$ is not a relationship and therefore cannot be plotted on a graph. However, if we impose a value on it we create a relationship. Suppose we say that the contribution shall be £420, then

$$60\ R + 70\ P = 420$$

which is a linear relationship and can be plotted. We see that it passes through $(0, 6)$ and $(7, 0)$ by using the $R = 0$ then $P = 0$ method. This is shown in Figure 16.3. If we had imposed a different contribution level we should have had another line; for example, £210 would pass the line through $(0, 3)$ and $(3\frac{1}{2}, 0)$. This is enough to show that the general relationship

$$60\ R + 70\ P = K$$

with K taking any value we please, is a family of parallel lines. One of them will have the largest value of K that the feasible area will allow, i.e. it will just touch the feasible area. We have seen from $K = 420$ and $K = 210$ that higher values of K drive the profit line upwards and to the right. Figure 16.3 shows that the £420 line is already too high for the feasible area. Moving it down parallel to itself will first touch the feasible area at corner C, and since moving the line in this direction reduces the profit involved, C is the mix that gives the greatest possible contribution to profit under the constraints laid down. Corner A, where the line would leave the feasible area if we continued it down, represents the minimum contribution from the firm's efforts.

We have found the mathematically optimum solution. Incidentally, we chose £420 as a number which made division easy by both 60 and 70. Any number would have done instead, but it is obviously preferable to ease the workload if possible.

Since corner C is on both the Timber A and the man-hours constraints, this solution utilizes both these resources to the full, though there is some Timber B to spare. If, for example, corner B had turned out to hit the profit line first, we should have used all our man-hours but had some spare Timber A. Evidently we have been able to use this additional A to some profitable purpose.

Reading from the graph, C corresponds to about $1\frac{1}{2}$ repairs and 3.1 new products per week. The contribution earned by these quantities is

$$(60 \times 1\tfrac{1}{2}) + (70 \times 3.1) \text{ or } £307$$

which is usefully higher than the £260 we found from our casually spotted solutions earlier. Mathematically this is fine, but if it does not correspond with reality we should have to accept a less-than-optimal solution and leave some resources unused. For instance, if only whole numbers of items could be handled per week, we should have to bring the profit line further in until it touched a point with a pair of integer co-ordinates. In this case we should hit (1, 3) first, i.e. one repair and 3 new products, yielding £270 contribution.

In our example, though, is this necessary? After all, $1\frac{1}{2}$ repairs per week means 3 in 2 weeks which may be fully realistic, and the problem was posed in terms of average repairs or products. Surely we could make up even 3.1 average-new-product-equivalents out of a mixture of pieces? Once the mathematical model has done its work, reality has to take over and we must interpret the mathematical solution in ways that make sense.

Algebraic simplex

Let us now go back and pretend that we have not begun the graphical simplex and therefore know neither the fairly precise solution nor even that Timber B is not a limiting factor. We happen to have spotted three answers of which ($P = 3, R = 1$) is the best and we shall now search for a best-of-all solution by algebra.

Inequalities as such cannot be solved algebraically as they cover too many possibilities. To stand a chance of producing an algebraic solution (which is likely to be more exact than one read off a graph), we first turn the inequalities into equations. This is done by bringing new variables into the constraints as follows:

Man-hours	$100\,R +$	$80\,P + S_1$		= 400
Timber A	$150\,R +$	$250\,P$	$+\,S_2$	= 1000
Timber B	$50\,R +$	$400\,P$	$+\,S_3$	= 1500

| Repairs | R | | $- S_4$ | $= 1$ |
| Products | | P | $- S_5 = 1$ | |

It is clearest if we lay the equations out with each variable in its own column.

These additional quantities are known as *slack variables* because they repre-sent the amount of resource unused, i.e. the slack in our demand for them. Note that a slack variable is added to bring a quantity up to its maximum (man-hours, A and B) but subtracted to bring one down to its minimum (repairs, products). Thus feasible solutions compel all the slack variables to be positive quantities (or zero, of course).

We have 5 equations but 7 unknowns, R, P and S_1 to S_5. Again, there is either no solution or an infinite number of them, and we know that it is the latter.

The simplex method that leads us to the desired best answer is merely organ-ized trial and error, which is formally called an *iterative* process. Each new solution is tested on the objective function to see whether it has led to an im-provement; if not, the last change was in the wrong direction and we try again. We have to begin by guessing a solution for the wanted variables R and P. Any solution will do and to show how the method works we shall not now choose the best one already spotted, but start with the minimum requirements of $R = 1$ and $P = 1$.

Inserting this first solution into all 5 equations we have:

$$100 + 80 + S_1 = 400 \qquad \text{so } S_1 = 220$$
$$150 + 250 + S_2 = 1000 \qquad \text{so } S_2 = 600$$
$$50 + 400 + S_3 = 1500 \qquad \text{so } S_3 = 1050$$
$$1 \qquad - S_4 = 1 \qquad \text{so } S_4 = 0$$
$$1 - S_5 = 1 \qquad \text{so } S_5 = 0$$

The values of the slack variables, let us repeat, are the unused amounts of the constraints if we make only 1 product and do only 1 repair. Moreover they are all positive or zero, hence this solution is confirmed as feasible. (If this were a case with no solution, we could not have a set of non-negative slack variables whatever guesses we tried. This is a clue to insoluble cases.) The contribution, i.e. the value of the objective function is $60 + 70$ or £130. Can we do better? The answer is yes, but only by taking up the slack, i.e. by decreasing the slack variables. Increasing R by 1, for instance, reduces S_1, S_2 and S_3, but increases S_4 by 1. (We do not mind S_4 becoming large, but like all the others it must not become negative.) Increasing P by 1 also reduces S_1, S_2 and S_3 while increasing S_5 by 1. It is helpful to look at these reductions or increases in tabular form especially when large numbers of variables are involved. We shall do so (in Table 16.1) for units of R and P separately, and for 1 of each simultaneously. The figures for R alone and P alone are, of course, the coefficients in the con-straints. We may increase R and P, separately or together, by any amounts so long as the slack variables do not become negative. We should like to take up as

Table 16.1

Increase of 1 in	R	P	Both R and P
Reduction in S_1	100	80	180
Reduction in S_2	150	250	400
Reduction in S_3	50	400	450
Increase in S_4	1	—	1
Increase in S_5	—	1	1

much slack as we can at one go (i.e. to reduce the slack variables as nearly to zero as possible), so let us try a unit of each, to make $R = 2$ and $P = 2$. We see that we cannot double this adjustment of one of each, for S_1 would then become negative.

There is no need to insert the new values of R and P in the original equations; we can act on the last values of the slack variables directly to find their new values.

With $R = 2$ and $P = 2$
$$S_1 = \ \ 220 - 180 = \ \ 40$$
$$S_2 = \ \ 600 - 400 = 200$$
$$S_3 = 1050 - 450 = 600$$
$$S_4 = \ \ \ \ 0 + \ \ 1 = \ \ \ \ 1$$
$$S_5 = \ \ \ \ 0 + \ \ 1 = \ \ \ \ 1$$

The value of the objective function is $(60 \times 2) + (70 \times 2) = £260$ which is an improvement, but it has to be so since slack has been converted into contribution.

Can we add more of R or P or both? We cannot add as much as a whole unit of each, as we have seen. Nor can we add a whole unit of either separately, for S_1 would be driven negative. We notice, however, that P is more effective than R at raising contribution, so favouring P at the expense of R should give better results. What happens if we add a unit of P and remove one of R at the same time? The changes would be:

$$
\begin{array}{c|l}
\begin{array}{c} P + 1 \\ R - 1 \end{array} &
\begin{array}{l}
\text{increase } S_1 \text{ by } \ 20 \\
\text{reduce } S_2 \text{ by } 100 \\
\text{reduce } S_3 \text{ by } 350 \\
\text{reduce } S_4 \text{ by } \ \ 1 \\
\text{increase } S_5 \text{ by } \ \ 1
\end{array}
\end{array}
$$

This is not too good for S_1, but helps enormously with the other, larger ones. However, S_3 prevents us from doing this twice over and we apply this change once.

With $R = 1$ and $P = 3$
$$S_1 = \ \ 40 + \ \ 20 = \ \ 60$$
$$S_2 = 200 - 100 = 100$$
$$S_3 = 600 - 350 = 250$$
$$S_4 = \ \ \ \ 1 - \ \ \ \ 1 = \ \ \ \ 0$$
$$S_5 = \ \ \ \ 1 + \ \ \ \ 1 = \ \ \ \ 2$$

and the objective function is $(60 \times 1) + (70 \times 3) = £270$, another improvement as we expected. Moreover this is the final solution if only integer numbers are permissible, since this is the direction of increased contribution and neither S_3 nor S_4 will allow another unit move in this direction. Note, incidentally, that we do not seek to reduce S_4 or S_5 to zero, but we persist in working with them as a defence against non-feasible answers.

If we may use fractions the process can continue, but more slowly as the range of choices is wider and we have to be careful. We aim again at reducing the slack variables to zero, as far as we can. 0.6 of a unit of R will do exactly this for S_1 and almost for S_2.

So with $R = 1.6$ and $P = 3$

$$S_1 = 60 - 60 = 0$$
$$S_2 = 100 - 90 = 10$$
$$S_3 = 250 - 30 = 220$$
$$S_4 = 1 + 0.6 = 1.6$$
$$S_5 = 1$$

The objective function is $(60 \times 1.6) + (70 \times 3) = £306$. However, P should bring more contribution than R. Suppose that we had changed from $(R = 1, P = 3)$ by adding a fraction of P instead of R. This would have the added virtue of attacking S_3, the largest slack variable, more heavily. Comparing the $(R = 1, P = 3)$ table values with the table of changes wrought by one unit of P, we see that S_2 limits the increase to 0.4 of a unit of P. Let us try it:

with $R = 1$ and $P = 3.4$

$$S_1 = 60 - 32 = 28$$
$$S_2 = 100 - 100 = 0$$
$$S_3 = 250 - 160 = 90$$
$$S_4 = 1$$
$$S_5 = 1 + 0.4 = 1.4$$

The objective function is $(60 \times 1) + (70 \times 3.4) = £298$, which is not quite so good as with $(R = 1.6, P = 3)$. This is because 0.4 of a unit of P is not as profitable as 0.6 of a unit of R. Nevertheless, since P is better than R, can we move from our best-so-far solution by replacing some R by P? The changes brought about by $+0.1\,P$ and $-0.1\,R$ together are of course one-tenth of those caused by unit changes, i.e.

$$
\begin{array}{c|l}
 & \text{increase } S_1 \text{ by } 2 \\
 & \text{reduce } S_2 \text{ by } 10 \\
P + 0.1 & \text{reduce } S_3 \text{ by } 25 \\
R - 0.1 & \text{reduce } S_4 \text{ by } 0.1 \\
 & \text{increase } S_5 \text{ by } 0.1 \\
\end{array}
$$

Looking at the £306 values above, S_2 will allow exactly one of these moves and must lead to an increase in contribution:

with $R = 1.5$ and $P = 3.1$

$$S_1 = \quad 0 \;+\; 2 \;=\; 2$$
$$S_2 = \quad 10 \;-\; 10 \;=\; 0$$
$$S_3 = 220 \;-\; 25 \;=\; 195$$
$$S_4 = \quad 1.6 \;-\; 0.1 \;=\; 1.5$$
$$S_5 = \quad 1 \;+\; 0.1 \;=\; 1.1$$

and the objective function is $(60 \times 1.5) + (70 \times 3.1) = £307$. We have achieved the answer that the graph gave us. It has taken longer, but there are two points to note:

1. This method works also for 3, 97 or any number of variables, while graphical simplex can cope with only two. We used the same example only to demonstrate the technique.

2. The algebraic method is more accurate. We thought from the graph that $(R = 1.5, P = 3.1)$ was at the intersection of the man-hours and Timber A constraints, but we now see that this is not quite so, for we have 2 man-hours unused (i.e. $S_1 = 2$). We also find not only that Timber B is not a limiting constraint, but also that we shall have 195 units unused; the graph did not tell us this so easily.

The graphical error in man-hours is a tiny one, it is true, but now that we know about it thanks to algebra, could we not convert the small slacks into still more contribution by fiddling with hundredths of a product? Undoubtedly we could. Any mix that involves removing R and adding P in proportions higher than 6/7 of a P to a unit of R will increase the contribution. You may care to return to the £306 answer and try, with unequal additions of P and removals of R, to do better. It is possible. However, to illustrate the method of algebraic simplex, the present £307 answer will suffice.

Restrictions on solvability

If we insist on making at least 4 new products each week, as well as doing at least one repair, Figure 16.2 is modified by the raising of the horizontal line from the 1 to the 4 level, as in Figure 16.4. The constraints are marked on their non-feasible sides and it is clear that there is no area feasible for all constraints at once. The graphical simplex thus gives us no worries about questions of feasibility.

Algebraic simplex, as we saw, starts with a guess and looks out for negative slack variables to show non-feasibility. If we can find no feasible solution by guesswork, we may suspect that the problem has no solution at all, but proving that there is none to be found is another matter. The checks are lengthy and it is easiest in practice to feed the problem into a computer; linear programming packages include the checks and print error messages as necessary.

Another kind of unsolvable problem has areas which are feasible but unlimited. Thus if the constraints on timbers and man-hours were removed, leaving only at least 4 new products and at least 1 repair, there are minimum limits but no maximum ones. The solution for greatest contribution will

Figure 16.4

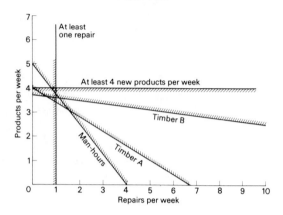

therefore be to produce an infinite number of each item. The presence of this kind of situation will quickly become clear from the working.

Computer solutions

The simplex method is an obvious candidate for the computer and there are scores of different packages available to apply it. The package is bound to need the following data:

> Number of variables
>
> Number of constraints
>
>> and for each constraint relationship:
>>
>> The coefficients
>>
>> Whether it is $\leqslant$, $=$ or $\geqslant$,
>>
>> The number to the right of that relation symbol
>
> The coefficients of the objective function
>
> Whether it is to be maximized or minimized.

Earlier we took pains to set out the constraint inequalities with a column for each variable. This has become standard practice because the coefficients, not forgetting zeros for absent items, can then be read straight into the computer, for which packages are invariably written to receive them in this order. The array of coefficients without variable names is called the *tableau*; positive signs are understood but negative ones have to be shown, as always.

Figure 16.5 shows in action a typical small package accessed through a time-sharing terminal; the printout has been annotated to show what was happening. The surplus and artificial variables were other introductions to suit the computer's way round the problem, the latter being in effect our slack variables S_4 and S_5 which did not need to be reduced but must not go negative.

Figure 16.5

```
GET-$LINPRO
9900 DATA 100,80,150,250,50,400,1,0,0,1,400,1000,1500,1,1,60,70
RUN                    THE CONSTRAINT RELATIONSHIP COEFFICIENTS
LINPRO                 AND OBJECTIVE FUNCTION ARE ENTERED IN
                       THE FORMAT REQUIRED BY THE PROGRAM.

* LINEAR PROGRAMMING *

IF MAX, TYPE '1'; IF MIN, TYPE '-1'?    1
TYPE: NUMBER OF CONSTRAINTS, NUMBER OF VARIABLES?  5,2
TYPE: NO. OF LESS THANS, NO. OF EQUALITIES, NO. OF GREATER THANS?  3,0,2


        YOUR VARIABLES 1     THROUGH 2
        SURPLUS VARIABLES 3     THROUGH 4
        SLACK VARIABLES 5     THROUGH 7
        ARTIFICIAL VARIABLES 8     THROUGH 9

TABLEAU AFTER Ø     ITERATIONS
  100     80     Ø     Ø     1     Ø     Ø     Ø     Ø     400
  150    250     Ø     Ø     Ø     1     Ø     Ø     Ø    1000
   50    400     Ø     Ø     Ø     Ø     1     Ø     Ø    1500
    1      Ø    -1     Ø     Ø     Ø     Ø     1     Ø       1
    Ø      1     Ø    -1     Ø     Ø     Ø     Ø     1       1
  -60    -70     Ø     Ø     Ø     Ø     Ø     Ø     Ø       Ø
   -1     -1     1     1     Ø     Ø     Ø     Ø     Ø      -2


    BASIS BEFORE ITERATION 1
    VARIABLE        VALUE
    5               400
    6              1000
    7              1500          VARIABLES 1 and 2 (i.e. R and P)
    8                 1          ARE GUESSED AT ZERO
    9                 1
    BASIS BEFORE ITERATION 2
    VARIABLE        VALUE
    5               320
    6               750
    7              1100
    8                 1          VARIABLE 2 HAS BEEN STEPPED UP BY 1
    2                 1
    BASIS BEFORE ITERATION 3
    VARIABLE        VALUE
    5               220
    6               600
    7              1050          BOTH VARIABLES ARE NOW 1 AND THE COMPUTER
    1                 1     }    HAS FOUND THE CHANGES IN SLACK VARIABLES
    2                 1          CAUSED BY UNIT CHANGES.
    BASIS BEFORE ITERATION 4
    VARIABLE        VALUE
    5                28
    4               2.4
    7                90
    1                 1
    2               3.4


ANSWERS:
    VARIABLE        VALUE
    3             .538462        SLACK VARIABLES 5 and 6 ARE ZERO. 7 IS
    4            2.07692         THE AMOUNT OF TIMBER B UNUSED.
    7            192.308
    1            1.53846    }  R = 1.538 REPAIRS, P = 3.077 NEW PRODUCTS PER WEEK
    2            3.07692

OBJECTIVE FUNCTION VALUE = 307.692
IN 4    ITERATIONS

TABLEAU AFTER 4     ITERATIONS
  Ø     Ø     1     Ø     .0192    -.0062    Ø    -1     Ø      .5385
  Ø     Ø     Ø     1    -.0115     .0077    Ø     Ø    -1     2.0769
  Ø     Ø     Ø     Ø    3.6538   -2.7692    1     Ø     Ø     192.308
  1     Ø     Ø     Ø     .0192    -.0062    Ø     Ø     Ø     1.5385
  Ø     1     Ø     Ø    -.0115     .0077    Ø     Ø     Ø     3.0769
  Ø     Ø     Ø     Ø    .3461     .1692     Ø     Ø     Ø     307.692
```

The whole job, including input of the data by a one-fingered typist, took about 4 minutes of terminal time. Printing of the output was continuous from the moment the last of the data went in, and CPU time was probably about 2 or 3 seconds only. Packages of this kind can handle up to 40 or 50 variables and up to a similar number of constraints; large packages in computers to match can handle many more.

Transportation

One particular sort of allocation problem arises so frequently that, although it is perfectly solvable by the simplex method, a special technique has been developed for it. This is the problem of transporting goods in the most economical way between m sources and n receiving-points, e.g. between 4 factories and 9 strategically-placed warehouses. The same case would arise, for example, in moving vehicles from m garages to n other points with minimum mileage.

Two features of the transportation situation are that only one commodity is involved, and that the tableau constraints are all equations. It is, of course, a condition of feasibility that the total amount of goods available must at least equal the total demand for them; this (possibly inequality) constraint is checked separately at the outset of solution rather than included in the tableau.

An advantage of using this special method of solution is that it requires less core store in a computer than does the ordinary simplex package. A given computer can therefore handle more variables and constraints with a transportation package than with a simplex one. The easiest way to describe the technique is through an example; a small one will suffice.

A motor accessory manufacturer has 3 factories and supplies his product to 4 car manufacturers. He is anxious to arrange his deliveries so that minimum unit-mileages are involved. The distances and factory capacities are as shown in Table 16.2. How should the deliveries be allocated to each factory?

We begin the solution by finding a feasible answer and a systematic approach develops quite a good first guess. We load the routes with as much as possible of their requirements, starting with the cheapest (or in this case, the shortest) and working upwards so that the dearest (longest) bears the least load. There is some spare capacity in the 3 plants and this is listed also as if it were another customer, but one a long way away so that it is supplied last of all. (The spare capacity is the slack variables.)

Table 16.2

Factory		Customer			
	Capacity (units)	A	B	C	D
1	1500	16	8	4	10
2	650	14	12	3	14
3	1350	18	4	7	14
Total needs (units)		1300	500	300	300

Table 16.3   Rank order

Factory		Customer				
Capacity		A	B	C	D	Spare capacity
1	1500	11 16	5 8	2 = 4	6 10	
2	650	8 = 14	7 12	1 3	8 = 14	
3	1350	12 18	2 = 4	4 7	8 = 14	
Total needs		1300	500	300	300	

We work with a tableau like the one in the statement of the problem. Ranking the mileages from the lowest gives us Table 16.3, with mileages being shown for reference at the lower left in each box. Now we load the customers with as many units as we can, starting with the law ranks, Route 2C is first. C needs 300 units altogether; 2 can supply them all so we allocate 300 to route 2C. Since C needs no more, 1C and C3 are allocated zero each. This is the position in Table 16.4. Next come two equal routes, 3B and 1C. The latter is already loaded with zero, however. B requires 500 units, 3 can supply them and we put 500 on route 3B with zero in 1B and 2B. Next in rank is route 1D. 1 can supply all 300 units needed by D and we load 300 into 1D with zero in 2D and 3D. 2A follows. A needs 1300 but the capacity of 2 leaves only 350 that can be supplied to A from there. 1A can receive the remaining 950 units for A, leaving zero for 3A. This fills in the tableau, and we see that 1 has 250 units of spare capacity, 2 has none and 3 has 850 units spare. This is the initial feasible solution in Table 16.5. The cost of this solution, measured in unit-miles, is found by multiplying the two figures on each real route and then totalling. It is 26 000 unit-miles.

The first solution is evidently a very reasonable first guess. The search for improvement consists of looking for interchanges between two factories and

Table 16.4   Start of loading

Factory		Customer				
Capacity		A	B	C	D	Spare capacity
1	1500	 16	 8	0 4	 10	
2	650	 14	 12	300 3	 14	
3	1350	 18	 4	0 7	 14	
Total needs		1300	500	300	300	

Table 16.5 First feasible solution

Factory		Customer				
	Capacity	A	B	C	D	Spare capacity
1	1500	950 \ 16	0 \ 8	0 \ 4	300 \ 10	250
2	650	350 \ 14	0 \ 12	300 \ 3	0 \ 14	0
3	1350	0 \ 18	500 \ 4	0 \ 7	0 \ 14	850
Total needs		1300	500	300	300	

two customers that could yield a saving. These must involve the same pairs of factories and customers, so we search for 4 corners of a rectangle within the tableau. For example, consider

$$1A \qquad 1C$$
$$2A \qquad 2C$$

The costs, written in the same way, are

$$16 \qquad 4$$
$$14 \qquad 3$$

Thus supplying A is shorter from 2 than from 1, but supplying B is longer from 2 than from 1, as we know. However, the difference is 2 miles for A and only 1 mile for B. If we effect a swap,

$$1A \qquad 1C$$
$$\downarrow \qquad \uparrow$$
$$2A \qquad 2C$$

with the arrows representing equal amounts of goods transferred from one pair of routes to the other, then a net saving of miles will follow without affecting factory capacities. Of course we must have some loads on the routes which are giving up certain quantities; in this case we have 950 on 1A and 300 on 2C. The maximum change is thus 300 units. Table 16.6 shows symbolically what we are doing and Table 16.7 shows the result.

Looking carefully at all other corners with loads, we see that no other changes are possible, since there is no way of shifting goods from a longer route to a shorter one without finding an absence of goods to swap, or alternatively without having at least as great an increase in exchange. We therefore have the final solution, at a cost of 25,700 unit-miles. We could see the saving of 300 coming from the net difference of 1 mile on the transfer of 300 units.

Table 16.6 Changing routes

Factory		Customer				
	Capacity	A	B	C	D	Spare capacity
1	1500	−300 16 ↓	8	+300 4 ↑	10	
2	650	+300 14	12	−300 3	14	
3	1350	18	4	7	14	
Total needs		1300	500	300	300	

Table 16.7 Final solution

Factory		Customer				
	Capacity	A	B	C	D	Spare capacity
1	1500	650 16	0 8	300 4	300 10	250
2	650	650 14	0 12	, 0 3	0 14	0
3	1350	0 18	500 4	0 7	0 14	850
Total needs		1300	500	300	300	

A theoretical point

We loaded only 5 of the possible 12 routes in the tableau. In fact, with m factories and n customers or vice versa (in general terms, with an $m \times n$ tableau) we should loan not more than $m + n - 1$ routes for the best solution. Our method of loading the cheapest first will ensure this.

In our example, $m + n - 1 = 3 + 4 - 1 = 6$. To load less than the formula states produces a solution called degenerate. However, a pejorative word need not worry us as there is no harm whatever in such a solution. It is more important not to use more than $(m + n - 1)$ and such cases tend to be found where a real-life pattern of transportation has evolved without much thought. Drawing the tableau of the existing pattern, which after all must be a feasible solution, allows this very quick check before the deeper attack is deemed necessary.

Obviously the computer will be used with large tableaux; our example was almost trivially small.

XVII
QUEUEING MODELS

A shop-counter queue forms and grows when the rate of arrival of customers is greater than their rate of being served and leaving the queue. It diminishes and may disappear when the rate of arrivals is less than the rate of service. A queue may thus be regarded as a buffer between an input process and an output process, for example, between demand (or arrivals) and supply (or service). By no means are all queues lines of people; here are some other examples:

1. An airfield handles incoming and outgoing aircraft and the associated traffic between runways and airfield buildings. At busy times, therefore, some traffic must wait before proceeding on its way.

2. At a taxi rank cabs arrive empty and may have to wait until a passenger arrives. On the other hand, at busy periods intending passengers must wait until an empty cab arrives.

3. Machines occasionally break down and must be repaired. Sometimes the repair mechanics will be unoccupied while all machines are running and at other times machines may be awaiting repair while each mechanic is busy.

4. Coal produced at a steady rate is delivered to the pithead, to be taken away by rail. Empty trains arrive only when the railways send them and a stockpile of coal builds up if there are longish gaps. On the other hand, a series of trains happening to arrive in quick succession could remove coal faster than the mines can deliver it. The queue (in this case the stockpile) then has another role, that of compensating for the deficiency of material arriving.

   If withdrawals continued to exceed arrivals until the stockpile was exhausted, a queue of trains could build up.

5. Rainfall varies both seasonally and annually, hence some form of storage is needed, so that water will always be available to consumers.

6. Long-distance telephone calls can be put through only when a line is free between the towns concerned. If more calls are demanded at a given moment than there are lines available, the excess of subscribers must wait. In fact the first attempts at a mathematical theory of queues came from telephone problems, studied in 1908 by Erlang for the Swedish Ericsson company.

A queue, then, is a dynamic condition with some special characteristics. The situation involves either demand waiting for service, or service facilities waiting for demand, and it does not matter which is considered as the input process and which the output. (Think of the taxis/people or the coal/trains examples above.) We shall find that the mathematics is the same from both aspects.

A queue copes with an out-of-balance condition between input and output processes, growing or shrinking according to which process is the larger of the two. However, the imbalance has to be temporary; if the input to the queue is permanently greater than the service, the queue must grow indefinitely, while in the alternative situation the queue will vanish. A temporary imbalance must imply that one process, or both of them, vary with time. An example of just one varying was the pithead, but both were varying in the taxis/people case. There need be no queue if both supply and demand are constant. Thus if a machine broke down regularly every 10 minutes and a repair always took just 10 minutes, one man could cope. If repairs took precisely 20 minutes each it would need 2 men to keep the machines running. With no queue, there is no queueing problem.

Queueing problems involve a search for optimal solutions. It costs someone money to have demand waiting for service and it also costs someone money to have service facilities idle for lack of demand. The optimal solution is the one that involves least total cost. Of course there are cases where the optimum is not sought; for example, hospitals arrange appointments so that doctors are not kept waiting, no matter how many patients wait for no matter how long at no matter what cost. Doctors are in such short supply that the cost of their time is considered (at least by the hospitals) as outweighing any cost of waiting patients. Similarly, the cost of a blast-furnace stopping for lack of iron ore and coke is so high that ironworks are usually prepared to pay for stocks (i.e. queues) of the raw materials sufficient to last for months without replenishment. However, more usual illustrations do seek optimal conditions.

1. A shopkeeper, hotelier or restaurateur must balance the cost of employing an idle staff in slack periods against the loss in busy periods if disgruntled customers, tired of waiting, go away unserved and resolve never to return.

2. The cost of employing mechanics to keep machines running must be weighed against the loss of production if broken-down machines are idle awaiting attention.

3. The stocks of raw materials or components that a factory carries can absorb a lot of its working capital and profits. The cost of holding stock must be balanced against the cost of lost production if there is a stockout. Much OR effort is devoted to finding optimum stock levels in different situations.

The search for optimal solutions leads us into a little mathematics.

The queueing problem

A queueing situation may be completely described by specifying:

1. The pattern of demand.
2. The pattern of service.

3. The number of service-points or channels.

4. The queue discipline.

The patterns of demand and service are their exact frequency distributions. The queue discipline is the set of rules imposed on those seeking service; obvious examples are first-come-first-served (i.e. new arrivals go to the back of the queue), or priorities for some (for instance, aircraft landing take precedence over those awaiting take-off from the same runways), and so on. There is a problem with multi-channel queues as to whether newcomers join the shortest queue, or any one they please, or whether they are directed so that each queue in turn receives a newcomer, for example.

As can be seen, the number of mathematically different possibilities is enormous and most can be very complicated. Only a few of the simplest cases have so far succumbed to an exact mathematical attack, despite the age of Erlang's work, but OR has developed an empirical method of solving all queueing problems, whatever their difficulty, in a readily understandable way. In all cases, whether by mathematics or by the OR technique of simulation, the problem is tackled by specifying the four factors listed above and then seeing what happens to the queue. If there is some choice, for example, if we could change the number of channels or the amount of service facilities, or if we could change the input pattern by an appointments system, we can solve the problem for each set of conditions put forward, see what the queues do, work out the costs and settle for the conditions that are most suitable all round. This is the real meaning of solving a queueing problem.

The mathematics of queues

Whatever the patterns of demand and service, a queue is ultimately a device that compares their averages. Slightly confusingly, these averages may be measured in two ways:

1. As average numbers arriving (or being served) per unit of time.

2. As the mean time between arrivals (or mean time per service).

Of course the two must be equivalent; for example, a mean arrival rate of 6 per hour is exactly the same as a mean time between arrivals of 1/6 hour or 10 minutes. Queueing theory could be developed from either point of view, and it turns out that the formulae are a little easier by method 1. It is therefore important to remember first to

> Turn all demand and supply rates into
> NUMBERS PER UNIT OF TIME

The time unit for both demand and service may be anything convenient, but must be the same for both in the same problem. Thus we speak of a mean of 40 aircraft landings or take-offs per hour (and not of one every $1\frac{1}{2}$ minutes on average) if an hour is a sensible time unit; if it takes on average 1 minute 20 seconds for each aircraft to clear the runway, leaving it available for the next user, we would have to say that the mean service time is 45 per hour. Again, it

3 minutes is the average interval between buses it may be best to say that the average arrival rate of passengers at a stop is 8.6 per 3 minutes. The mean service rate will then be the average number of people who can get on a bus when it arrives, for example, 10.4 per 3 minutes.

For the general case, let us call the mean arrival rate λ (the Greek lower-case lambda) and the mean service rate μ (we have already met mu) per unit of time. It is the relative sizes of λ and μ that will fix the behaviour of the queue, for if λ is greater than μ there is more demand than service and the queue must grow indefinitely. However, if μ is greater than λ, any queue will disappear in the long run for there is more than enough service to meet the demand. Short-term bursts of demand may build up the queue, but it must vanish in time.

Of course, with more service than demand, there will be idle spells for the service facilities and these cost money. One therefore thinks in terms of making $\mu = \lambda$, i.e. of providing service of which the average just meets the average demand. Surprisingly and regrettably, this would also mean that queues would grow indefinitely. The formulae will show this, but meanwhile suppose that, with $\lambda = \mu$, there is a temporary lull in demand and further that this enables the service facilities to dispose of the entire queue and be idle for a spell. The service has not asked to be kept idle; this was forced on it by the short-term lack of demand. We know that later there will be compensatory periods of heavy demand to maintain the overall average at λ, but the service cannot catch up with its own average in this way. Its idle time is lost to it. To say, for instance, that the service can handle an average of 10 clients per hour means that the average client demands 6 minutes. Any loss of time through lack of demand cannot alter the service-times needed when demand returns again, and the queue will therefore grow. I do not pretend that this explanation is rigorous, but I hope that it is at least plausible. The point to remember is that, if uncontrollably growing queues are to be avoided, there has to be more than enough service to meet average demand and some idle service facilities have to be accepted. It only remains to ask how much idle capacity we must maintain, and the answer depends on costs.

The ratio λ/μ is named ρ (the Greek lower-case rho, as for correlation coefficients) and is called either the *traffic intensity* after Erlang's work on telephone systems, or the *utilization*. Thus, as we have seen,

> If $\rho < 1$ the queues are manageable;
> if $\rho \geqslant 1$ the queues become infinite.

We shall therefore confine our considerations to cases where $\rho < 1$.

The first deduction we can make is that if $\rho = 0.8$, for example, then there is demand for 80% of the time, i.e. the service facilities are in use 80% of the time and idle 20%. (This is where the name utilization stems from.) The chance that the next arrival will find no queue and will therefore be served without waiting is 20%. In other words,

> The probability of at least one unit of demand
> being present $= \rho$.

and

> The probability of no queue $= P = 1 - \rho$.

We shall look at average queue sizes and average times spent waiting, omitting the theory and merely producing and using the answers. We have to decide on various definitions and for us the queue is made up of those waiting without yet being served. We define the *system* as the queue plus the individual being served.

Single-channel Poisson queues

The simplest queueing situations arise, of course, when there is only one channel or service-point, i.e. only a single queue. Within this category, the simplest kind of variation that can apply to the patterns of demand and service is random variation. This means that the Poisson distribution applies, giving rise to what are called Poisson queues.

With Poisson arrivals at an average rate of λ per unit time, the chances of 0, 1, 2, 3 . . . arrivals in the next unit of time are given by the Poisson formula (see Chapter VIII)

$$\text{Probability } (c) = \frac{e^{-\lambda} \lambda^c}{c!}$$

with c as the 0, 1, 2 or 3. . . . With μ for λ this would also be true for Poisson service. However, people sometimes prefer to speak of the average time per service rather than the mean number of services per unit of time, and of the pattern of service times rather than the pattern of numbers of services. This viewpoint of the Poisson leads to the negative exponential distribution and it does not matter whether we refer to Poisson or to negative exponential service times (or just to exponential ones); the situation is the same. We may meet, then

	Pattern of Arrivals	Service
1	Poisson (or exponential)	Poisson (or exponential)
2	Poisson (or exponential)	constant
3	constant	Poisson (or exponential)

As we have seen, the constant/constant case is not one for queueing. Cases 2 and 3 are mathematically identical. We need only think of the pithead situation with coal waiting for trains or trains waiting for coal; which is the demand and which the service? Really, then, we are left with only the two basic cases where either both arrivals and service are Poisson or one of them is Poisson and the other constant. We have already specified a single channel; the fourth factor for complete definition, the queue discipline, fortunately does not matter with these Poisson queues. Any queue discipline will do.

Poisson arrivals and service
The average queue length, Q, turns out to be

$$Q = \frac{\rho^2}{1 - \rho}$$

with ρ, of course $= \lambda/\mu$, i.e. mean arrival rate/mean service rate. The average number in the system, S, is

$$S = \frac{\rho}{1 - \rho}$$

The difference between these two is, of course, the individual being served. Subtracting to find this difference, we have

$$S - Q = \frac{\rho}{1 - \rho} - \frac{\rho^2}{1 - \rho} = \frac{\rho - \rho^2}{1 - \rho} = \frac{\rho(1 - \rho)}{1 - \rho} = \rho$$

Alternatively, then

$$S = Q + \rho$$

This difference is not 1, as might loosely be thought, for there is not always someone being served. Indeed, on average ρ people are being served, since this is the proportion of time that the facilities are being used.

Q is the average queue length overall, including times when there is a queue and times when there is not. If we wish to disregard empty systems, the average queue length when there is a queue, R, is

$$R = \frac{1}{1 - \rho}$$

How long must one wait? The mean time in the queue, W, i.e. before beginning to be served, is

$$W = \frac{\rho}{\mu(1 - \rho)}$$

which can also be put

$$W = \frac{Q}{\lambda}$$

The mean time in the system, V, i.e. both waiting and being served, is

$$V = \frac{1}{\mu(1 - \rho)}$$

which can also be put

$$V = \frac{S}{\lambda}$$

These two times are not surprising, for dividing queue or system lengths by arrival rates ought to give us the times spent in each.

Let us see what these formulae mean in an example. Suppose that on average 40 aircraft per hour seek to land or take off at a certain airport, while the mean time for an aircraft to be served, i.e. to occupy the runway, is 80 seconds, so that μ is 45 services per hour.

$$\rho = \frac{\lambda}{\mu} = \frac{40}{45} = \frac{8}{9}$$

It often pays to work in fractions rather than decimals.

The chance of an aircraft coming in or leaving without having to wait is thus

$$P = 1 - \rho \text{ or } 1/9$$

Thus an aircraft would have to wait 8 times out of each 9 takeoffs or landings, on average.

The mean queue length (both in the air and off-runway on the ground) is

$$Q = \frac{\rho^2}{1 - \rho} = \frac{8/9 \times 8/9}{1/9} = 7\,1/9 \text{ aircraft}$$

Excluding times of no queue, the mean queue length when a queue exists is

$$R = \frac{1}{1 - \rho} = \frac{1}{1/9} = 9 \text{ aircraft}$$

Some of these will be queueing to take off, others will be circling somewhere overhead.

Finally, the mean number in the system, i.e. queueing or actually on the runway, is

$$S = \frac{\rho}{1 - \rho} = \frac{8/9}{1/9} = 8 \text{ aircraft}$$

It must be remembered that these are averages. Sometimes there will be smaller queues, at other times they will be longer.

An aircraft will be queueing, awaiting clearance to enter the runway, or average for

$$W = \frac{Q}{\lambda} = \frac{64/9}{40} = \frac{16}{90} \text{ hours or 10 minutes and 40 seconds}$$

Adding the mean service time of 80 seconds gives 12 minutes, which should be the mean time in the system; let us check this from the formula for V.

$$V = \frac{S}{\lambda} = \frac{8}{40} = \frac{1}{5} \text{ hour} = 12 \text{ minutes}$$

Note that all calculations are worked in terms of the unit time quoted for λ and μ.

Here are two final formulae, both probabilities. The chance of waiting for a time longer than t, T, is

$$\boxed{T = \rho e^{-t(\mu - \lambda)}}$$

Thus the chance of having to wait at all is T with a value of zero for t, i.e.

$$T = \rho e^{-0} = \rho$$

which confirms the conclusion that the chance of someone being in the system is ρ. The chance of more than C customers in the queue, U, is

$$\boxed{U = \rho^{C+1}}$$

The chance in our example of an aircraft having to wait more than 30 minutes (or rather, $\frac{1}{2}$-hour) is thus

$$T = \rho e^{-t(\mu - \lambda)} = \frac{8}{9} e^{-\frac{1}{2}(45-40)} = \frac{8}{9} e^{-2.5} = \frac{8}{9} \times 0.0821 = 0.073$$

i.e. over 7% of all flights would have these extreme waits. The chance of an aircraft having to join a queue of over 10 aircraft is

$$U = \rho^{C+1} = \left(\frac{8}{9}\right)^{11} = 0.274$$

i.e. over a quarter of all aircraft movements would be so affected.

These results explain the congestion at busy international airports. While the facilities can more than cope on average with the demand, there is not enough slack in the system to avoid delays. As a rule of thumb, the utilization of any system should not exceed about 0.7 or 70% if queues are to be kept reasonably short. The cost of airport facilities on this scale would frighten anyone; instead governments (who must pay) seem to prefer having the airlines and their passengers bear the costs of delays.

Let us remind ourselves that the formulae work only if $\lambda < \mu$ or $\rho < 1$. If we try them with $\lambda = \mu$ or $\rho = 1$, infinite or indefinite results emerge, as stated earlier.

Lastly, it remains to point out that these formulae are valid for our example only if aircraft movements are at random times and if they also take random lengths of time on the runways. Can this be so when aircraft fly to schedules? Strangely, observation has shown that both are approximately random. Times on the runway vary with the type of aircraft, the extent to which it happens to be loaded and the strength of gusts of wind. The overall mixture seems to produce a near-Poisson result. The clock times of arrivals are affected very much by the weather (bearing in mind that the planes come from all over the world), and by delays at the airports of departure. Take-off times are affected partly by landing times of the same aircraft (themselves a mixture of arrival times and queueing delays) and partly by such accidental events as breakdowns and maintenance; these also fit Poisson quite well. In fact it is surprising how many commercial and industrial situations are near enough to Poisson in pattern, i.e. random, so that our simple theoretical model can be applied to them.

Poisson arrivals, constant service time or vice versa
Yet another surprise in the field of queueing theory is that this case of random/constant rates is actually more complicated to analyze than the random/random situation. The pithead illustration is of this type, as is its converse, the blast furnace whose daily consumption of raw materials is constant while arrivals tend to be random. Examples are harder to find than of the random/random case, but as more service tends to be provided by automatic machines the importance of this type of queue is growing.

The formulae are a little different from those of the first case; here are some of them. The average length of queue, Q, is

$$Q = \frac{\rho^2}{2(1 - \rho)}$$

The average number in the system, S, is again ρ more than Q:

$$S = Q + \rho \qquad \text{or} \qquad S = \frac{\rho^2}{2(1 - \rho)} + \rho$$

As before, the lengths of queue and system are divided by the arrival rates to find the times. Thus we have the mean waiting time in the queue, W, as

$$W = \frac{Q}{\lambda}$$

and the mean time in the system, V, as

$$V = \frac{S}{\lambda}$$

Multi-channel queues have been fully solved only in the simplest case of Poisson input and Poisson (or negative exponential) service. Rather than have complicated formulae, it is easier to use the graph of Figure 17.1, which applies to this Poisson/Poisson case.

Figure 17.1   Poisson queue with multi-channel service. The graph shows Q, the mean queue length, for C channels and various values of utilization L $(=\rho/C)$. For conversion to other parameters use $W = Q/\lambda$, $S = Q + \rho$, $V = S/\lambda$.

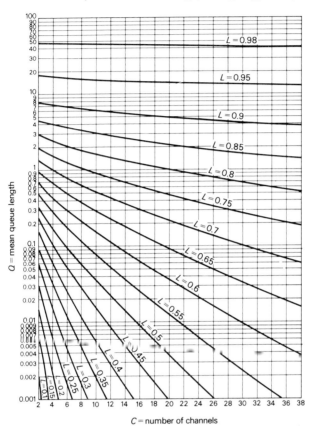

C = number of channels

Our discussion has implicitly assumed that whenever we looked at a queue it had settled down and the position was stable. It is in fact common for the start of any queueing process to be highly unstable and the formulae will not then apply.

Nor can these formulae work where queues are of artificially limited length; if there are only 8 chairs in a barber's shop or only a limited storage capacity for stock, any excess arrivals may not join the queue and are lost to the system. Yet another complexity to nullify the use of our formulae would be extraordinary departures, those who have joined the queue but leave it before their turn for service arrives, whether through tiring of waiting or for any other reason.

All in all, the mathematical theory of queueing is so hedged in with restrictions and conditions that the vast majority of real-life queueing problems are outside its scope. Nevertheless, there is a brilliantly simple way of solving them all.

Simulation

If we could somehow get representations, in other forms, of the input and output processes, the service-points and the queue-discipline, it might be possible to play them off against each other and see what happens. True, mathematical equations are representations, but of the relationships in the processes rather than of their events. When the maths fails we seek more realistic models of the events themselves, actual arrivals and services rather than an overall picture. This is what simulation sets out to do.

In the early 1950s I was slightly involved with the blast furnace stock problem described earlier. Because of the enormous costs incurred if a blast furnace should be extinguished, ironworks traditionally devoted large tracts of expensive land to holding huge stocks of iron ore, coke and limestone, ensuring at least that the catastrophe would not occur for lack of raw materials. In consequence they ran out of land for expansion while at the same time some stockpiles were so old that mature trees were growing on them. When the managements awoke to this they sought OR aid to find the optimum amount of stock to carry. They could instead have managed without theoretical help and simply have reduced stock levels until they hit trouble, but they knew the OR way to be quicker, safer and cheaper.

It was clear that this was a queueing problem, with a constant daily rate of demand. The supply side was observed over a period and it was found that the materials arrived only in whole rail truckloads. To the astonishment of the investigators (these were early days in the applications of queueing theory outside the telephone networks) it was found that deliveries were almost perfectly at random—the Poisson model was an excellent fit. The constant rate of demand was known; the average rate of deliveries obviously had to equal the demand in the long term; there was in effect one service point and as it did not matter which of the material was used first, any convenient queue discipline could be assumed. However, this was a finite queue situation: once the stockyard was full any further arrivals had to be turned away and were lost.

Existing theory was not able to cope, and while an approximate theoretical way of finding the optimum stockyard size was developed (by D. G. Nickols of the British Iron and Steel Research Association), it was felt necessary to build a model to simulate the situation. The model was an electrical analogue (Figure 17.2) which represented material by electricity. The stockyard was simulated by a capacitor that could store electricity until it was full, then no more. Deliveries in truckloads were represented by a Poisson generator of electric pulses comprising a radioactive source (a luminous light-switch button), followed by a Geiger counter and an amplifier. The blast furnace was a circuit that drained a steady current from the capacitor whatever its state of charge. A pen recorder monitored the electrical stock-in-hand. The various elements were adjustable so that different combinations could be tried out, and another circuit, detecting when the store became empty, could instantly refill it

Figure 17.2

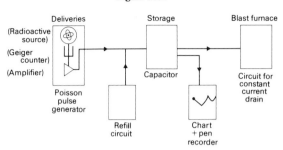

to a predetermined level so that the same situation could be run through repeatedly. Of course these refills showed up clearly on the chart produced by the pen recorder so that afterwards the distances (i.e. times) to emptiness could be measured and converted into the probability of running out of stock in the given set of conditions.* From these runs, which simulated years of blast furnace operation in a few hours, it was possible to find a size of stockyard that gave an acceptably small chance of being emptied while costing a suitable amount in land and other items. Meanwhile the cost of the simulation study was only a couple of thousand pounds, but it saved millions.

Simulation has come a long way since then, thanks particularly to the computer. Nevertheless the principles remain the same:

1. Find out by observation, prolonged if necessary, what the exact patterns of demand and service are.

2. Decide on the queue discipline, the number of service points and any special conditions. Generally speaking, the aim is to find what service facilities ought to be provided, so these are the items to be tried out in various mixes.

3. Find suitable representations in detail of all the above, put them together and observe the results.

4. Cost the consequences and make the managerial decisions.

Suppose new loading facilities for lorries are to be provided at a warehouse and it has to be decided how many loading bays should be built. Since the lorries belong to customers it is bad policy to have them wait a long time, yet bays cost a fortune to build and to man, so no unnecessary ones are to be contemplated. We would have to find through observation the current arrival pattern of the lorries, as timings. The pattern of service times, i.e. the pattern of times it takes to load lorries now, must also be noted. Suppose we find that there are different patterns for each main size of lorry (as is reasonable); we should then need to note the lorry sizes as well as their timings in the arrivals, with a set of loading times for each size in the service pattern. All in all, a complicated picture is likely to appear, possibly along the lines of Table 17.1.

* The equipment was described in *Proceedings of the Isotope Techniques Conference, Oxford*, July 1951, Volume II (HMSO) in the paper by H. Herne, its designer.

Table 17.1 Distribution of lorry arrivals and loading times

17.1A Mean numbers of arrivals per hour:

Time	8.00–9.00	9.01–10.00	10.01–11.00	11.01–12.00	13.01–14.00
Mean arrivals per hour	14.2	8.6	5.8	10.0	7.7

Time	14.01–15.00	15.01–16.00	16.01–17.00
Mean arrivals per hour	5.5	5.6	6.0

17.1B Deviations from average

Observation shows that actual numbers of arrivals within any hour vary from day to day in an approximately Normal pattern, with a standard deviation about 25% of the hourly average. Thus, between 8 and 9 a.m. the number-of-arrivals pattern may be taken as Normal with mean 14.2 and standard deviation 3.55.

17.1C Moments of arrival

Within the hourly numbers of arrivals, there are equal chances of a lorry arriving at any given minute of the hour. In other words, for any specified hour there is a uniform pattern of moments of arrival over a period of days.

17.1D Pattern of lorry sizes

Up to 2-tonners	3-tonners	4-tonners	5-tonners	Over 5-tonners
24%	28%	21%	16%	11%

The order of arrivals is random throughout, i.e. the chance of the next lorry being a 4-tonner is 21% or 0.21.

17.1E Pattern of loading times

	10–15 mins	16–20 mins	21–25 mins	26–30 mins	31–40 mins	41–60 mins
Up to 2-tonners	30%	23%	27%	16%	4%	—
3-tonners	22%	28%	20%	18%	10%	2%
4-tonners	16%	23%	28%	19%	11%	3%
5-tonners	6%	15%	24%	27%	20%	8%
Over 5-tonners	—	7%	19%	33%	26%	15%

Sorting out these patterns from the observations normally requires some simplification, but in the end something like this will emerge, a clear enough picture of what is happening now.

Would the same patterns continue once the new facilities were installed? Someone has to clarify this point, and if changes are to be expected the tables should be modified as foresight indicates. Since the method of simulation will not be affected by such changes, we shall assume that the Table 17.1 data is expected to hold good.

The next step is to convert all the figures into percentage patterns like those of lorry sizes (17.1D) and loading times (17.1E). The reason for this is the method of simulation. Let us look at this for the lorry sizes. Imagine two packs of playing cards, i.e. 104 in all, with four cards removed to leave exactly 100. We then associate each card of our super-pack with a particular size of lorry so that shuffling and drawing makes a simulated lorry size generator. Suppose we remove one king of each suit from the 104; we could then, for example, associate cards with lorry sizes as in Table 17.2. Note that the total number of cards in each group is exactly the same as the percentage of lorries in that group. To simulate the next arrival, draw a card from the shuffled pack, replacing it and reshuffling immediately. Thus if a 10 is drawn the lorry is a 5-tonner and the chances next time are the same as this time, and are as observed in real life. Also as in real life, the exact order of lorry sizes arriving will be dictated by chance.

Table 17.2

	Up to 2-tonners	3-tonners	4-tonners	5-tonners	Over 5-tonners
%	24	28	21	16	11
Associated cards	aces 2s 3s	4s 5s 6s black 7s	red 7s 8s 9s king (spades)	10s jacks	queens kings (hearts) (diamonds) (clubs)

Because of the ease with which playing cards, roulette wheels, dice and the like generate chance quantities for us, this technique of simulation is sometimes called the *Monte Carlo method*. Obviously, random numbers are also ideal chance quantities, being available in streams as rapidly as needed. When associating random numbers with percentages it is easier if we work with cumulative percentages. Thus, with the same figures for lorry sizes, we would have the results of Table 17.3 and working in this way the digits (even including 0 if we regard it as 100) correspond precisely to the cumulative percentages. Thus if 26 turns up this means that the lorry is a 3-tonner. Where we work to one place of decimals in percentages, e.g. 21.8%, 3-digit random numbers from 001 to 999 and 000 can be allocated in just the same way. Where we have awkward totals instead of round 100s or 1000s we can still use random numbers, however. For example, the 60 minutes of the hour may be simulated by random digit pairs from 00 to 59, while 60 or over would be discarded if they appeared. Converting all the parts of Table 17.1 into cumulative percentages gives us Table 17.4 There is no need to allocate random numbers since the cumulative percentages

Table 17.3

	Up to 2-tonners	3-tonners	4-tonners	5-tonners	Over 5-tonners
Cumulative %	24	52	73	89	100
Associated random numbers	01 to 24	25 to 52	53 to 73	74 to 89	90 to 99 and 00

do this automatically. All in all, these patterns are quite complicated and certainly not Poisson.

Now we decide on the hypothetical facilities and queue disciplines to try out. Suppose we provide two loading bays, each capable of handling all sizes of lorries, and rule that bay 1 will be used before bay 2 if the choice is available.

Table 17.4 Cumulative distribution of arrivals and service

17.4A Numbers of lorries arriving within the hour

No. of lorries	8.00 to 9.00	9.01 to 10.00	10.01 to 11.00	11.01 to 12.00	12.01 to 13.00	13.01 to 14.00	14.01 to 15.00	15.01 to 16.00	16.01 to 17.00
0		00.01	00.01		00.01	00.01	00.01	00.01	00.01
1	00.01	00.03	00.05	00.02	01.20	00.03	00.06	00.05	00.04
2	00.03	00.11	00.44	00.07	30.11	00.15	00.55	00.51	00.39
3	00.08	00.46	02.68	00.26	88.82	00.73	03.46	03.18	02.28
4	00.20	01.63	10.72	00.82	99.84	02.73	13.77	12.66	09.12
5	00.48	04.71	29.06	02.28	100.00	08.04	35.81	33.42	25.24
6	01.04	11.34	55.49	05.48		18.86	64.19	61.24	50.00
7	02.12	22.85	79.59	11.51		35.82	86.23	84.13	74.76
8	04.09	39.01	93.53	21.19		56.17	96.54	95.67	90.88
9	07.16	57.37	98.62	33.46		75.01	99.45	99.24	97.72
10	11.84	74.26	99.81	50.00		88.39	99.94	99.92	99.61
11	18.40	86.77	99.98	66.54		95.67	100.00	99.99	99.96
12	26.77	94.31	100.00	78.81		99.01		100.00	99.99
13	36.77	97.96		88.49		99.70			100.00
14	47.77	99.40		94.52		99.95			
15	58.91	99.85		97.72		99.99			
16	69.39	99.97		99.18		100.00			
17	78.49	100.00		99.93					
18	85.78			99.98					
19	91.18			100.00		*Note:*			
20	94.88					These are calculated from the			
21	97.22					normal distribution with the			
22	98.60					means given in Table 17.1A			
23	99.33					with standard deviations res-			
24	99.71					pectively equal to a quarter o			
25	99.88					the means.			
26	99.95								
27	99.98								
28	99.99								
29	100.00								

17.4B Moments of arrival—take random pairs from 00 to 59

17.4C Pattern of lorry sizes

Up to 2-tonners	3-tonners	4-tonners	5-tonners	Over 5-tonners
24	52	73	89	100

17.4D Pattern of loading times

	10–15 mins	16–20 mins	21–25 mins	26–30 mins	31–40 mins	41–60 mins
Up to 2-tonners	30	53	80	96	100	—
3-tonners	22	50	70	88	98	100
4-tonners	16	39	67	86	97	100
5-tonners	6	21	45	72	92	100
Over 5-tonners	—	7	26	59	85	100

At this stage we do not limit the size of possible queue. The queue-discipline is established as first come, first served.

To carry through the simulation manually, we need a quantity of random numbers and a worksheet with a number of columns. Simulated lorry arrivals need random numbers, as follows in our example:

	Example
1. 4 digits to give the number of arrivals in a given hour	2864
Then, for each lorry,	
2. 2 digits not exceeding 59, to give the minute of arrival	09
3. 2 digits to give the size of the lorry	56
4. 2 digits to give its loading time	31

We start the day at 08.00 hours and our first random number, 2864, is in the bracket for 13 arrivals in the first column of Table 17.4A. Thus 13 lorries are going to arrive between 8 and 9 a.m. on this particular simulated day and we have to generate 13 sets of the 2-digit random numbers to find the details for all of them. First come the numbers not exceeding 59 to fix the moments of arrival, and these must of course be sorted into ascending order. Suppose our 09 is the smallest of these. The first lorry therefore arrives at 08.09 and its next random numbers 56 and 31 tell us that it is a 4-tonner (56 is in this group) and will take between 16 and 20 minutes to load. The exact loading time should be proportional to the position of 31 between 17 and 39, the extremities of the random numbers in this sector. Working to the nearest minute gives us 19 minutes to load this lorry. Starting with both bays empty, this first lorry will go into Bay 1 when it arrives at 8.09; it will vacate the bay 19 minutes later at 8.28, as recorded on the first row of the worksheet in Figure 17.3. We can see as each lorry arrives whether or not a bay is free and if not, how long it must wait. Where a bay is idle we can see and record the idle time up to the moment a lorry enters it. The worksheet might continue as in Figure 17.4, and so on. The work may become quite

Figure 17.3 Start of worksheet.

LOADING BAY SIMULATION—WORKSHEET

Lorry no.	Arrival time	Size (tons)	Loading time (mins)	Bay 1 Time in	Bay 1 Time out	Bay 2 Time in	Bay 2 Time out	Bay 1 idle time	Bay 2 idle time	Lorry waiting time
1	08.09	4	19	08.09	08.28			9		0
2										
3										
4										
5										

Figure 17.4

LOADING BAY SIMULATION—WORKSHEET

Lorry no.	Arrival time	Size (tons)	Loading time (mins)	Bay 1 Time in	Bay 1 Time out	Bay 2 Time in	Bay 2 Time out	Bay 1 idle time	Bay 2 idle time	Lorry waiting time
1	08.09	4	19	08.09	08.28			9		0
2	08.12	>5	29			08.12	08.41		12	0
3	08.14	3	35	08.28	09.03					14
4	08.15	4	22			08.41	09.03			26
5	08.19	5	46	09.03	09.49					44
6	08.26	2	14			09.03	09.17			37
7	08.34	3	12			09.17	09.29			43
8	08.35	2	30			09.29	09.59			54
9	08.39	5	23	09.49	10.12					70
10	08.39									
11										

lengthy, but it is nevertheless interesting because we get the feel of the real events we are simulating.

At the end of the day's run we shall have total lorry waiting times and total bay idle times, both of which can be costed. This exercise should be repeated 3 or 4 times at least, to smooth out fluctuations and provide realistic daily average figures for the conditions chosen. The process is then repeated with any other set of conditions that we care to try.

Even carried through manually as above (a procedure which is strongly recommended as good experience of simulation) it is very clear that this is both much quicker and enormously cheaper than experimenting in the real situation. The computer can obviously duplicate what we have done at a much faster rate, either printing out all the details if we want them or giving us only the totals of queueing and idle times if these are all we need. There is no special problem in programming a computer for these in standard languages like FORTRAN, ALGOL or BASIC, but such is the importance of simulation that special languages and compilers have been devised to make it even easier to program this kind of problem. Table 17.5 shows a printout, produced on a multi-access terminal working interactively, of a loading bay simulation rather more complicated than our present example. Two runs are shown, one with full detail and one with summaries only.

With the simulation method of solving queueing problems there are no restrictions on the kind of input or service patterns, the number of service

Table 17.5

```
RUN
SIMULA

HOW MANY BAYS? 3
FULL PRINTOUT? YES
```

LORRY NO.	ARRIVAL TIME	LOAD SIZE	UNLOAD TIME	B	A	Y	TIME IN	TIME OUT	WAIT TIME
1	7.51	7	54	1			7.51	8.45	0
2	7.54	4	23		2		7.54	8.17	0
3	7.57	4	14			3	7.57	8.11	0
4	8.02	5	20			3	8.11	8.31	9
5	8.07	2	60		2		8.17	9.17	10
6	8.18	4	21			3	8.31	8.52	13
7	8.37	4	20	1			8.45	9.05	8
8	8.37	2	50			3	8.52	9.42	15
9	8.41	6	35	1			9.05	9.40	24
10	8.51	3	28		2		9.17	9.45	26
11	9.32	3	20	1			9.40	10.00	8
12	9.49	3	17		2		9.49	10.06	0
13	9.51	3	18			3	9.51	10.09	0
14	10.49	3	21	1			10.49	11.10	0
15	11.02	2	10		2		11.02	11.12	0
16	11.10	6	28	1			11.10	11.38	0
17	11.44	3	70	1			11.44	12.54	0
18	13.25	7	36	1			13.25	14.01	0
19	13.59	2	30		2		13.59	14.29	0
20	14.02	7	62	1			14.02	15.04	0
21	14.12	7	74			3	14.12	15.26	0
22	14.39	2	19		2		14.39	14.58	0
23	14.40	3	14		2		14.58	15.12	18
24	14.53	4	14	1			15.04	15.18	11
25	15.07	3	25		2		15.12	15.37	5
26	15.34	4	19	1			15.34	15.53	0
27	15.42	7	31		2		15.42	16.13	0
28	15.57	5	21	1			15.57	16.18	0

```
.. LORRIES WAITED A TOTAL OF  147 MINUTES,
   OR  17.9% OF UNLOADING TIME AND A MEAN OF  . OF MINS EACH,
```

BAY	LORRIES	OVERTIME MINS	% BASIC	IDLE TIME MINS	% TOTAL
1	12	18	3.3	158	28.3
2	10	13	2.4	296	53.5
3	6	0	0.0	343	63.5
TOT	28	31	1.9	797	48.3

```
ANOTHER RUN? YES
HOW MANY BAYS? 3
FULL PRINTOUT? NO


25 LORRIES WAITED A TOTAL OF   81 MINUTES,
   OR  11.0% OF UNLOADING TIME AND A MEAN OF  3.24 MINS EACH.
```

BAY	LORRIES	OVERTIME MINS	% BASIC	IDLE TIME MINS	% TOTAL
1	12	15	2.8	148	26.7
2	8	2	0.4	322	59.4
3	5	0	0.0	416	77.0
TOT	25	17	1.0	886	54.1

```
ANOTHER RUN?NO
```

points or queue discipline or any other special conditions. It is only necessary to be able to specify the patterns as cumulative percentages and this is always possible, though it may take prolonged observation to establish the underlying data. If there is nothing to observe because the queueing system is totally in the future, one can test any postulates desired. Thus London's Heathrow Airport was first designed in the late 1940s to cope with projected air traffic. Unfortunately all the projections made by the transport authorities, even the highest conceivable, were rapidly surpassed by the growth of civil aviation once the airport was built, and the facilities have never failed to be overloaded (i.e. with ρ approaching 1) despite all additions and improvements. Of course, no one can blame the simulation techniques, only the forecasting. Later airports (or some of them at least) have been analyzed on the basis of better forecasts of usage.

Conclusion

In more everyday applications, queueing problem situations are often recognizable because one or more of the following can be seen: persistently high stocks; frequent production stoppages for lack of some material or other; frequent production delays while broken down machines await repair; persistent production difficulties at known bottlenecks; transportation bottlenecks; workers or machines with excessive spare time, and so on. An analysis of these problems as input/output processes subject to variability (i.e. as queueing problems) almost always yields a quick, practical and often inexpensive solution, since when the utilization is near 1 even a small reduction in it can make a huge difference to the queues which form. On the other hand, underused service facilities are just as readily assessed and the true needs discovered. The aim of queueing theory, let us recall, is to minimize the total cost of idle facilities and time lost waiting for them.

XVIII
DECISION TREE MODELS
OF AN UNCERTAIN FUTURE

My wife has decided to buy a coat and has asked me to accompany her to the shops. However, knowing my distaste for shopping she does not insist on this. I know from past experience that if I go with her she will certainly find a coat and it will cost £25. If I do not go she will either buy a coat for £50 or fail to find one at all. In this last event she might abandon the idea altogether, or she might insist that I go with her in which case we should undoubtedly find a coat, but it will cost £35.

I now have to decide whether or not to join her on the first search. Looking only at the financial effects and ignoring personal aspects, what should I do?

This is a realistic if trivial illustration of a type of problem that faces managers all the time. The future is always uncertain, though we have so far tried to make it less so by basing our vision of it on something known, namely the past. Our forecasting techniques have dealt with a continuous spectrum of possibilities (for example, sales could take any value within reason), but could not tackle the problem above, which involves discrete outcomes rather than continuous ones. My wife will either find a coat or she will not; there is no intermediate stage. Managerial examples of this situation are numerous; our new product will be a success or a failure; we shall either gain or lose a certain export contract; if we drill a hole in the ground we either shall or shall not strike oil. There are also no gradations in the decisions open to us in advance, i.e. the ones that will put these outcomes to the test. Either we drill the hole/launch the product/quote for the order/accompany our wives, or we do not. The difference between these situations and the ones discussed so far is thus the difference between *attributes* and *variables*, i.e. between classifications and measurements. The question is, always, which decision of several alternatives is the best one to take now?

Let us face facts. Any decision of the kind is a gamble. The prudent manager will therefore wish to back the decision likely to be the most rewarding. Since managers are accustomed to measuring everything in money terms, we can look at the costs and rewards as sums of money. Let us do so for my wife's shopping expedition.

The decision tree of Figure 18.1 is a map of all possible decisions and their outcomes. In this case there is only one decision as such, mine at the outset. My wife's choices of coat or of action are not regarded as decisions in this context because nothing can be done now to influence them; they are seen merely as possible outcomes flowing (or not flowing, as the case may be) from my initial decision. Note the convention that decision branch-points are

Figure 18.1 Shopping decision tree.

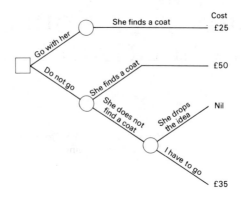

marked as squares, outcome branch-points as circles. We shall adhere to this throughout.

The possible eventualities are thus:

		Cost
1.	I accompany my wife and she finds a coat	£25
2.	I do not accompany her and she finds a coat	£50
3.	I do not accompany her, she does not find a coat and takes no further action	0
4.	I do not accompany her, she does not find a coat and she drags me along with her next time	£35

Note how much clearer is the diagram than the verbal description.

Which decision is going to be the best, i.e. the most rewarding, or rather the least costly? I will incur on the one hand a definite £25 cost or on the other hand unknown risks of nil, £35 or £50. To see how to assess these risks, let us consider an even simpler example.

A horse is running in a race at odds of 10 to 1. Should I put £1 on it to win?

Obviously, I should only bet if I think the horse has a good chance of winning, a better chance than the odds tell me. It may seem strange to compare a management decision with playing the horses, but to be consistently successful a punter has to be no less scientific in his approach than a manager. Let us draw the decision tree for the horserace (Figure 18.2). As we said, the decision depends on our assessment of the horse's chances of winning or not winning. If we put these at 50/50, we stand a 50% chance of winning £10 and a 50% chance of losing £1. How much would one pay for a 50% chance of winning? Clearly it is worth half the amount to be won. We may therefore value these chances respectively at half of £10 and half of £(−1), i.e. at £5 and £(−0.50).

Figure 18.2 Horserace decision tree.

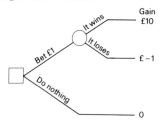

Together they are worth a net £4.50 and to obtain this value I have to risk £1. Is it worthwhile? The answer is, obviously, yes.

However, suppose we estimate the horse's probability of winning at 10%, with a 90% chance of not winning. We then value our potential gain at 10% of £10, or £1, and our potential loss at 90% of £(−1) or £(−0.90). We should think carefully before risking £1 for a net expected gain of £0.10.* Incidentally, each-way bets were excluded purely for simplicity; you might like to try their consequences for yourself.

It is the idea of valuing our gains or losses according to their likelihood of occurring that solves our problems. We define the *expected value* of an outcome as its actual gain or cost multiplied by the expectation of it happening. This expectation is measured as a probability, but a subjective one; it is no more accurate than the best guess we can make.

The forecast gains or losses are also subjective to some extent. This is not so when betting on a horse at fixed odds, but when betting at starting price the return for a winning £1 is usually a matter of guesswork. The prices my wife will pay for a coat have been declared categorically, but in truth they are only the amounts I think she will pay. The same is true of profits on export contracts or from striking oil, or of virtually every financial forecast in management. With this in mind, let us return to my wife and her shopping.

There is only one outcome if I accompany her and no probability judgements are needed. If I do not go, what is the chance that she will find a coat? Suppose I guess this (based on experience or on anything) at 40% or 0.4, then the chance of her coming home empty-handed is judged to be 0.6. Then, as a follow-up to the latter eventuality, what is the chance of her dropping the whole idea? Again, making the best guess I can, I say 50%. The decision tree is then as in Figure 18.3. The last two expected values, nil and £17.50, both belong to the branch after no coat being found and their total of £17.50 is thus the total expected value of that outcome. This total is conveniently written (abbreviated to 17.5) inside the circle symbol at the branch-point. Working back to the next branch, the expected value is 0.4 × £50 from one outcome and 0.6 × £17.50 from the other, a total of £20 + £10.50 or £30.50 which is inserted (as 30.5) in its branch-point symbol. This completes the calculations. The expected cost of

* Probability footnote: those who were surprised that the expected gain was not exactly zero had forgotten that odds of 10 to 1 correspond to chances of 1 in 11 and 10 in 11. Try the calculation with $\frac{1}{11}$ and $\frac{10}{11}$ if in doubt.

Figure 18.3   Shopping decision tree.

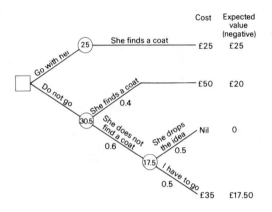

accompanying my wife is £25; the expected cost of not doing so is £30.50. If minimum expected cost is the only criterion, my decision must be to go with her first time out.

It is perhaps unfortunate that the name expected value or cost is given to something which cannot occur, i.e. which is not expected in the everyday use of the word. Thus we expect a cost of 0 or £25 or £35 or £50 if I do not go with my wife; the expected cost of £50.50 could not possibly arise. We must be careful not to confuse the meanings; we have a special technical sense for the word, which we have defined.

The considerations of the decision tree force us to recognize things for what they are, and in particular to see what is called experience as organized routine guesswork. An advantage of doing so is that we are compelled to make better guesses if we can, perhaps worthy of being called estimates. Then, when the simple calculations let us compare the consequences of our guesses, we have to think about the criteria we wish to apply to them. Like all OR, this technique is basically simple yet has great power. Let us look at a more realistic example:

A car-hire firm changes its cars every year and is about to renew its fleet of 20. The managing director is trying to plan the firm's future in an uncertain economic climate. He estimates that, if the firm buys 30 cars, it could earn a profit of £30 000 with them next year given an economic upswing, could earn £16 000 if things stay about as they are and could lose £2000 if there is a recession. If he buys 20 cars to keep the firm at its present size, the earnings will be respectively £22 000, £19 000 and £4000. Buying only 15 cars would earn £17 000, £15 000 and £10 000. He estimates the chance of an economic upswing at 0.3, of staying level at 0.4 and of a recession at 0.3. How many cars should the firm buy?

It is easy enough to write out the problem in these terms, but in real life it is extremely hard for any manager to quantify the subjective probabilities and profits in this way. Incidentally, the discrete situation described, with only 3 levels of cars instead of any number between the desired limits, and only 3 levels of economic activity with consequent steps rather than gradations in earnings, is very much a simplification of the real situation. Posing the full problem would involve a family of irregular surfaces in 3 dimensions (the 3 being cars, economic activity and earnings, with the family connection being probability levels) that would be impossible to solve. By using discrete steps the problem has been brought within bounds.

The decision tree would look like Figure 18.4: the manager's decision now rests on the criterion applied to its results. If we look for *maximum expected value*, the choice would be 20 cars again, for their expected value is £15 400 as against £14 800 for 30 cars and £14 100 for 15. If the criterion is *maximax*, i.e. absolute optimism, we choose the action that can lead to the greatest profit if all goes well. We therefore buy 30 cars as this is the only way we could make as much as £30 000 profit. The *minimax* criterion is that of absolute pessimism. It leads to the decision which would involve the least loss if everything went wrong. Buying 15 cars would be the answer in this case: we might never do brilliantly, but the very lowest profit that could flow from this decision is more than the lowest profit from either of the other decisions. The *minimax regret* criterion

Figure 18.4

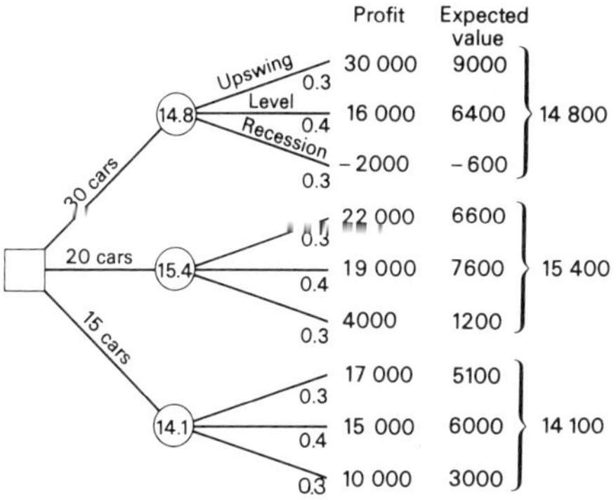

also expects the worst, but our feelings if this happens would be relief that in the circumstances we have come as close as we can to the best possible result of our same decision. This is a complicated idea to express but simple in effect: if we buy 30 cars and the economy turns sour we should be £32 000 below the best that this decision could have given us. With 20 cars the worst would be £18 000 below its best. With 15 cars the difference would be £7000 and this is the one to choose if we look for minimax regret. Having taken the decision we naturally hope for the best from it, but if the worst arrives our hopes will be dashed to the least possible extent.

There are numerous other criteria we could apply, depending on circumstances and on our psychological attitude to life and business. However, in my opinion the best all-round criterion is maximum expected value, or its corollary, minimum expected cost. From now on we shall use this and opt to buy 20 cars.

So far we have considered next year in isolation, but there are often implications in a decision which go on beyond the next period. Let us continue the problem, looking ahead also into the second year.

The managing director considers that a firm which has grown to 30 cars ought not suddenly descend to only 15 in the following year, while one which has 15 cars next year should not consider buying 30 for the year after. He feels that the year after next will probably be economically poorer than next year in that a recession next year would probably tend to get worse, a boom would tend to level off and if today's levels continue into next year, the year after would tend to have a recession. He estimates the probabilities and the profits from 30, 20 and 15 cars in the year after next to be as in Table 18.1.

Table 18.1

| If next year has | The year after may have | Prob. | Earnings the year after next | | |
			30 cars	20 cars	15 cars
Boom	More boom	0.1	32 000	24 000	20 000
	Same as next year	0.6	30 000	22 000	17 000
	Recession	0.3	18 000	20 000	15 000
Same as this year	Boom	0.2	29 000	23 000	17 000
	Same as next year	0.3	16 000	19 000	15 000
	Recession	0.5	0	5 000	11 000
Recession	Boom	0.1	15 000	17 000	14 000
	Same as next year	0.3	−2 000	4 000	10 000
	Deeper recession	0.6	−8 000	−3 000	2 000

The decision tree, Figure 18.5, shows the very many possibilities for the year after next. The problem is to decide between 30, 20 or 15 cars now so that, taken in conjunction with the decision that will have to be made in 12 months' time, the maximum expected value will be achieved over the two years. The principles of the calculation are the same as in the 1-year case; let us work through the topmost branch only.

There are 3 possible outcomes from that next decision to buy 30 cars, respectively yielding £32 000, £30 000 and £18 000 with associated probabilities of 0.1, 0.6 and 0.3. The expected value at the topmost circle is thus

$$(0.1 \times £32\ 000) + (0.6 \times £30\ 000) + (0.3 \times £18\ 000)$$

or £3200 + £18 000 + £5400 , i.e. £26 600

26.6 has been written into the circle. Below it is an expected value of £21 600 for the alternative 20-car decision. The maximum expected value at the decision-point was thus £26 600 and 26.6 has been written below it. (There is no sense in considering a worse decision any longer.)

This decision-point would have been reached only if a boom (probability 0.3) followed the decision now to buy 30 cars. If the economy stayed as it is now

Figure 18.5

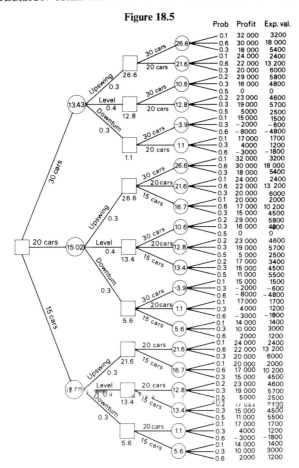

Prob	Profit	Exp. val.
0.1	32 000	3200
0.6	30 000	18 000
0.3	18 000	5400
0.1	24 000	2400
0.6	22 000	13 200
0.3	20 000	6000
0.2	29 000	5800
0.3	16 000	4800
0.5	0	0
0.2	23 000	4600
0.3	19 000	5700
0.5	5000	2500
0.1	15 000	1500
0.3	-2000	-600
0.6	-8000	-4800
0.1	17 000	1700
0.3	4000	1200
0.6	-3000	-1800
0.1	32 000	3200
0.6	30 000	18 000
0.3	18 000	5400
0.1	24 000	2400
0.6	22 000	13 200
0.3	20 000	6000
0.1	20 000	2000
0.6	17 000	10 200
0.3	15 000	4500
0.2	29 000	5800
0.3	16 000	4800
0.5	0	0
0.2	23 000	4600
0.3	19 000	5700
0.5	5 000	2500
0.2	17 000	3400
0.3	15 000	4500
0.5	11 000	5500
0.1	15 000	1500
0.3	-2000	-600
0.6	-8000	-4800
0.1	17 000	1700
0.3	4000	1200
0.6	-3000	-1800
0.1	14 000	1400
0.3	10 000	3000
0.6	2000	1200
0.1	24 000	2400
0.6	22 000	13 200
0.3	20 000	6000
0.1	20 000	2000
0.6	17 000	10 200
0.3	15 000	4500
0.2	23 000	4600
0.3	19 000	5700
0.5	5000	2500
0.2	17 000	3400
0.3	15 000	4500
0.5	11 000	5500
0.1	17 000	1700
0.3	4000	1200
0.6	-3000	-1800
0.1	14 000	1400
0.3	10 000	3000
0.6	2000	1200

(probability 0.4) after this first decision, there would be a maximum expected value of £12 800 for next year's decision. Had there been a slump the expected value would be only £1100, with a probability of 0.3. The expected value of these 3 outcomes together is thus

$$(0.3 \times £26\,600) + (0.4 \times £12\,800) + (0.3 \times £1100)$$

or   £7980   £5120   £330   = £13 430

This, then, is the expected value of the decision to buy 30 cars now. (On the one-year-only view it was £14 800; see Figure 18.4). Similarly, we have £15 020 as the expected value of buying 20 cars now and £13 520 for 15 cars. Again, then, we buy 20 cars.

The restrictions on next year's buying have changed the relative positions of the three expected values. Fifteen is now in second place with 30 cars last. However, we have not moved 20 cars from first place and the decision is the same as on the one-year view. Note that next year's decisions are also clear, provided the managing director's views on the economic climate do not change. If there is a boom in the year about to start, we buy 30 cars next year. If not, we buy 15 cars.

Despite the formidable problems of making managers produce figures for the anticipated earnings and their probabilities, we see how the decision tree provides a sort of map of the future and how a few simple calculations put the hills and valleys on this map. The landscape is slightly more rugged than it appears; for example, we might have taken discounted values of the various sums involved, but even at the present level of simplification we have met another powerful OR tool.

XIX
NETWORK MODELS IN PROBLEMS OF CO-ORDINATION

Anyone who has seen a major building being built and has thought about how the work was organized and co-ordinated must have realized that there was method in the way one team of men and machines demolished the old structure, another team dug the big hole, another drove piles, then foundations were laid, steel was erected and so on, ending with electricians, glaziers, decorators and flooring specialists. Meanwhile the future occupant has been able to plan his move to fit a closely forecast date.

Perhaps the good organization could be put down to experience? After all, people have been putting up buildings for a long time and know what to do; it is obvious that drains have to be laid before the roofs are put on, and so forth. In fact, it is only the smaller builders who rely on experience alone to plan their work and to control it (i.e. to see that it proceeds according to plan if possible, and if not, to take the right corrective actions). Any large building project is almost bound to be different from all previous projects, probably in major as well as minor respects. While there is no doubt that drains come before roofing, who is to say off-hand whether the air-conditioning plant should be installed before or after the prefabricated wall sections? Before this particular question can be categorically answered the planners have to ascertain various facts:

1. Should the walls be erected first, to protect the plant from the weather?

2. Should the equipment at least be placed on the right floors first, as otherwise there will be no openings big enough to allow it into the building? (This condition might split the task of installing the plant into two parts; bring in and install).

3. Is there really no priority, since either is technically possible?

Hundreds of decisions of this kind have to be made at some time, preferably at a planning stage before any physical work is begun on the project.

Builders and civil engineers, apart perhaps from the smallest ones, all use an OR technique to help them make the right decisions first time. Even if this were all it did the technique would be widely used, but in fact it goes on to help the planners in many areas, such as

1. Forecasting the time that the whole project will take to complete.

2. Providing starting and completion dates for subsections of the project.

3. Identifying in advance all the stages where timing is critical or even difficult.

4. Deciding in advance exactly what resources (men, machines, etc.) are going to be needed, and when.

5. Finding, even before work has commenced, ways of overcoming timing or resource problems.

6. Monitoring progress as the project proceeds so that all the consequences of any delays or difficulties can be forecast as soon as the causes arise.

7. Deciding easily on the best corrective action when things go off the rails. (These last two may be summed up as allowing the managers to control the project.)

8. Maintaining 2-way communication throughout the project with operatives and all levels of management.

This is why the use of the technique is universal in the construction industries. It is also very widely used for all manner of other projects which, like construction, share the characteristics of being new (i.e. never done before in exact detail), complicated, and of taking some time to complete. Examples of such projects are:

1. Producing any complex product for the first time, whether it is to be the only one of its kind (for example, a ship) or merely the first of many (for instance, a new model car or suite of furniture).

2. Getting a Bill through Parliament.

3. Moving a business from one office to another, or a department from one factory to another.

4. Taking a newly-trained army and its equipment from Texas to Normandy by ship and getting it effectively into battle as quickly as possible.

It was to solve military problems like this last one that the technique was invented during World War II, independently on both sides of the Atlantic. As it developed after the war it was variously christened

program evaluation and review technique	or PERT
critical path method	or CPM
critical path analysis	or CPA
graphes et ordonnancements, which translates to	
networks and scheduling	

Assorted other names have also been put forward. Since the heart of the technique is a model of the project, looking like the map of a network of paths, we shall here refer to it as networking, a generic name that covers all aspects.

The stages of network modelling
To tackle the planning and control of a project by networking, we must proceed through the following stages:

Stage 1. We first break down the project into a list of separate steps called *activities*. It is characteristic for an activity that it is complete in itself and it takes some time. Thus in the project Bake a loaf of bread, the step Leave dough for 1 hour is an activity even though the baker has to do nothing. The list of activities must be complete and the discipline of having to think of everything so far in advance is most useful. However, later stages will force us to fill in any accidental gaps. The level of detail needed will become apparent from our examples.

Stage 2. We decide on the order in which the activities take place. The technical word is *dependency*. Erecting the wall panels is said to depend on bringing in the air conditioning plant if the latter must be done first. In general terms, activity A depends on activity B if B must be completed before A can begin. It is possible for one activity to depend on several, all of which must finish before the one can begin. Thus Road-test new car depends (among others) on Fit road wheels, Fit engine and Put petrol in tank. All of these are independent of one another, but the road test cannot take place until the very last of them is complete. Similarly, several otherwise independent activities may all depend on just one other activity. This stage will certainly help to find any activities missing from the list at Stage 1.

Stage 3. We now draw up a model of the activities as a network which shows their dependencies. There are two main ways of doing this; we shall look at both later by means of an example. This stage will help to fill in any gaps left after Stages 1 and 2 and will also bring out an important feature of dependency, namely that it has two possible kinds of cause. One is technical and unavoidable (for example, one cannot allow paint to dry unless it has first been applied) and the other is policy (for example, we may bring in the air conditioning plant before erecting the wall panels, not for technical reasons, but because the architect likes it that way). Policy decisions will thus alter the appearance of a network, which is a statement of the logical and policy decisions on the sequence of activities. Yet another advantage of using network models is that they force management's policy decisions to be taken rather than avoided and also to be seen explicitly for what they are; illogical ones show up as such but, happily, can be corrected long before they can give trouble. Of course, activities which are independent of all others appear as such in the network.

Stage 4. It is now time to decide how long each activity will take and put these *durations* on the network. This is the hard part, for all the activities for which durations are being decided are to take place in the future. Some are well-known and can be accurately assessed, but others have never been seen before and can only be guessed at. The most realistic guesses possible are needed, neither optimistic nor pessimistic. There will be many consultations between planners and management while the network is being drawn up; most of them will be about dependencies and durations.

Stage 5. Analysis of the network takes place next, to find the total time for the project and the chain(s) of activities which add up to give this total. These are the *critical paths* which gave the alternative names critical path method and critical path analysis to networking. We shall see from our examples how to perform this and the subsequent steps.

Stage 6. We derive a detailed timetable from the analyzed network. This timetable and the network are the main means of communication between all concerned, as well as being the prime planning documents.

Stage 7. Using a graphical form of the timetable, we check whether resources can be available as necessary. This completes the planning with networks; the project could now begin.

Stage 8. Finally, we use the timetable and network to monitor and control the project as it runs. Since the accuracy of the original timetable can be no better than the guesses of activity durations, some things are almost bound to depart from the plan. As soon as such departures become known, or even if we learn that there is going to be a departure, the network and derived timetable should be revised accordingly. If the changes prove undesirable, the model will guide management in formulating plans for corrective action.

Stages 1 to 7 form a very attractive intellectual exercise (as we shall see), so much so that many people then forget Stage 8 and nine-tenths of the value of the method is lost. Sometimes, Stages 5, 6 and 7 are thought of as a single stage, called analysis, leaving only six main stages. This is only a matter of labelling.

Let us now turn to an example to see how networking models are built and used. Without living through the actual situation we cannot go through the motions of drawing up the list of activities from life, nor of finding the durations by questioning those who could know. Instead we shall assume that these stages (1 and 4) have been done and we quote the results.

An expanding firm has decided to move to a new factory in a development area, taking advantage of government grants. Some new plant and machinery will be needed, in addition to some of the present equipment which will be moved with the firm. There is ample housing and no problem about moving the key staff when necessary. The activities involved are:

	Duration
Choose new site	12 weeks
Obtain planning permission and approval of grants	26 weeks
Choose and instruct architects	2 weeks
Prepare architectural drawings	4 weeks
Choose builder	1 week
Build new factory	50 weeks
Phase out production in old factory	8 weeks
Plan layout of plant in new factory	2 weeks
Choose, order and obtain some new machines	45 weeks
Move old machines to new factory	2 weeks
Recruit new staff	3 weeks
Train new staff	6 weeks
Start up new factory	2 weeks

It has been decided that, to avoid the risk of incurring unnecessary costs, all permissions and approval for government grants must be received before the architect can begin designing. The builder will insist that the drawings must be complete before he will commence any building work whatever.

We must first ascertain how long it will take until the new factory is running properly and also where the bottlenecks are likely to be. Other questions will be raised when the model has been developed, to show its power.

We now proceed to Stages 2 and 3, looking first at the order in which the activities must take place. However, it is very helpful when doing so to begin drawing the network also. We shall therefore adopt one of the two main ways of drawing it, this being to have each activity as a labelled rectangle, with dependencies shown as arrows pointing from the earlier activities towards the dependent ones (see Figure 19.1). We draw networks generally from left to right so that their time sequence, while not to scale, reads generally as time does on a graph.

Figure 19.1

| Activity 1 | → | Activity 2 (dependent on activity 1) |

We begin by looking for activities that can take place from the very start and see that Choose new site and Choose and instruct architects could both come at the beginning of the project. An architect friend of mine disagrees with this view, holding that the architect should be chosen first so that he can offer professional advice on the choice of site, thus we have Figure 19.2. (Note that labels are often abbreviated.) However, a policy decision is immediately forced on us: do we or do we not want an architect to help (or interfere, depending on our point of view) when we choose the site? The consequences would be different and the network models would look different to reflect this. If we decide to choose the site for ourselves, the network would now begin as Figure 19.3. To have a uniform beginning and, as we shall see later, to help in the analysis, we insist on a single start to any network, and we make all our earliest activities depend on an imaginary activity called Start of project.

Figure 19.2

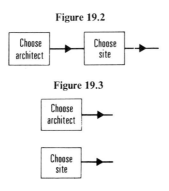

Figure 19.3

Figure 19.4

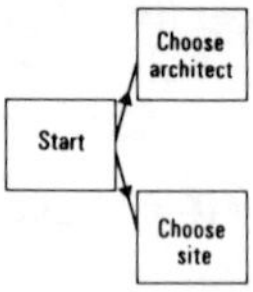

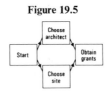

Similarly, we shall have a single final activity called End of project. So far, then, the network looks like Figure 19.4. These appear to be all the initial activities, though if we are wrong we shall find this out and be able to make corrections.

Next we look for activities depending on those we have drawn in. Obtain planning permission and approval of grants must depend on having the site and also on having at least an outline plan of the building we want. It therefore depends on both of the initial activities, as in Figure 19.5. We have another activity, Prepare architectural drawings, which, we are told, must be finished before any building will commence, but must not be started before planning permission and approval of grants have been received. Clearly, these outlines cannot be the main drawings, but have to be understood as part of the 26-week procedure for obtaining permissions and grants.

Figure 19.5

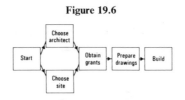

Since the main drawings depend on having the planning permission, they automatically depend on having the site and the architect. Figure 19.6 shows this, and also shows the building operation depending on the drawings. However, as yet we have no builder. We could have chosen him independently at the outset, and could still add him as an initial activity if we so decide. However, let us instead have the architect help us choose the builder and, furthermore, let us not have him involved until the permission and grants are assured (Figure 19.7).

Figure 19.6

Choose architect / Start / Obtain grants / Prepare drawings / Build / Choose site

When going through a list of activities in this way, it pays to mark or cross out each one as it is built into the network. We might manage our tiny 13-activity example without doing this but when several hundred activities are involved, as often happens in life, this small action is important.

Figure 19.7

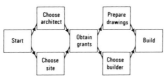

We are aware that the task of finding new machines will be a lengthy one, but obviously cannot commence until we know which machines we want, which in turn depends on the layout plan of machines in the new factory. We can prepare the layout plan as soon as the drawings of the building are ready, which gives us Figure 19.8. By redrawing completely at each stage, we are able to achieve fairly economical layout of the network for these pages, but in practice it would not be redrawn as here but would tend to sprawl a bit. This does not matter; the important thing is to get the logic right. Networks always have to be redrawn tidily once they are complete.

Figure 19.8

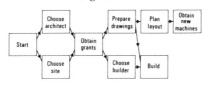

We are now left with five activities, of which Phase out production is still difficult to fit into the network. Let us therefore leave it for the moment; such activities can always be fitted in later, and will not be forgotten so long as we mark those that have been dealt with. In order to Train new staff we must first have recruited them, which could be done (if we so chose) as soon as the layout is fixed, for we should then know the machines and also the people we need. However, let us say that the training calls for the machines to be in place in the new building. (If this were not so in reality we would know it and would draw a different network. Our present policy decision is as stated.) Figure 19.9 shows these activities in the network and also shows the dependency of Move old

Figure 19.9

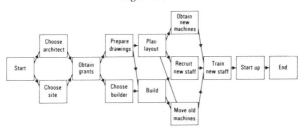

machines on the completion of the building. The purchase of new machines and the recruitment of new staff (as distinct from their training) do not depend on the building being up, however. Once training is ended we can start up the factory, which completes the project apart from Phase out. This must of course be finished before the project can be considered complete, i.e. the End of project artificial activity depends on it. Where does the phasing out begin, though? The answer is at any suitable time once we are committed to the move, i.e. once building has begun. On the network, the commencement of building is, of course, at the termination of the activities it depends on, so Phase out, like Build, depends on both Prepare drawings and Choose builder. Figure 19.10 now shows the complete network, redrawn and with durations inserted, ready for analysis. Note that the rectangles have become more elaborate, Figure 19.11 showing what the spaces are for. The meanings of Earliest start, Latest start and Float will be explained shortly.

Figure 19.10

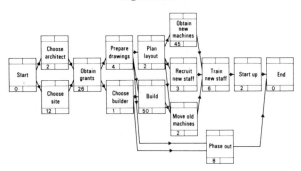

The network as now drawn is clearly a model of the future project. Moreover, it is a model in the time dimension, though it is not drawn to scale and, indeed, could not be so unless the durations were freakish. It has been drawn without regard to problems of resources; for example, one person might in reality have to choose both architect and site, jobs so different that they cannot be done simultaneously. We ignore this when preparing the network and assume that

Figure 19.11

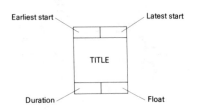

we have as many men and machines, as much money and material as could be desired. We shall come back later to deal with the practicalities of lack of resources.

Stage 5 is tackled next, and we begin by establishing how long the entire project will take to be completed. The total time for the 13 activities is 163 weeks. It was obvious even before we began that some of them could take place at the same time, bringing the project duration down to less than this, but by how much? The network shows us and our analysis will bring out the answer.

During our discussions on drawing the network it will have been clear that some activities, while certainly impossible to begin until others had finished, nonetheless allowed some choice: they might not have to begin at their earliest possible moments. Indeed, if Phase out production in old factory, which lasts 8 weeks, were to begin as soon as the drawings were ready and the builder chosen, a year or thereabouts might have to pass with no output for us at all. On the other hand, we can also see that some activities have to be done as soon as ever possible. Our analysis will tell us which activities are in which group.

The analysis runs as follows: the Start and End, being artificial or *dummy* activities, have zero duration as shown in their lower left-hand boxes in Figure 19.10. The upper left-hand boxes are used for carrying the earliest times at which their activities can begin, the *earliest starts*. We begin finding these with Start set at time 0, and of course Choose architect and Choose site can also begin at zero. At this point we imagine that every activity starts as early as it can.

Obtain grants can only begin after the end of both the activities on which it depends. Of these Choose architect can start at zero and lasts for 2 weeks, hence could end at 2 which is $(0 + 2)$, its start time plus its duration. Choose site similarly will not end earlier than $(0 + 12)$ or week 12. The earliest start for Obtain grants is thus 12 (see Figure 19.12). Note, by the way, that this means after the end of week 12; there will be no confusion, though, since the zero in Start means 'after the end of week zero' and the use of numbers is consistent throughout. Obtain grants can end not before $(12 + 26)$ or 38 which is thus the earliest start for both Prepare drawings and Choose builder. Plan layout depends only on Prepare drawings. It can therefore start not earlier than $(38 + 4)$

Figure 19.12

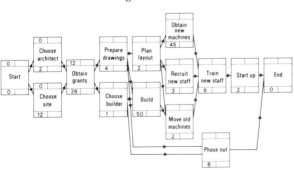

or 42. Build, however, depends on both Prepare drawings and Choose builder, so its earliest start is the later of $(38 + 4)$ or $(38 + 1)$; it is also 42. We may now spot that Phase out has the same pair of dependencies and therefore the same earliest start. This is the position in Figure 19.13.

Figure 19.13

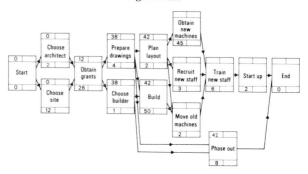

Obtain new machines and Recruit new staff depend only on Plan Layout, $42 + 2 = 44$. Move old machines depends on both Plan layout and Build. The later of $(42 + 2)$ and $(42 + 50)$ is 92. Train new staff cannot start before the last of $(44 + 45)$ or $(44 + 3)$ or $(92 + 2)$, i.e. 94. Start up is at $(94 + 6)$ or 100, and End at the later of $(100 + 2)$ from Start up or $(42 + 8)$ from Phase out. The end of the project is thus reached after 102 weeks at the earliest (Figure 19.14).

Figure 19.14

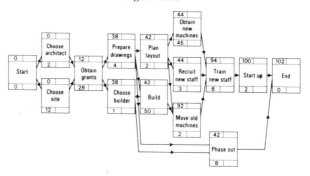

This answers the first question that was posed with the problem. The simple additions that we have done constitute what is called a *forward pass* through the network, and a reader looking for it could have spotted the particular path in this example in which the durations added up to the 102 weeks of the project.

However, there is no need to look out for this path during the forward pass, which is just as well since it is difficult or even impossible to spot with a realistic network of hundreds of activities. We shall find it as we go on.

The next step is a *backward pass* through the network. We now imagine that every activity is going to begin as late as it possibly can, consistent with not delaying the project beyond its 102 weeks. In other words we seek the *latest starts* of all activities. As the name of the pass implies, we start at the dummy activity End. Its latest start has of course to be the same as its earliest and we write 102 in its upper right-hand box. Moving backwards, we have two paths to Start up and to Phase out. Since Phase out takes 8 weeks and it is to start as late as possible, it must begin no later than (102 − 8) or 94, which goes into its latest-start box. The next activities back from here have other paths also leading back into them so we follow instead the path through Start up. This must begin not later than (102 − 2) = 100 if it is to be completed in time to reach End by 102. Train new staff must begin no later than that last 100 less its duration of 6, i.e. 94. Three activities follow directly from this: Obtain new machines could start no later than (94 − 45) or 49; for Recruit new staff the latest start is (94 − 3) or 91; Move old machines takes 2 weeks and could thus start at 92. This is the position shown in Figure 19.15.

Figure 19.15

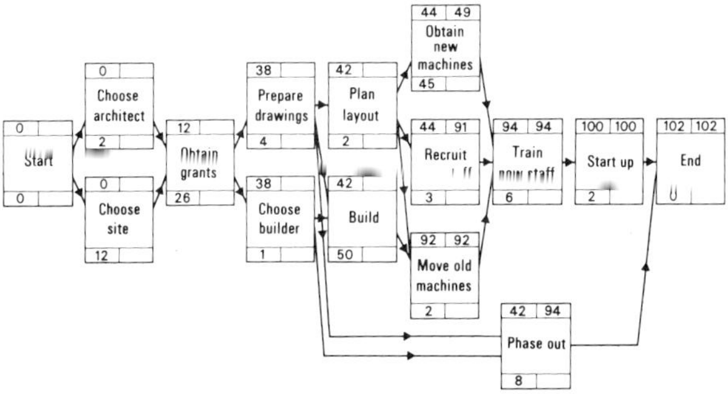

We can already see that some activities have equal latest and earliest starts, i.e. they must begin as soon as they can begin, while others leave us some choice about their exact moments of starting. Continuing backwards, Build derives only from Move old machines, (92 − 50) = 42. Plan layout has three activities to consider. Lasting 2 weeks, it must begin not later than the earliest of:

(49 − 2), to allow Obtain new machines to be completed on time,

or   (91 − 2), so that Recruit new staff can meet its deadline,

or   (92 − 2), for Move old machines.

Its latest start is thus 47.

Note that in both the forward and backward passes we have had to take the most difficult case whenever there are two or more activities leading into the one we are working on. Here in the backward pass it is the earliest of the possible latest starts that is the most stringent requirement; in a forward pass where an activity cannot begin until the end of each of those it depends on, the earliest start is the latest of the possibilities.

Continuing the backward pass, the latest start for Choose builder is either $(42 - 1)$ from Build, or $(93 - 1)$ from Phase out which we put aside earlier but can now pick up again. The answer is, of course, 41. Prepare drawings will have $(42 - 4)$ or $(94 - 4)$ as above, or $(47 - 4)$ from Plan layout. It is 38. Obtain grants is $(38 - 26)$ or $(41 - 26)$, giving 12; Choose architect is $(12 - 2)$ which is 10; Choose site is $(12 - 12)$, which is 0. Finally, Start has $(0 - 0)$ or $(10 - 0)$ i.e. 0. This is a check on our arithmetic throughout both passes, for if this final latest start is not zero, we have made an error somewhere and must recheck. As it is, all is well. The completed picture is in Figure 19.16.

Figure 19.16

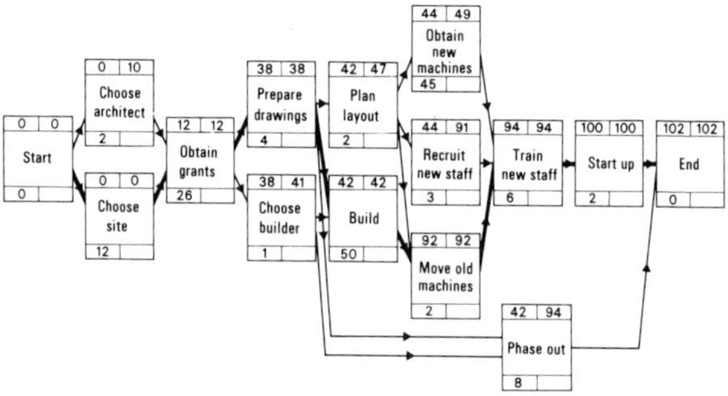

There happens to be just one path along which the earliest and latest starts are the same. (Sometimes there are several, but there must be at least one or else there has been an arithmetical slip.) This is the *critical path* and has been heavily drawn for emphasis. It is the longest time of passage from start to end, since all other paths offer spare time somewhere and therefore have shorter total durations.

We see now why the most realistic estimates we could find were needed for the durations. An optimistic or pessimistic builder or clerk in the borough surveyor's department could easily put us weeks out in our calculations. As it is we are not sure of being right, but corrective measures will flow from the model.

As a planning instrument the network model has already provided the overall timing, not easy to arrive at otherwise. If this timing proves unacceptably long the model helps further, for it has identified the critical activities that must be shortened to achieve savings. Often one is surprised to find which activities are critical and which are not, for instance there is usually a tendency to put pressure on suppliers of equipment subject to long delivery dates, yet in this example the activity Obtain new machines is not critical and energy spent on shortening its duration would be wasted. If instead the critical building stage, or the grant procedures, or (more under our own control) the choice of site could be speeded up we should certainly be able to save some time. There is less scope for saving with activities of shorter duration, though they are no less critical.

Sometimes a policy change can take time out of the critical path, and the model will make it clear where this is feasible. We might, in the present case, be glad that we decided to choose the site without first taking two weeks to choose the architect, as these are weeks that would add to the critical path. However, if with the architect's help the search for the site could be cut to less than 10 weeks there would be a net saving from the change of tactics.

The second question posed with the problem was: where are the likely bottlenecks? We have now found the answer; they are on the critical path.

To continue with our example, let us proceed to Stages 6 and 7 and assume that the 102 week duration is acceptable. The timetable is clear as far as the critical activities are concerned (they follow one another without delay), but off the critical path there is spare time. This is measured by the difference between the earliest and latest starts for an activity and is called its *float*. The floats may conveniently be recorded in the remaining boxes at the lower right as in Figure 19.17. Of course, activities with no float are critical ones.

Figure 19.17

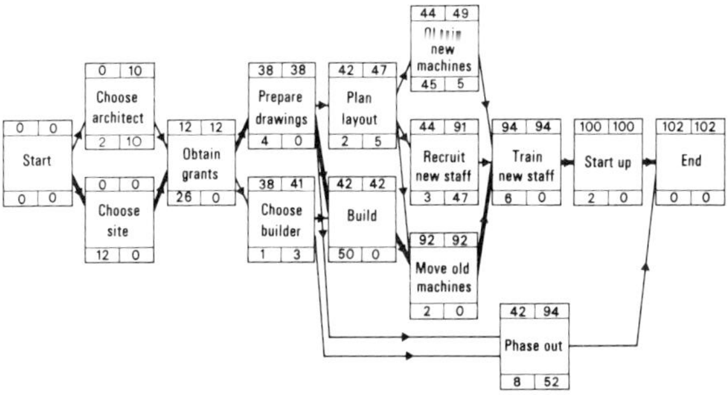

Some non-critical activities can take up their estimated durations, plus their floats in addition, without causing trouble. Others cannot do so. Thus if we began at time 0 to choose an architect, we could take 12 weeks over this task (duration 2 plus float 10) and still keep up with the project. However, if Plan layout took the full 7 weeks instead of its estimated 2, it would finish at week 49 even if it began at its earliest start. The dependent Obtain new machines would then be unable to begin before its latest start; its float would have been consumed elsewhere. When a sequence of activities must share a float in this way, we speak of it as their *total float*. Non-sequenced activities like Choose architect may have *free float*.

The position can be seen even more clearly if we construct a scale model of our findings. A *bar chart* is used for this. The critical activities may be shown as a chain of bars on a horizontal time scale, with the other activities shown independently or in their chains as appropriate. Conventionally, all are drawn at their earliest starts with any float (preferably shaded for clarity) stretching away to the right. Figure 19.18 is such a bar chart.

Figure 19.18 Bar chart of project.

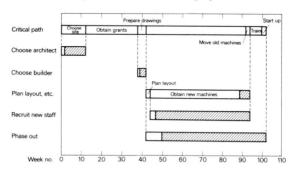

We may imagine that the activities can slide along the bars that show their float, and one can buy planning boards or charting boards which allow this to happen. We see at once where activities have free float, and also that Plan layout and its dependent Obtain new machines have to share 5 weeks of total float between them.

The vertical dotted links show dependencies. Thus the link at week 94 says that Train depends on both Obtain new machines and Recruit new staff. Its third dependency on Move old machines comes with the critical path of course. If any non-critical activity is prolonged or delayed so that it reaches the limit of its float it becomes critical, since activities on the critical path depend on it. Extension beyond the end of the float, like prolongation of any critical activity, must lengthen the total time for the project unless something can be done to shorten critical activities still to come.

The planning decisions on timing the non-critical activities are now fairly easy. For one thing, their extreme time limits are clearly visible. The main point, though, is that we can build our actual resources into this model and adjust the times to suit them. (The network was drawn assuming unlimited resources.) Consider, for example, the activity Phase out. Commonsense tells us that it should be delayed as long as possible, to keep some output going. Its latest start is the end of week 94, i.e. the beginning of week 95 so that its 8-week duration finishes at the end of week 102. If we put it at the tail of the project like this it will coincide with Train and Start up (see the bar chart, Figure 19.18). This is fine if they do not all call for the same resources, but suppose the same key staff are needed for both. (These are the people who, according to the problem can move as necessary.) Since the staff cannot be in both places at once, we must move Phase out forward to avoid the clash, for example to start at the end of week 86. If these people are also concerned in moving the old machines the phasing-out will be set still further forward, to start at 84 and end at 92. There will be implications flowing from 10 weeks without production, but we know this already and the 10 weeks in question are about 2 years away, which is ample time to build up stocks to cover the gap.

The answers will not always come so easily. For example, we note that Choose builder overlaps Prepare drawings. What if the architect must be personally involved in both, so deeply that he can do only one of them at a time? This is typical of the problems that arise only when the project is under way, in this case when the architect has been chosen and is putting his point of view. This problem has two possible solutions:

1. A change of policy so that the architect is not involved in both activities at once. We might insist that he delegates at least one week's worth of drawings to someone else, involving the use of extra resources. Or we might persuade him to trust us to choose the builder without him.

2. Where no further resources are available and policies cannot or will not be altered, there is no choice but to extend the time for the project. In this case there would be a one-week extension by choosing the builder before proceeding with the drawings, or vice versa. In effect the network is modified to bring Choose builder into the critical path.

So far we have acted as if time was the most important factor in planning, but the model reflects the fact that time and resources are equally important, one being able within limits to replace the other. The planner's task has always been to strike the best balance between the two and we see why network modelling is such a powerful aid.

With more realistic networks having many activities, one uses float to balance resources by adding up the demand for each resource, period by period, comparing the totals with what is available, and juggling the activities within their float to try to bring demands to within the resources one has. There is no routine way to do this; it is systematic trial and error, and the sliding charting boards are of help. In our small example there are no special difficulties; we shall assume that a suitable timetable has been prepared and go on to consider Stage 8, control of the project once it has begun.

As we said earlier, the analysis of a network is a fascinating mental exercise, very satisfying to complete. It is too easy afterwards to forget that the network and its timetable are no more accurate than the forecast durations of the individual activities. Thus there will almost inevitably be departures from the plan as the project goes ahead. The network and the bar chart can be excellent means of monitoring progress and adapting actions or plans to the situation as it develops, but only if all relevant information is fed to the planners as soon as it becomes known, wherever it arises.

Suppose that a spell of atrocious weather around week 50 of our project tells the builder that his work must take at least 52 weeks instead of the 50 expected. A builder accustomed to networking will not just keep quiet and hope for the best but will at once declare what he knows. The planners will then see either that the project will have to take a further 2 weeks and will save money by adjusting the dates for recruiting, moving machines, phasing out and so forth, or else they will look for ways to make up time if possible. They might, for example, look into the effects of moving the old machinery before the building is complete and possibly save a week over that activity. This is not to say that there is always a way round every delay; the point is that the best available decisions will be made possible through advance warning applied to the network model. If it does not become clear until near the old completion date that a 2-week building delay is looming, the phasing-out might come too early for example, and recruiting might take place for work to start at an impossible date, both with considerable loss of money.

The time consequences of any departures from plan are put into the bar chart. It will be seen whether formerly non-critical activities have become critical or whether, because of trouble off the old critical path, there is a new path and formerly critical activities now have some float. Good news of early completion of activities will also be put in. Where policy changes are the planners' answer to trouble it may also be necessary to modify and re-analyse the network, producing an entirely new bar chart. Whatever the changes, their effects are easily calculated, and of course the prints of the network and bar chart are splendid means of communication with all the supervisors and managers involved. In particular they will all be able to keep an eye on any activities that are using up their float; they have early warning of impending trouble and will often be able to devote attention to preventing a setback rather than compensating for it afterwards.

The computer in network analysis

Any procedure as routine and repetitive (in a word, as programmable) as the forward and backward passes through a network is made-to-order for the computer to tackle. All that is needed is a package program which will accept into the computer the list of activities. These are reference-numbered for brevity and clarity, and for each activity the computer is told the following:

1. Reference number.

2. Short title (to be stored and printed out only; it has no meaning for the computer).

3. List of dependencies (i.e. the reference numbers of the activities it depends on).

4. Duration.

5. Resources required (if desired; these will be in coded form).

The analysis package will first check that the network is consistent and has been correctly described, and that it is free from errors of logic such as loops (Figure 19.19) and danglers which are activities depending from something but leading nowhere (only the End may do this). If all is well it will produce a table (see Table 19.1) giving all the earliest and latest starts and the floats. Next it can produce a bar-chart, though it cannot show the vertical links of our manual version. If provided with a calendar start-date for the project and details of days or weeks off for holidays, some packages can give a full calendar version of the output instead of using Week 23, and so on. Where resourcing is desired, larger packages go on to give a list of the required resources, period by period, but I believe that so far there has been no fully successful program which uses the float to balance resources. This juggling stage requires a measure of managerial decision beyond the abilities of the machine. Equally, the computer cannot draw the original network from a description of the problem; this requires human judgement, as we have seen.

Figure 19.19   A loop: B depends on A, C depends on B, A depends on C.
This is logical nonsense.

The computer is obviously a major aid to speedy analysis, but its main advantage arises during the control stage. Any serious project will give rise to so much control information, i.e. so many notifications of departures from plan, that the analysis must be reassessed many times before the project is complete. The computer stores the original data, so it would only be necessary to call for the amendment section of the package program, feed in the alterations and wait briefly for the new analysis to emerge as a basis for planning decisions. The amount of human work is minimal, which helps to encourage full use of the power of the model.

Alternative ways of drawing the network
As we have seen, a network is an assembly of alternating arrows and shapes. We have made the shapes represent the activities and the arrows the dependencies. Simple though this idea is, it is a recent development. The classical networks were organized the other way round, with the activities on the arrows. To separate one activity from the next, each began and ended with circles (as in Figure 19.20), which were referred to as *events* because they represented the

Figure 19.20

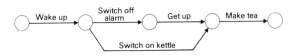

Table 19.1

```
GET-$CPATH
9900    DATA 12,5,10,15,20,25,30,35,40,45,50,55,60
9901    DATA 17
9902    DATA 5,10,2,5,15,12,10,15,0
9903    DATA 15,20,26,20,25,4,20,30,1
9904    DATA 25,30,0,25,35,2,30,40,50
9905    DATA 35,40,0,35,45,45,35,50,3
9906    DATA 40,50,2,45,50,0,50,55,6
9907    DATA 55,60,2,30,60,8

RUN
CPATH

*   CRITICAL PATH   *


DO YOU WISH TO ENTER DATA FROM THE TELETYPE AS IT BECOMES NECESSARY,
OR TO ENTER IT INTERNALLY WITH 'DATA'-STATEMENTS?  (ENTER 'T' FOR
TELETYPE, 'D' OTHERWISE)? D
HAS THE DATA ALREADY BEEN ENTERED? ('Y' FOR YES, 'N' FOR NO.)?Y
```

```
*********************************************************************
                  ***   EVENT TIMES   ***
        EVENT       EARLIEST TIME  LATEST TIME

        5           0              0              CRITICAL PATH
        10          2              12
        15          12             12             CRITICAL PATH
        20          38             38             CRITICAL PATH
        25          42             42             CRITICAL PATH
        30          42             42             CRITICAL PATH
        35          44             49
        40          92             92             CRITICAL PATH
        45          89             94
        50          94             94             CRITICAL PATH
        55          100            100            CRITICAL PATH
        60          102            102            CRITICAL PATH


                  ***  ACTIVITY TIMES  ***

  PREDECESSOR    SUCCESSOR      ACTUAL TIME   MAXIMUM TIME

        5           10             2              12
        5           15             12             12             CRITICAL PATH
        10          15             0              10
        15          20             26             26             CRITICAL PATH
        20          25             4              4              CRITICAL PATH
        20          30             1              4
        25          30             0              0              CRITICAL PATH
        25          35             2              7
        30          40             50             50             CRITICAL PATH
        35          40             0              48
        35          45             45             50
        35          50             3              50
        40          50             2              2              CRITICAL PATH
        45          50             0              5
        50          55             6              6              CRITICAL PATH
        55          60             2              2              CRITICAL PATH
        30          60             8              60


*********************************************************************
```

Figure 19.21

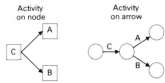

end of one activity and the start of the next. Because of the negative aspect of this definition, the word *node* also became accepted as the name for a circle. Our method of drawing the network is thus called *activity-on-node*, the classic way being *activity-on-arrow*.

There is more to this difference than merely transposing labels, as special conventions have to be used to describe some dependencies. Figure 19.21 shows activities A and B depending on C. Figure 19.22 has A and B each depending on both C and D. So far there is no difficulty. It is a different matter when we wish to represent:

A depends on C

B depends on C and D

It is easy in activity-on-node (Figure 19.23) but can be achieved in activity-on-arrow only by introducing a dummy activity, drawn as a dotted arrow (Figure 19.24). The dependency of B on C passes through the dummy, which of course

Figure 19.22

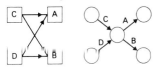

Figure 19.23

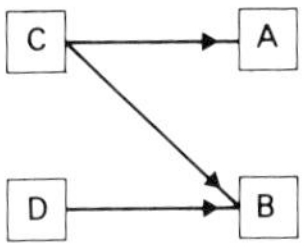

Figure 19.24

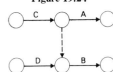

Figure 19.25

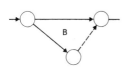

has zero duration, but the direction of the dummy prevents A from depending on D. This is the *logical* use of the dummy, to achieve a logical statement impossible without it. There is also a *grammatical* use for it, to avoid ambiguities where two or more activities begin and end at the same pair of nodes. Figure 19.25 shows such a situation at A, and we cannot describe either activity unambiguously to a computer, or even to people. At B the dummy, plus an extra node, overcomes this difficulty.

The activity-on-arrow network for our problem can be drawn quite straightforwardly by arguing as we did before. It has four dummy activities, two being logical and two grammatical, and is seen in Figure 19.26.

Figure 19.26

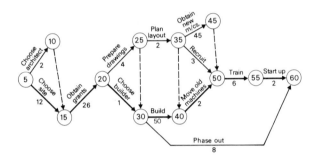

Note three conventions:

1. As with activity-on-node diagrams, there is only a single start node and finish node for the project, to make the analysis possible.

2. The nodes are numbered for ease of communication, so that one can tell a computer that an activity starting at node 20 and finishing at node 25 has a duration of 4. This convention also makes it clearer when communicating with people, for numbered nodes are found more easily than named arrows in a large network. (The same is true of activity-on-node networks.) We may use any node numbers we please, as long as there is no duplication and as long as we comply with any restrictions imposed by the computer, for example concerning the first and last nodes.

3. The activity names are written above their arrows and the durations below them.

Analysis proceeds exactly as for activity-on-node diagrams, the forward pass finding the earliest start and the backward pass the latest starts. Conventionally these are inserted above and below the nodes respectively. The analysed arrow diagram is as Figure 19.27. Derivation of the bar chart and the remaining uses of the model are carried out as before.

Figure 19.27

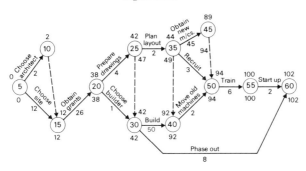

It is difficult to decide which is the better type of network diagram. Both give the same results and anyone practised in using networks can handle either without difficulty. However, those who have used both tend to say that activity-on-node diagrams are marginally better. The main advantage claimed for activity-on-node is that it is easier to learn from scratch (primarily because there are no dummies apart from Start and End) and networks are easier to draw with it. Against it is mainly the fact that activity-on-arrow was very well established before the newcomer arrived and those who had become accustomed to it are naturally unwilling to change for only a slight benefit. Allied to this is the plentiful supply of computer packages for activity-on-arrow diagrams and a dearth of them for activity-on-node networks: the example in Table 19.1 was produced via a multi-access terminal, using an arrow package because this was the easiest to obtain.

A short-cut, called card networking, can be used with activity-on-node methods. A piece of card for each activity is marked up like the boxes used in the network diagram (or Figure 19.11). The pack is arranged and re-arranged on a large table or board until the shape of the desired network has been achieved through thought and discussion. Only then is it committed to paper. This can save a lot of time. Unfortunately it does not work for activity-on-arrow networks because of the dummies needed.

It is impossible to measure the savings brought about by networking. As it is essentially a tool for tasks which are performed only once, there can be no 'with' and 'without' comparisons. However, major building firms say that on a project worth 2 or 3 million pounds they will typically spend about £25 000 on network analysis, including computer time, and consider that by doing so they will have saved ten times this amount in avoided difficulties.

APPENDIX A
PASCAL'S PYRAMID

```
                                                                              1
                                                                          1
                                                                      1       19
                                                                  1       18
                                                              1       17   171
                                                          1       16   153
                                                      1       15   136   969
                                                  1       14   120   816
                                              1       13   105   680   3876
                                          1       12   91    560   3060
                                      1       11   78    455   2380   11628
                                  1       10   66    364   1820   1365?
                              1       9    55    286   1001   1365   27132
                          1       8    45    220   715    1001   3003
                      1       7    36    165   495    792    2002   50388
                  1       6    28    120   330    462    924    3003
              1       5    21    84    210    252    462    1716   75582
          1       4    15    56    126    126    210    792    3432
      1       3    10    35    70     56     84     330    1716   92378
  1       2    6     20    35     21     28     120    495    3003
      1       3    10    35     15     56     462    1287   92378
          1       4    15    21     84     210    924    6435
              1       5    10     28    126    210    2002  75582
                  1       6     36    120    252    792    6435
                      1      8     45    330    462    1716  50388
                          9     55    165    495    924    5005
                      10     66    220    495    1716   8008  27132
                  11     78    286    715    1287   3003  12376
              12     91    364    1001   2002   3003  18564  11628
          13     105   455    1365   3003   4368  12376  31824
      14     120   560    1820   4368   6188   8008  19448  3876
  15     136   680    2380   6188   8568  11440  24310  43758
      153   816    3060   8568  18564  19448  24310  48620  969
      969    3876  11628  27132 31824  43758  43758  92378
          11628  27132 50388 50388 75582 75582  92378       171
                  50388 75582 92378 92378                          19
```

APPENDIX B

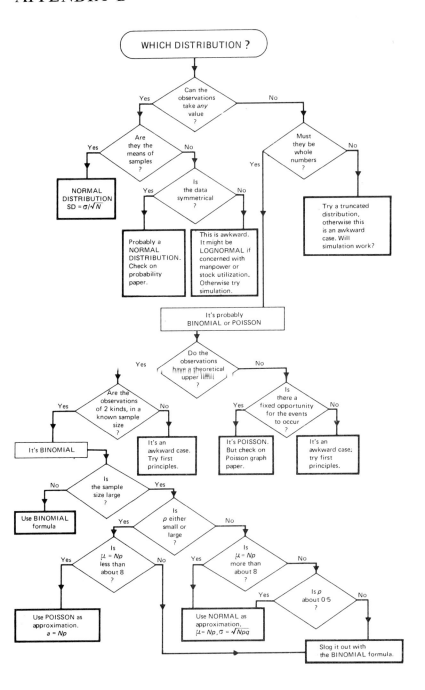

APPENDIX C
THE NORMAL DISTRIBUTION

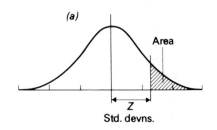

(a)

Area

Z
Std. devns.

STD DEVNS FROM MEAN	.00	.01	.02	.03	.04	.05	.06	.07	.08	.09
0.0	.50000	.49601	.49202	.48803	.48405	.48006	.47608	.47210	.46812	.46414
0.1	.46017	.45621	.45224	.44828	.44433	.44038	.43644	.43251	.42858	.42466
0.2	.42074	.41683	.41294	.40905	.40517	.40129	.39743	.39358	.38974	.38591
0.3	.38209	.37828	.37448	.37070	.36693	.36317	.35942	.35569	.35197	.34827
0.4	.34458	.34010	.33724	.33350	.32997	.32636	.32276	.31918	.31561	.31207
0.5	.30854	.30503	.30153	.29806	.29460	.29116	.28774	.28434	.28096	.27760
0.6	.27425	.27093	.26763	.26435	.26109	.25785	.25463	.25143	.24824	.24510
0.7	.24196	.23885	.23576	.23270	.22965	.22663	.22363	.22065	.21760	.21476
0.8	.21186	.20897	.20611	.20327	.20045	.19766	.19489	.19215	.18943	.18673
0.9	.18406	.18141	.17879	.17619	.17361	.17106	.16853	.16602	.16354	.16109
1.0	.15866	.15625	.15386	.15151	.14917	.14686	.14457	.14231	.14117	.13786
1.1	.13567	.13350	.13136	.12924	.12714	.12507	.12302	.12100	.11900	.11702
1.2	.11507	.11314	.11123	.10935	.10749	.10565	.10383	.10204	.10027	.09853
1.3	.09680	.09510	.09342	.09176	.09012	.08851	.08691	.08534	.08379	.08226
1.4	.08076	.07927	.07780	.07636	.07593	.07353	.07214	.07078	.06944	.06811
1.5	.06681	.06652	.06426	.06301	.06178	.06057	.05938	.05821	.05705	.05592
1.6	.05480	.05370	.05262	.05155	.05050	.04947	.04846	.04756	.04648	.04551
1.7	.04457	.04363	.04272	.04182	.04093	.04006	.03920	.03836	.03754	.03673
1.8	.03593	.03515	.03438	.03363	.03288	.03216	.03144	.03074	.03005	.02938
1.9	.02872	.02807	.02743	.02680	.02619	.02559	.02500	.02442	.02385	.02330
2.0	.02275	.02222	.02169	.02118	.02068	.02018	.01970	.01923	.01876	.01831
2.1	.01786	.01743	.01700	.01659	.01618	.01578	.01539	.01500	.01463	.01426
2.2	.01390	.01355	.01321	.01287	.01255	.01222	.01191	.01160	.01130	.01101
2.3	.01072	.01044	.01017	.00990	.00964	.00939	.00914	.00889	.00866	.00842
2.4	.00820	.00798	.00776	.00755	.00734	.00714	.00695	.00676	.00657	.00639
2.5	.00621	.00604	.00587	.00570	.00554	.00539	.00523	.00508	.00494	.00480
2.6	.00466	.00453	.00440	.00427	.00415	.00402	.00391	.00379	.00368	.00357
2.7	.00347	.00336	.00326	.00317	.00307	.00298	.00289	.00281	.00272	.00264
2.8	.00256	.00248	.00241	.00233	.00226	.00219	.00212	.00205	.00199	.00193
2.9	.00187	.00181	.00175	.00169	.00164	.00159	.00154	.00149	.00144	.00139
3.0	.00135	.00131	.00126	.00122	.00118	.00114	.00111	.00107	.00103	.00100
3.1	.00097	.00094	.00090	.00087	.00084	.00082	.00079	.00076	.00074	.00071
3.2	.00069	.00066	.00064	.00062	.00060	.00058	.00056	.00054	.00052	.00050
3.3	.00048	.00047	.00045	.00043	.00042	.00040	.00039	.00038	.00036	.00035
3.4	.00034	.00032	.00031	.00030	.00029	.00028	.00027	.00026	.00025	.00024
3.5	.00023	.00022	.00022	.00020	.00020	.00019	.00019	.00018	.00017	.00017
3.6	.00016	.00015	.00015	.00014	.00014	.00013	.00013	.00012	.00012	.00011
3.7	.00011	.00010	.00010	.00010	.00009	.00009	.00009	.00008	.00008	.00008
3.8	.00007	.00007	.00007	.00006	.00006	.00006	.00006	.00005	.00005	.00005
3.9	.00005	.00005	.00004	.00004	.00004	.00004	.00004	.00004	.00003	.00003
4.0	.00003	.00003	.00003	.00003	.00003	.00003	.00002	.00002	.00002	.00002
4.1	.00002	.00002	.00002	.00002	.00002	.00002	.00002	.00002	.00001	.00001
4.2	.00001	.00001	.00001	.00001	.00001	.00001	.00001	.00001	.00001	.00001
4.3	.00001	.00001	.00001	.00001	.00001	.00001	.00001	.00001	.00001	.00001
4.4	.00001	.00001								

APPENDIX D
TABLE OF RANDOM NUMBERS

50880	74277	53411	62067	13362	86504	74153	18655	98167	21619
25051	69918	91164	15437	00663	77227	77823	55587	79920	36737
05488	99356	89461	05232	07318	32110	36808	18983	62017	55397
00973	76311	48608	52092	44617	92593	16889	29957	90492	52804
69532	13383	12185	77828	94240	76942	53831	64298	61618	99527
66467	04016	04665	56940	41835	95700	46626	35490	72939	06817
53368	96846	02560	66441	14010	77460	54389	04435	34369	25747
26643	85514	03134	10625	90924	93354	53933	58581	66543	88727
35211	73853	04266	44804	44669	49271	88828	41067	30753	68315
49072	94855	26992	69725	92171	37691	97006	72017	39889	30545
04060	22346	90567	83682	64363	74298	04198	38591	77416	09341
39572	33834	89084	98612	62069	43184	41526	11219	21093	31716
83409	54984	11928	48331	85826	07030	56134	83964	61428	33653
27849	43044	68672	18828	17160	32709	08497	65762	67595	86013
77873	97333	42989	23007	41090	21007	15356	10407	53869	94467
52991	30201	25445	51448	42530	80049	70862	18887	51302	10443
84720	66833	03016	78725	72565	37584	32895	11602	18100	30820
52337	42844	11671	43483	27051	35604	40184	44216	79073	26504
62806	33730	09388	19965	90653	74942	44111	69252	55551	31911
99599	24961	78859	33197	32424	52537	15993	59347	10044	89608
99066	63001	32696	85587	30180	19542	72215	76752	50703	87160
48310	64876	66557	34332	22489	59170	47108	64356	19991	10604
88089	48179	86951	86630	21851	62029	58203	14101	91730	93547
54154	00675	53450	52836	10070	02814	20358	10374	76341	07569
32085	49895	87289	10071	46622	27227	89364	84127	78458	01765
90656	48306	52072	89164	65584	96151	94958	98026	47662	75447
30324	21036	18108	38869	54019	77653	95043	56257	89049	01668
57048	21189	89762	32151	39355	39420	58413	10376	59312	77037
70851	51998	17849	90919	74309	11740	69920	27455	23509	34501
80234	00011	66013	57782	54029	08804	41705	40841	20596	09337
32497	52028	42591	80469	28566	37923	88232	90530	33016	19743
59186	66001	54158	74778	70409	55375	75988	69459	99857	35163
97490	09700	01703	86225	42658	37506	85864	78767	08667	03688
33479	17505	08837	21151	08803	61593	82591	53999	16688	63470
45117	04967	94479	81107	78200	82042	29683	44013	91793	93926
97892	86073	91265	10865	02996	37804	45761	68184	81998	78102
24739	64481	24065	47320	50719	91520	02492	12255	17794	43973
44693	72686	74185	04031	22109	60476	60223	70373	04616	60983
02507	91680	24037	38535	34021	79262	64179	29516	69687	71468
04913	29951	20767	46187	53707	37902	55740	75662	30996	92489
85542	09503	04418	70156	32319	85503	98571	58736	25162	32456
12916	07255	83406	18126	61771	32476	40958	56899	28363	41307
24222	54901	53649	46699	43958	33002	67064	37839	05955	49886
15106	33788	81457	70331	66225	03365	37263	39126	97887	49044
23735	27883	12223	43746	32448	55520	97081	11075	65487	88873
95228	66972	47314	25343	48829	73898	25440	62130	54662	51850
06155	20550	62932	87045	14229	60823	50761	00969	23599	15485
02516	58058	97452	42088	51339	74614	83391	41486	41750	39818
71871	18110	53340	87396	85042	64208	09647	98189	51934	08439
90664	42591	98856	68001	36692	81810	10723	72560	06591	09262
64474	09971	68474	05683	64336	42501	16387	63446	64208	71940
31537	02122	66223	57765	52672	61925	04530	92063	72432	29064
01954	65829	22078	17729	27146	63575	08359	51995	15165	04958
81735	03048	23636	65009	87314	88216	66099	96606	01354	80349
36422	46244	35311	58392	19211	43594	09913	75771	91460	56251

APPENDIX E
THE t-DISTRIBUTION

DEGS OF FRDM	PROBABILITY						
	50%	30%	10%	5%	2%	1%	0.1%
1	1.000	1.963	6.314	12.706	31.821	63.657	636.619
2	.816	1.386	2.920	4.303	6.965	9.925	31.598
3	.765	1.250	2.353	3.182	4.541	5.841	12.941
4	.741	1.190	2.132	2.776	3.747	4.604	8.610
5	.727	1.156	2.015	2.571	3.365	4.032	6.859
6	.718	1.134	1.943	2.447	3.143	3.707	5.959
7	.711	1.119	1.895	2.365	2.998	3.499	5.405
8	.706	1.108	1.860	2.306	2.896	3.355	5.041
9	.703	1.100	1.833	2.262	2.821	3.250	4.781
10	.700	1.093	1.812	2.228	2.764	3.169	4.587
11	.697	1.088	1.796	2.201	2.718	3.106	4.437
12	.695	1.083	1.782	2.179	2.681	3.055	4.318
13	.694	1.079	1.771	2.160	2.650	3.012	4.221
14	.692	1.076	1.761	2.145	2.624	2.977	4.140
15	.691	1.074	1.753	2.131	2.602	2.947	4.073
16	.690	1.071	1.746	2.120	2.583	2.921	4.015
17	.689	1.069	1.740	2.110	2.567	2.898	3.965
18	.688	1.067	1.734	2.101	2.552	2.878	3.922
19	.688	1.066	1.729	2.093	2.539	2.861	3.883
20	.687	1.064	1.725	2.086	2.528	2.845	3.850
21	.686	1.063	1.721	2.080	2.518	2.831	3.819
22	.686	1.061	1.717	2.074	2.508	2.819	3.792
23	.685	1.060	1.714	2.069	2.500	2.807	3.767
24	.685	1.059	1.711	2.064	2.492	2.797	3.745
25	.684	1.058	1.708	2.060	2.485	2.787	3.725
26	.684	1.058	1.706	2.056	2.479	2.779	3.707
27	.684	1.057	1.703	2.052	2.473	2.771	3.690
28	.683	1.056	1.701	2.048	2.467	2.763	3.674
29	.683	1.055	1.699	2.045	2.462	2.756	3.659
30	.683	1.055	1.697	2.042	2.457	2.750	3.646
INF.	.674	1.036	1.645	1.960	2.326	2.576	3.291

This is a table of the 2-tailed family of distributions, i.e. it gives the numbers of standard deviations from the mean if *both tails together* are to contain 50%, 30%, 10% . . . . of the distributions.

For significance tests where only one tail is relevant, halve the probabilities.

Example: On 10 Degrees of Freedom, a t-value of 2·9 corresponds to a probability between 1% and 2% if the observed difference between samples might have occurred in either direction, or between ½% and 1% if only one direction is being considered.

APPENDIX F

THE *F*-TEST OF SIGNIFICANCE

DEGREES OF FREEDOM OF LARGER VARIANCE (columns) vs **DEGREES OF FREEDOM OF SMALLER VARIANCE** (rows)

DF (smaller)	PROB	INF	100	60	40	30	24	20	16	14	12	10	9	8	7	6	5	4	3	2	1
1	10%	63.33	63.02	62.79	62.53	62.26	62.00	61.74	61.55	61.18	60.71	60.19	59.86	59.44	58.91	58.20	57.24	55.83	53.59	49.50	39.86
	5%	254.3	253.1	252.2	251.1	250.1	249.1	248.0	246.3	245.2	243.9	241.9	240.5	238.9	236.8	234.0	230.2	224.6	215.7	199.5	161.4
	1%	6366	6334	6313	6287	6261	6235	6209	6169	6142	6106	6056	6022	5981	5928	5859	5764	5625	5403	4999	4052
	0.1%	636600	633400	631300	628700	626100	623500	620900	617050	614600	610700	605600	602300	598150	592900	585950	576400	562500	540400	500000	405300
2	10%	9.49	9.48	9.47	9.47	9.46	9.45	9.44	9.43	9.42	9.41	9.39	9.38	9.37	9.35	9.33	9.29	9.24	9.16	9.00	8.53
	5%	19.50	19.49	19.48	19.47	19.46	19.45	19.45	19.43	19.42	19.41	19.39	19.38	19.37	19.35	19.33	19.30	19.25	19.16	19.00	18.51
	1%	99.50	99.49	99.48	99.47	99.47	99.46	99.45	99.44	99.43	99.42	99.40	99.39	99.37	99.36	99.33	99.30	99.25	99.17	99.00	98.49
	0.1%	999.5	999.5	999.5	999.5	999.5	999.5	999.4	999.4	999.4	999.4	999.4	999.4	999.4	999.4	999.3	999.3	999.2	999.2	999.0	998.5
3	10%	5.13	5.14	5.15	5.16	5.17	5.18	5.18	5.20	5.21	5.22	5.23	5.24	5.25	5.27	5.28	5.31	5.34	5.39	5.46	5.54
	5%	8.53	8.56	8.57	8.59	8.62	8.64	8.66	8.69	8.71	8.74	8.78	8.81	8.85	8.89	8.94	9.01	9.12	9.28	9.55	10.13
	1%	26.13	26.23	26.32	26.41	26.50	26.60	26.69	26.83	26.92	27.05	27.23	27.35	27.49	27.67	27.91	28.24	28.71	29.46	30.82	34.12
	0.1%	123.5	124.1	124.5	125.0	125.4	125.9	126.4	127.2	127.9	128.3	129.2	129.9	130.6	131.6	132.8	134.6	137.1	141.1	148.5	167.0
4	10%	3.76	3.78	3.79	3.80	3.82	3.83	3.84	3.86	3.88	3.90	3.92	3.94	3.96	3.98	4.01	4.05	4.11	4.19	4.32	4.54
	5%	5.63	5.66	5.69	5.72	5.75	5.77	5.80	5.84	5.87	5.91	5.96	6.00	6.04	6.09	6.16	6.26	6.39	6.59	6.94	7.71
	1%	13.46	13.57	13.65	13.75	13.84	13.93	14.02	14.15	14.24	14.37	14.55	14.66	14.80	14.98	15.21	15.52	15.98	16.69	18.00	21.20
	0.1%	44.05	44.47	44.75	45.09	45.43	45.77	46.10	46.50	46.88	47.41	48.05	48.47	49.00	49.66	50.53	51.71	53.44	56.18	61.25	74.14
5	10%	3.10	3.12	3.14	3.16	3.17	3.19	3.21	3.23	3.25	3.27	3.30	3.32	3.34	3.37	3.40	3.45	3.52	3.62	3.78	4.06
	5%	4.36	4.40	4.43	4.46	4.50	4.53	4.56	4.60	4.64	4.68	4.74	4.77	4.82	4.88	4.95	5.05	5.19	5.41	5.79	6.61
	1%	9.02	9.13	9.20	9.29	9.38	9.47	9.55	9.68	9.77	9.89	10.05	10.16	10.29	10.46	10.67	10.97	11.39	12.06	13.27	16.26
	0.1%	23.97	24.08	24.33	24.60	24.87	25.14	25.39	25.70	26.02	26.42	26.92	27.24	27.64	28.16	28.84	29.75	31.09	33.20	37.12	47.18
6	10%	2.72	2.75	2.76	2.78	2.80	2.82	2.84	2.86	2.88	2.90	2.94	2.96	2.98	3.01	3.05	3.11	3.18	3.29	3.46	3.78
	5%	3.67	3.71	3.74	3.77	3.81	3.84	3.87	3.92	3.96	4.00	4.06	4.10	4.15	4.21	4.28	4.39	4.53	4.76	5.14	5.99
	1%	6.88	6.99	7.06	7.14	7.23	7.31	7.40	7.52	7.60	7.72	7.87	7.98	8.10	8.26	8.47	8.75	9.15	9.78	10.92	13.75
	0.1%	15.75	16.00	16.21	16.44	16.67	16.89	17.12	17.45	17.70	17.99	18.41	18.69	19.03	19.46	20.03	20.81	21.92	23.70	27.00	35.51
7	10%	2.47	2.49	2.51	2.54	2.56	2.58	2.59	2.62	2.64	2.67	2.70	2.72	2.75	2.78	2.83	2.88	2.96	3.07	3.26	3.59
	5%	3.23	3.28	3.30	3.34	3.38	3.41	3.44	3.49	3.52	3.57	3.64	3.68	3.73	3.79	3.87	3.97	4.12	4.35	4.74	5.59
	1%	5.65	5.75	5.82	5.91	5.99	6.07	6.16	6.28	6.36	6.47	6.62	6.71	6.84	6.99	7.19	7.46	7.85	8.45	9.55	12.25
	0.1%	11.70	11.93	12.12	12.33	12.53	12.73	12.93	13.22	13.42	13.71	14.08	14.33	14.63	15.02	15.52	16.21	17.19	18.77	21.69	29.25
8	10%	2.29	2.32	2.34	2.36	2.38	2.40	2.42	2.45	2.47	2.50	2.54	2.56	2.59	2.62	2.67	2.73	2.81	2.92	3.11	3.46
	5%	2.93	2.98	3.01	3.04	3.08	3.12	3.15	3.20	3.23	3.28	3.35	3.39	3.44	3.50	3.58	3.69	3.84	4.07	4.46	5.32
	1%	4.86	4.96	5.03	5.12	5.20	5.28	5.36	5.48	5.56	5.67	5.81	5.91	6.03	6.18	6.37	6.63	7.01	7.59	8.65	11.26
	0.1%	9.33	9.56	9.73	9.92	10.11	10.30	10.48	10.76	10.92	11.19	11.54	11.77	12.04	12.40	12.86	13.49	14.39	15.83	18.49	25.42
9	10%	2.16	2.19	2.21	2.23	2.25	2.28	2.30	2.33	2.36	2.38	2.42	2.44	2.47	2.51	2.55	2.61	2.69	2.81	3.01	3.36
	5%	2.71	2.75	2.79	2.83	2.86	2.90	2.94	2.98	3.02	3.07	3.14	3.18	3.23	3.29	3.37	3.48	3.63	3.86	4.26	5.12
	1%	4.31	4.41	4.48	4.57	4.65	4.73	4.81	4.92	5.00	5.11	5.26	5.35	5.47	5.61	5.80	6.06	6.42	6.99	8.02	10.56
	0.1%	7.81	8.03	8.19	8.37	8.55	8.72	8.90	9.16	9.33	9.57	9.89	10.11	10.37	10.70	11.13	11.71	12.56	13.90	16.39	22.86
10	10%	2.06	2.09	2.11	2.13	2.16	2.18	2.20	2.23	2.25	2.28	2.32	2.35	2.38	2.41	2.46	2.52	2.61	2.73	2.92	3.29
	5%	2.54	2.59	2.62	2.66	2.70	2.74	2.77	2.82	2.86	2.91	2.98	3.02	3.07	3.14	3.22	3.33	3.48	3.71	4.10	4.96
	1%	3.91	4.01	4.08	4.17	4.25	4.33	4.41	4.52	4.60	4.71	4.85	4.94	5.06	5.21	5.39	5.64	5.99	6.55	7.56	10.04
	0.1%	6.76	6.96	7.12	7.30	7.47	7.64	7.80	8.05	8.12	8.45	8.75	8.96	9.20	9.52	9.92	10.48	11.28	12.55	14.91	21.04
11	10%	1.97	2.01	2.03	2.05	2.08	2.10	2.12	2.15	2.18	2.21	2.25	2.27	2.30	2.34	2.39	2.45	2.54	2.66	2.86	3.23
	5%	2.40	2.45	2.49	2.53	2.57	2.61	2.65	2.70	2.74	2.79	2.85	2.90	2.95	3.01	3.09	3.20	3.36	3.59	3.98	4.84
	1%	3.60	3.70	3.78	3.86	3.94	4.02	4.10	4.21	4.29	4.40	4.54	4.63	4.74	4.89	5.07	5.32	5.67	6.22	7.21	9.65
	0.1%	6.00	6.21	6.35	6.52	6.68	6.85	7.01	7.25	7.40	7.63	7.92	8.12	8.35	8.66	9.05	9.58	10.35	11.56	13.81	19.69

DEGREES OF FREEDOM OF SMALLER VARIANCE (rows) × DEGREES OF FREEDOM OF LARGER VARIANCE (columns)

df (smaller)	PROB	1	2	3	4	5	6	7	8	9	10	12	14	16	20	24	30	40	60	100	INF
12	10%	3.18	2.81	2.61	2.48	2.39	2.33	2.28	2.24	2.21	2.19	2.15	2.12	2.09	2.06	2.04	2.01	1.99	1.96	1.94	1.90
	5%	4.75	3.88	3.49	3.26	3.11	3.00	2.92	2.85	2.80	2.76	2.69	2.64	2.60	2.54	2.50	2.46	2.42	2.38	2.35	2.30
	1%	9.33	6.93	5.95	5.41	5.06	4.82	4.65	4.50	4.39	4.30	4.16	4.05	3.98	3.86	3.78	3.70	3.61	3.54	3.46	3.36
	0.1%	18.64	12.97	10.80	9.63	8.89	8.38	8.00	7.71	7.48	7.29	7.00	6.79	6.64	6.40	6.25	6.09	5.93	5.76	5.61	5.42
13	10%	3.14	2.76	2.56	2.43	2.35	2.28	2.23	2.20	2.16	2.14	2.10	2.07	2.05	2.01	1.98	1.96	1.93	1.90	1.88	1.85
	5%	4.67	3.80	3.41	3.18	3.02	2.92	2.84	2.77	2.72	2.67	2.60	2.55	2.51	2.46	2.42	2.38	2.34	2.30	2.26	2.21
	1%	9.07	6.70	5.74	5.20	4.86	4.62	4.44	4.30	4.19	4.10	3.96	3.85	3.78	3.67	3.59	3.51	3.42	3.34	3.27	3.16
	0.1%	17.81	12.31	10.21	9.07	8.35	7.86	7.49	7.21	6.98	6.80	6.52	6.32	6.16	5.93	5.78	5.63	5.47	5.30	5.16	4.97
14	10%	3.10	2.73	2.52	2.39	2.31	2.24	2.19	2.15	2.12	2.10	2.05	2.02	1.99	1.96	1.94	1.91	1.89	1.86	1.83	1.80
	5%	4.60	3.74	3.34	3.11	2.96	2.85	2.77	2.70	2.65	2.60	2.53	2.48	2.44	2.39	2.35	2.31	2.27	2.22	2.19	2.13
	1%	8.86	6.51	5.56	5.03	4.69	4.46	4.28	4.14	4.03	3.94	3.80	3.70	3.62	3.51	3.43	3.34	3.26	3.18	3.11	3.00
	0.1%	17.14	11.78	9.73	8.62	7.92	7.43	7.08	6.80	6.58	6.40	6.13	5.93	5.78	5.56	5.41	5.25	5.10	4.94	4.79	4.60
15	10%	3.07	2.70	2.49	2.36	2.27	2.21	2.16	2.12	2.09	2.06	2.02	1.99	1.96	1.92	1.90	1.87	1.85	1.82	1.79	1.76
	5%	4.54	3.68	3.29	3.06	2.90	2.79	2.70	2.64	2.59	2.54	2.48	2.43	2.38	2.33	2.29	2.25	2.21	2.16	2.12	2.07
	1%	8.68	6.36	5.42	4.89	4.56	4.32	4.14	4.00	3.89	3.80	3.67	3.56	3.48	3.36	3.29	3.20	3.12	3.05	2.97	2.87
	0.1%	16.59	11.34	9.34	8.25	7.57	7.09	6.74	6.47	6.26	6.08	5.81	5.61	5.46	5.25	5.10	4.95	4.80	4.64	4.48	4.31
16	10%	3.05	2.67	2.46	2.33	2.24	2.18	2.13	2.09	2.06	2.03	1.99	1.96	1.93	1.89	1.87	1.84	1.81	1.78	1.75	1.72
	5%	4.49	3.63	3.24	3.01	2.85	2.74	2.66	2.59	2.54	2.49	2.42	2.37	2.33	2.28	2.24	2.20	2.16	2.11	2.07	2.01
	1%	8.53	6.23	5.29	4.77	4.44	4.20	4.03	3.89	3.78	3.69	3.55	3.45	3.37	3.25	3.18	3.10	3.01	2.93	2.86	2.75
	0.1%	16.12	10.97	9.00	7.94	7.27	6.81	6.46	6.19	5.98	5.81	5.55	5.35	5.20	4.99	4.85	4.70	4.54	4.39	4.24	4.06
17	10%	3.03	2.64	2.44	2.31	2.22	2.15	2.10	2.06	2.03	2.00	1.96	1.92	1.89	1.86	1.84	1.81	1.78	1.75	1.72	1.69
	5%	4.45	3.59	3.20	2.96	2.81	2.70	2.62	2.55	2.50	2.45	2.38	2.33	2.29	2.23	2.19	2.15	2.11	2.06	2.02	1.96
	1%	8.40	6.11	5.18	4.67	4.34	4.10	3.93	3.79	3.68	3.59	3.45	3.35	3.27	3.16	3.08	3.00	2.92	2.83	2.76	2.65
	0.1%	15.72	10.66	8.73	7.68	7.02	6.56	6.22	5.96	5.75	5.58	5.32	5.13	4.98	4.78	4.63	4.48	4.33	4.18	4.03	3.85
18	10%	3.01	2.62	2.42	2.29	2.20	2.13	2.08	2.04	2.00	1.98	1.93	1.90	1.87	1.84	1.81	1.78	1.75	1.72	1.70	1.66
	5%	4.41	3.55	3.16	2.93	2.77	2.66	2.58	2.51	2.46	2.41	2.34	2.29	2.25	2.19	2.15	2.11	2.07	2.02	1.98	1.92
	1%	8.28	6.01	5.09	4.58	4.25	4.01	3.84	3.71	3.60	3.51	3.37	3.27	3.19	3.07	3.00	2.91	2.83	2.75	2.68	2.57
	0.1%	15.38	10.39	8.49	7.46	6.81	6.35	6.02	5.76	5.56	5.39	5.13	4.95	4.80	4.59	4.45	4.30	4.15	4.00	3.85	3.67
19	10%	2.99	2.61	2.40	2.27	2.18	2.11	2.06	2.02	1.98	1.96	1.91	1.87	1.85	1.82	1.79	1.76	1.73	1.70	1.68	1.63
	5%	4.38	3.52	3.13	2.90	2.74	2.63	2.55	2.48	2.43	2.38	2.31	2.26	2.21	2.15	2.11	2.07	2.02	1.98	1.94	1.88
	1%	8.18	5.93	5.01	4.50	4.17	3.94	3.77	3.63	3.52	3.43	3.30	3.19	3.12	3.00	2.92	2.84	2.76	2.67	2.60	2.49
	0.1%	15.08	10.16	8.28	7.26	6.62	6.18	5.85	5.59	5.39	5.22	4.97	4.77	4.63	4.43	4.29	4.14	3.99	3.84	3.69	3.51
20	10%	2.97	2.59	2.38	2.25	2.16	2.09	2.04	2.00	1.96	1.94	1.89	1.84	1.82	1.79	1.77	1.74	1.71	1.68	1.65	1.61
	5%	4.35	3.49	3.10	2.87	2.71	2.60	2.52	2.45	2.40	2.35	2.28	2.23	2.18	2.12	2.08	2.04	1.99	1.95	1.90	1.84
	1%	8.10	5.85	4.94	4.43	4.10	3.87	3.70	3.56	3.45	3.37	3.23	3.13	3.05	2.94	2.86	2.77	2.69	2.61	2.53	2.42
	0.1%	14.82	9.95	8.10	7.10	6.46	6.02	5.69	5.44	5.24	5.08	4.82	4.63	4.48	4.29	4.15	4.00	3.86	3.70	3.55	3.38
21	10%	2.96	2.57	2.36	2.23	2.14	2.08	2.02	1.98	1.95	1.92	1.87	1.84	1.81	1.78	1.75	1.72	1.69	1.66	1.63	1.59
	5%	4.32	3.47	3.07	2.84	2.68	2.57	2.49	2.42	2.37	2.32	2.25	2.20	2.15	2.09	2.05	2.00	1.96	1.92	1.87	1.81
	1%	8.02	5.78	4.87	4.37	4.04	3.81	3.65	3.51	3.40	3.31	3.17	3.07	2.99	2.88	2.80	2.72	2.63	2.55	2.47	2.36
	0.1%	14.59	9.77	7.94	6.95	6.32	5.88	5.56	5.31	5.11	4.95	4.70	4.52	4.37	4.17	4.03	3.88	3.74	3.58	3.44	3.26
22	10%	2.95	2.56	2.35	2.22	2.13	2.06	2.01	1.97	1.93	1.90	1.86	1.82	1.80	1.76	1.73	1.70	1.67	1.64	1.61	1.57
	5%	4.30	3.44	3.05	2.82	2.66	2.55	2.47	2.40	2.35	2.30	2.23	2.18	2.13	2.07	2.03	1.98	1.93	1.89	1.84	1.78
	1%	7.94	5.72	4.82	4.31	3.99	3.76	3.59	3.45	3.35	3.26	3.12	3.02	2.94	2.83	2.75	2.67	2.58	2.50	2.42	2.31
	0.1%	14.38	9.61	7.80	6.81	6.19	5.76	5.44	5.19	4.99	4.83	4.58	4.39	4.24	4.06	3.92	3.78	3.63	3.48	3.33	3.15

DEGREES OF FREEDOM OF LARGER VARIANCE

Smaller df	PROB	1	2	3	4	5	6	7	8	9	10	12	14	16	20	24	30	40	60	100	INF
23	10%	2.94	2.55	2.34	2.21	2.11	2.05	1.99	1.95	1.92	1.89	1.84	1.81	1.78	1.74	1.72	1.69	1.66	1.62	1.59	1.55
	5%	4.28	3.42	3.03	2.80	2.64	2.53	2.45	2.38	2.32	2.28	2.20	2.14	2.10	2.04	2.00	1.96	1.91	1.86	1.82	1.76
	1%	7.88	5.66	4.76	4.26	3.94	3.71	3.54	3.41	3.30	3.21	3.07	2.97	2.89	2.78	2.70	2.62	2.53	2.45	2.37	2.26
	0.1%	14.19	9.47	7.67	6.69	6.08	5.65	5.33	5.09	4.89	4.73	4.48	4.30	4.15	3.96	3.82	3.68	3.53	3.38	3.23	3.05
24	10%	2.93	2.54	2.33	2.19	2.10	2.04	1.98	1.94	1.91	1.88	1.83	1.79	1.76	1.73	1.70	1.67	1.64	1.61	1.57	1.53
	5%	4.26	3.40	3.01	2.78	2.62	2.51	2.43	2.36	2.30	2.26	2.18	2.13	2.09	2.02	1.98	1.94	1.89	1.84	1.80	1.73
	1%	7.82	5.61	4.72	4.22	3.90	3.67	3.50	3.36	3.25	3.17	3.03	2.93	2.85	2.74	2.66	2.58	2.49	2.40	2.33	2.21
	0.1%	14.03	9.34	7.55	6.59	5.98	5.55	5.23	4.99	4.80	4.64	4.39	4.24	4.07	3.87	3.74	3.59	3.45	3.29	3.15	2.97
25	10%	2.92	2.53	2.32	2.18	2.09	2.02	1.97	1.93	1.89	1.87	1.82	1.78	1.75	1.72	1.69	1.66	1.63	1.59	1.56	1.52
	5%	4.24	3.38	2.99	2.76	2.60	2.49	2.41	2.34	2.28	2.24	2.16	2.11	2.06	2.00	1.96	1.92	1.87	1.82	1.77	1.71
	1%	7.77	5.57	4.68	4.18	3.85	3.63	3.46	3.32	3.21	3.13	2.99	2.89	2.81	2.70	2.62	2.54	2.45	2.36	2.29	2.17
	0.1%	13.88	9.22	7.45	6.49	5.88	5.46	5.15	4.91	4.71	4.56	4.31	4.13	3.98	3.79	3.66	3.52	3.37	3.22	3.06	2.89
30	10%	2.88	2.49	2.28	2.14	2.05	1.98	1.93	1.88	1.85	1.82	1.77	1.73	1.70	1.67	1.64	1.61	1.57	1.54	1.50	1.46
	5%	4.17	3.32	2.92	2.69	2.53	2.42	2.34	2.27	2.21	2.16	2.09	2.04	1.99	1.93	1.89	1.84	1.79	1.74	1.69	1.62
	1%	7.56	5.39	4.51	4.02	3.70	3.47	3.30	3.17	3.06	2.98	2.84	2.74	2.66	2.55	2.47	2.38	2.29	2.21	2.13	2.01
	0.1%	13.29	8.77	7.05	6.12	5.53	5.12	4.82	4.58	4.39	4.24	4.00	3.82	3.68	3.49	3.36	3.22	3.07	2.92	2.77	2.59
40	10%	2.84	2.44	2.23	2.09	2.00	1.93	1.87	1.83	1.79	1.76	1.71	1.67	1.64	1.61	1.57	1.54	1.51	1.47	1.43	1.38
	5%	4.08	3.23	2.84	2.61	2.45	2.34	2.25	2.18	2.12	2.07	2.00	1.95	1.90	1.84	1.79	1.74	1.69	1.64	1.59	1.51
	1%	7.31	5.18	4.31	3.83	3.51	3.29	3.12	2.99	2.88	2.80	2.66	2.56	2.49	2.37	2.29	2.20	2.11	2.02	1.94	1.81
	0.1%	12.61	8.25	6.60	5.70	5.13	4.73	4.44	4.21	4.02	3.87	3.64	3.47	3.34	3.15	3.01	2.87	2.73	2.57	2.41	2.23
60	10%	2.79	2.39	2.18	2.04	1.95	1.87	1.82	1.77	1.74	1.71	1.66	1.62	1.58	1.54	1.51	1.48	1.44	1.40	1.35	1.29
	5%	4.00	3.15	2.76	2.52	2.37	2.25	2.17	2.10	2.04	1.99	1.92	1.86	1.81	1.75	1.70	1.65	1.59	1.53	1.48	1.39
	1%	7.08	4.98	4.13	3.65	3.34	3.12	2.95	2.82	2.72	2.63	2.50	2.40	2.32	2.20	2.12	2.03	1.93	1.84	1.74	1.60
	0.1%	11.97	7.76	6.17	5.31	4.76	4.37	4.09	3.87	3.69	3.54	3.31	3.15	3.02	2.83	2.69	2.55	2.41	2.25	2.09	1.89
100	10%	2.76	2.35	2.14	1.99	1.91	1.83	1.78	1.73	1.68	1.65	1.60	1.57	1.53	1.48	1.45	1.42	1.37	1.33	1.27	1.20
	5%	3.94	3.09	2.70	2.46	2.30	2.19	2.10	2.03	1.97	1.92	1.85	1.79	1.75	1.68	1.63	1.57	1.51	1.43	1.39	1.28
	1%	6.90	4.82	3.98	3.51	3.20	2.99	2.82	2.69	2.59	2.51	2.36	2.26	2.19	2.06	1.98	1.89	1.79	1.69	1.59	1.43
	0.1%	11.42	7.35	5.82	4.98	4.45	4.07	3.80	3.58	3.41	3.27	3.05	2.88	2.75	2.56	2.43	2.29	2.14	1.98	1.77	1.58
INF	10%	2.71	2.30	2.08	1.94	1.85	1.77	1.72	1.67	1.63	1.60	1.55	1.51	1.47	1.42	1.38	1.34	1.30	1.24	1.18	1.00
	5%	3.84	2.99	2.60	2.37	2.21	2.09	2.01	1.94	1.88	1.83	1.75	1.69	1.64	1.57	1.52	1.46	1.40	1.32	1.24	1.00
	1%	6.64	4.60	3.78	3.32	3.02	2.80	2.64	2.51	2.41	2.32	2.18	2.07	1.99	1.87	1.79	1.69	1.59	1.47	1.36	1.00
	0.1%	10.83	6.91	5.42	4.62	4.10	3.74	3.47	3.27	3.10	2.96	2.74	2.58	2.45	2.27	2.13	1.99	1.84	1.66	1.47	1.00

Left-margin labels: DEGREES OF FREEDOM OF SMALLER VARIANCE.

APPENDIX G
THE χ^2-DISTRIBUTION

DEGS OF FRDM	PROBABILITY						
	99%	95%	90%	10%	5%	1%	0.
1	.00016	.0039	.016	2.71	3.84	6.63	10.
2	.020	.103	.211	4.61	5.99	9.21	13.
3	.115	.352	.584	6.25	7.81	11.34	16.
4	.297	.711	1.06	7.78	9.49	13.28	18.
5	.554	1.15	1.61	9.24	11.07	15.09	20.
6	.872	1.64	2.20	10.64	12.59	16.81	22.
7	1.24	2.17	2.83	12.02	14.07	18.48	24.
8	1.65	2.73	3.49	13.36	15.51	20.09	26.
9	2.09	3.33	4.17	14.68	16.92	21.67	27.
10	2.56	3.94	4.87	15.99	18.31	23.21	29.
11	3.05	4.57	5.58	17.28	19.68	24.73	31.
12	3.57	5.23	6.30	18.55	21.03	26.22	32.
13	4.11	5.89	7.04	19.81	22.36	27.69	34.
14	4.66	6.57	7.79	21.06	23.68	29.14	36.
15	5.23	7.26	8.55	22.31	25.00	30.58	37.
16	5.81	7.96	9.31	23.54	26.30	32.00	39.
17	6.41	8.67	10.09	24.77	27.59	33.41	40.
18	7.01	9.39	10.86	25.99	28.87	34.81	42.
19	7.63	10.12	11.65	27.20	30.14	36.19	43.
20	8.26	10.85	12.44	28.41	31.41	37.57	45.
21	8.90	11.59	13.24	29.62	32.67	38.93	46.
22	9.54	12.34	14.04	30.81	33.92	40.29	48.
23	10.20	13.09	14.85	32.01	35.17	41.64	49.
24	10.86	13.85	15.66	33.20	36.42	42.98	51.
25	11.52	14.61	16.47	34.38	37.65	44.31	52.
26	12.20	15.38	17.29	35.56	38.89	45.64	54.
27	12.88	16.15	18.11	36.74	40.11	46.96	55.
28	13.56	16.93	18.94	37.92	41.34	48.28	56.
29	14.26	17.71	19.77	39.09	42.56	49.59	58.
30	14.95	18.49	20.60	40.26	43.77	50.89	59.

APPENDIX H
USEFUL FORMULAE

(For algebraic formulae see p. 19.)

Means:

Arithmetic	Geometric	Harmonic

$$\bar{X} = \frac{\sum x}{N} \quad \text{or} \quad \frac{\sum fx}{\sum f} \qquad \sqrt[N]{x_1 . x_2 . x_3 \ldots x_N} \qquad \frac{N}{\dfrac{1}{x_1} + \dfrac{1}{x_2} + \cdots + \dfrac{1}{x_N}}$$

Standard deviation: (Variance $= \sigma^2$)

$$\sigma = \sqrt{\frac{\sum(x - \bar{x})}{N}} = \sqrt{\frac{\sum x^2}{N} - \left(\frac{\sum x}{N}\right)^2}$$

i.e. mean of squares minus square of mean

Correlation coefficient:

$$r = \frac{\sum(x - \bar{x})(y - \bar{y})}{N\sigma_x\sigma_y} = \frac{\sum xy - N\bar{x}\bar{y}}{N\sigma_x\sigma_y}. \quad \text{Spearman's } R = 1 - \frac{6\sum d^2}{N^3 - N}$$

tested for significance by $t = \dfrac{r\sqrt{N - 2}}{\sqrt{1 - r^2}}$ on $(N - 2)$ degrees of freedom.

Regression:

The line of y on x is

$$(y - \bar{y}) = \frac{r\sigma_y}{\sigma_x}(x - \bar{x}) \qquad \text{(for } x \text{ on } y \text{ interchange } x \text{ and } y \text{ throughout)}$$

Alternatively, $y = mx + c$ where

$$m = \frac{N\sum xy - (\sum x)(\sum y)}{N\sum x^2 - (\sum x)^2} \quad \text{and} \quad c = \frac{(\sum x)(\sum xy) - (\sum y)(\sum x^2)}{(\sum x)^2 - N\sum x^2}$$

Binomial distribution:

$$\text{Pr}(r) = {}^N C_r p^r q^{N-r}$$
$$\text{Mean} = Np$$
where ${}^N C_r = \dfrac{N!}{r!(N - r)!}$ and $q = 1 - p$

$$\text{Standard deviation} = \sqrt{Npq}$$

(See Appendix A for values of ${}^N C_r$)

Poisson distribution:

$$\text{Pr}(c) = \frac{e^{-a}a^c}{c!}$$

Mean $= a$; Standard deviation $= \sqrt{a}$

Standard errors:

Mean $\sigma/\sqrt{N}$ Standard deviation $\sigma/\sqrt{2N}$ Median $1.43\sigma/\sqrt{N}$

Accuracy of a percentage:

$P\% \pm L$ (95% confidence)

$$L^2 = \frac{4P(100-P)}{N} \quad \text{or} \quad N = \frac{4P(100-P)}{L^2}$$

Significance tests:

$$t = \frac{\text{Difference between means}}{\text{Standard error of difference}}$$

$$= \frac{\bar{x}-\bar{y}}{\sqrt{\left(\dfrac{N_x\,\sigma_x^2 + N_y\,\sigma_y^2}{N_x + N_y - 2}\right)\left(\dfrac{N_x + N_y}{N_xN_y}\right)}} \qquad \begin{array}{l} \text{on } (N_x + N_y - 2) \text{ DoF} \\ \text{(Unequal sample sizes)} \end{array}$$

$$\text{or} \quad \frac{\bar{x}-\bar{y}}{\sqrt{\dfrac{\sigma_x^2 + \sigma_y^2}{(N-1)}}} \qquad \begin{array}{l} \text{on } (2N - 2) \text{ DoF} \\ \text{(Equal sample sizes)} \end{array}$$

$$\chi^2 = \sum\frac{(O-E)^2}{E}$$

APPENDIX I 261

TABLES OF e^x and e^{-x}

x	.00	.01	.02	.03	.04	.05	.06	.07	.08	.09
0.0	1.00000	.99005	.98020	.97045	.96079	.95123	.94176	.93239	.92312	.91393
0.1	0.90484	.89583	.88692	.87810	.86936	.86071	.85214	.84366	.83527	.82696
0.2	0.81873	.81058	.80252	.79453	.78663	.77880	.77105	.76338	.75578	.74826
0.3	0.74082	.73345	.72615	.71892	.71177	.70469	.69768	.69073	.68386	.67706
0.4	0.67032	.66365	.65705	.65051	.64404	.63763	.63128	.62500	.61878	.61263
0.5	0.60653	.60050	.59452	.58860	.58275	.57695	.57121	.56553	.55990	.55433
0.6	0.54881	.54335	.53794	.53259	.52729	.52205	.51685	.51171	.50662	.50158
0.7	0.49659	.49164	.48675	.48191	.47711	.47237	.46767	.46301	.45841	.45384
0.8	0.44933	.44486	.44043	.43605	.43171	.42741	.42316	.41895	.41478	.41066
0.9	0.40657	.40252	.39852	.39455	.39063	.38674	.38289	.37908	.37531	.37158
1.0	0.36788	.36422	.36059	.35701	.35345	.34994	.34646	.34301	.33960	.33622
1.1	0.33287	.32956	.32628	.32303	.31982	.31664	.31349	.31037	.30728	.30422
1.2	0.30119	.29820	.29523	.29229	.28938	.28650	.28365	.28083	.27804	.27527
1.3	0.27253	.26982	.26714	.26448	.26185	.25924	.25666	.25411	.25158	.24908
1.4	0.24660	.24414	.24171	.23931	.23693	.23457	.23224	.22993	.22764	.22537
1.5	0.22313	.22091	.21871	.21654	.21438	.21225	.21014	.20805	.20598	.20393
1.6	0.20190	.19989	.19790	.19593	.19399	.19205	.19014	.18825	.18637	.18452
1.7	0.18268	.18087	.17907	.17728	.17552	.17377	.17204	.17033	.16864	.16696
1.8	0.16530	.16365	.16203	.16041	.15882	.15724	.15567	.15412	.15259	.15107
1.9	0.14957	.14808	.14661	.14515	.14370	.14227	.14086	.13946	.13807	.13670
2.0	0.13534	.13399	.13266	.13134	.13003	.12873	.12745	.12619	.12493	.12369
2.1	0.12246	.12124	.12003	.11884	.11765	.11648	.11533	.11418	.11304	.11192
2.2	0.11080	.10970	.10861	.10753	.10646	.10540	.10435	.10331	.10228	.10127
2.3	0.10026	.09926	.09827	.09730	.09633	.09537	.09442	.09348	.09255	.09163
2.4	0.09072	.08982	.08892	.08804	.08716	.08629	.08543	.08458	.08374	.08291
2.5	0.08208	.08127	.08046	.07966	.07887	.07808	.07730	.07654	.07577	.07502
2.6	0.07427	.07353	.07280	.07208	.07136	.07065	.06995	.06925	.06856	.06788
2.7	0.06721	.06654	.06587	.06522	.06457	.06393	.06329	.06266	.06204	.06142
2.8	0.06081	.06020	.05961	.05901	.05843	.05784	.05727	.05670	.05613	.05558
2.9	0.05502	.05448	.05393	.05340	.05287	.05234	.05182	.05130	.05079	.05029
3.0	0.04979	.04929	.04880	.04832	.04783	.04736	.04689	.04642	.04596	.04550
3.1	0.04505	.04460	.04416	.04372	.04328	.04285	.04243	.04200	.04159	.04117
3.2	0.04076	.04036	.03996	.03956	.03916	.03877	.03839	.03801	.03763	.03725
3.3	0.03688	.03652	.03615	.03579	.03544	.03508	.03474	.03439	.03405	.03371
3.4	0.03337	.03304	.03271	.03239	.03206	.03175	.03143	.03112	.03081	.03050
3.5	0.03020	.02990	.02960	.02930	.02901	.02872	.02844	.02816	.02788	.02760
3.6	0.02732	.02705	.02678	.02652	.02625	.02599	.02573	.02548	.02522	.02497
3.7	0.02472	.02448	.02423	.02399	.02375	.02352	.02328	.02305	.02282	.02260
3.8	0.02237	.02215	.02193	.02171	.02149	.02128	.02107	.02086	.02065	.02045
3.9	0.02024	.02004	.01984	.01964	.01945	.01925	.01906	.01887	.01869	.01850
4.0	0.01832	.01813	.01795	.01777	.01760	.01742	.01725	.01708	.01691	.01674
4.1	0.01657	.01641	.01624	.01608	.01592	.01576	.01561	.01545	.01530	.01515
4.2	0.01500	.01485	.01470	.01455	.01441	.01426	.01412	.01398	.01384	.01370
4.3	0.01357	.01343	.01330	.01317	.01304	.01291	.01278	.01265	.01253	.01240
4.4	0.01228	.01216	.01203	.01191	.01180	.01168	.01156	.01145	.01133	.01122
4.5	0.01111	.01100	.01089	.01078	.01067	.01057	.01046	.01036	.01025	.01015
4.6	0.01005	.00995	.00985	.00975	.00966	.00956	.00947	.00937	.00928	.00919
4.7	0.00910	.00900	.00892	.00883	.00874	.00865	.00857	.00848	.00840	.00831
4.8	0.00823	.00815	.00807	.00799	.00791	.00783	.00775	.00767	.00760	.00752
4.9	0.00745	.00737	.00730	.00723	.00715	.00708	.00701	.00694	.00687	.00681
5.0	0.00674	.00667	.00660	.00654	.00647	.00641	.00635	.00628	.00622	.00616
5.1	0.00610	.00604	.00598	.00592	.00586	.00580	.00574	.00568	.00563	.00557
5.2	0.00552	.00546	.00541	.00535	.00530	.00525	.00520	.00514	.00509	.00504
5.3	0.00499	.00494	.00489	.00484	.00480	.00475	.00470	.00465	.00461	.00456
5.4	0.00452	.00447	.00443	.00438	.00434	.00430	.00425	.00421	.00417	.00413
5.5	0.00409	.00405	.00401	.00397	.00393	.00389	.00385	.00381	.00377	.00374
5.6	0.00370	.00366	.00362	.00359	.00355	.00352	.00348	.00345	.00341	.00338
5.7	0.00335	.00331	.00328	.00325	.00321	.00318	.00315	.00312	.00309	.00306
5.8	0.00303	.00300	.00297	.00294	.00291	.00288	.00285	.00282	.00279	.00277
5.9	0.00274	.00271	.00269	.00266	.00263	.00261	.00258	.00255	.00253	.00250
6.0	0.00248	.00245	.00243	.00241	.00238	.00236	.00233	.00231	.00229	.00227
6.1	0.00224	.00222	.00220	.00218	.00215	.00213	.00211	.00209	.00207	.00205
6.2	0.00203	.00201	.00199	.00197	.00195	.00193	.00191	.00189	.00187	.00185
6.3	0.00184	.00182	.00180	.00178	.00176	.00175	.00173	.00171	.00170	.00168
6.4	0.00166	.00165	.00163	.00161	.00160	.00158	.00156	.00155	.00153	.00152
6.5	0.00150	.00149	.00147	.00146	.00144	.00143	.00142	.00140	.00139	.00137
6.6	0.00136	.00135	.00133	.00132	.00131	.00129	.00128	.00127	.00126	.00124
6.7	0.00123	.00122	.00121	.00119	.00118	.00117	.00115	.00114	.00114	.00112
6.8	0.00111	.00110	.00109	.00108	.00107	.00106	.00105	.00104	.00103	.00102
6.9	0.00101	.00100	.00099	.00098	.00097	.00096	.00095	.00094	.00093	.00092
7.0	0.00091	.00090	.00089	.00088	.00088	.00087	.00086	.00085	.00084	.00083

	.00	.01	.02	.03	.04	.05	.06	.07	.08	.09
0.0	1.0000	1.0101	1.0202	1.0305	1.0408	1.0513	1.0618	1.0725	1.0833	1.0942
0.1	1.1052	1.1163	1.1275	1.1388	1.1503	1.1618	1.1735	1.1853	1.1972	1.2092
0.2	1.2214	1.2337	1.2461	1.2586	1.2712	1.2840	1.2969	1.3100	1.3231	1.3364
0.3	1.3499	1.3634	1.3771	1.3910	1.4049	1.4191	1.4333	1.4477	1.4623	1.4770
0.4	1.4918	1.5068	1.5220	1.5373	1.5527	1.5683	1.5841	1.6000	1.6161	1.6323
0.5	1.6487	1.6653	1.6820	1.6989	1.7160	1.7333	1.7507	1.7683	1.7860	1.8040
0.6	1.8221	1.8404	1.8589	1.8776	1.8965	1.9155	1.9348	1.9542	1.9739	1.9937
0.7	2.0138	2.0340	2.0544	2.0751	2.0959	2.1170	2.1383	2.1598	2.1815	2.2034
0.8	2.2255	2.2479	2.2705	2.2933	2.3164	2.3396	2.3632	2.3869	2.4109	2.4351
0.9	2.4596	2.4843	2.5093	2.5345	2.5600	2.5857	2.6117	2.6379	2.6645	2.6912
1.0	2.7183	2.7456	2.7732	2.8011	2.8292	2.8577	2.8864	2.9154	2.9447	2.9743
1.1	3.0042	3.0344	3.0649	3.0957	3.1268	3.1582	3.1899	3.2220	3.2544	3.2871
1.2	3.3201	3.3535	3.3872	3.4212	3.4556	3.4903	3.5254	3.5609	3.5966	3.6328
1.3	3.6693	3.7062	3.7434	3.7810	3.8190	3.8574	3.8962	3.9354	3.9749	4.0149
1.4	4.0552	4.0960	4.1371	4.1787	4.2207	4.2631	4.3060	4.3492	4.3929	4.4371
1.5	4.4817	4.5267	4.5722	4.6182	4.6646	4.7115	4.7588	4.8066	4.8550	4.9037
1.6	4.9530	5.0028	5.0531	5.1039	5.1552	5.2070	5.2593	5.3122	5.3656	5.4195
1.7	5.4739	5.5290	5.5845	5.6407	5.6973	5.7546	5.8124	5.8709	5.9299	5.9895
1.8	6.0496	6.1104	6.1719	6.2339	6.2965	6.3598	6.4237	6.4883	6.5535	6.6194
1.9	6.6859	6.7531	6.8210	6.8895	6.9588	7.0287	7.0993	7.1707	7.2427	7.3155
2.0	7.3891	7.4633	7.5383	7.6141	7.6906	7.7679	7.8460	7.9248	8.0045	8.0849
2.1	8.1662	8.2482	8.3311	8.4149	8.4994	8.5849	8.6711	8.7583	8.8463	8.9352
2.2	9.0250	9.1157	9.2073	9.2999	9.3933	9.4877	9.5831	9.6794	9.7767	9.8749
2.3	9.974	10.074	10.176	10.278	10.381	10.486	10.591	10.697	10.805	10.913
2.4	11.023	11.134	11.246	11.359	11.473	11.588	11.705	11.822	11.941	12.061
2.5	12.182	12.305	12.429	12.554	12.680	12.807	12.936	13.066	13.197	13.330
2.6	13.464	13.599	13.736	13.874	14.013	14.154	14.296	14.440	14.585	14.732
2.7	14.880	15.029	15.180	15.333	15.487	15.643	15.800	15.959	16.119	16.281
2.8	16.445	16.610	16.777	16.945	17.116	17.288	17.462	17.637	17.814	17.993
2.9	18.174	18.357	18.541	18.728	18.916	19.106	19.298	19.492	19.688	19.886
3.0	20.086	20.287	20.491	20.697	20.905	21.115	21.328	21.542	21.758	21.977
3.1	22.198	22.421	22.646	22.874	23.104	23.336	23.571	23.807	24.047	24.288
3.2	24.533	24.779	25.028	25.280	25.534	25.790	26.050	26.311	26.576	26.843
3.3	27.113	27.385	27.660	27.938	28.219	28.503	28.789	29.079	29.371	29.666
3.4	29.964	30.265	30.569	30.877	31.187	31.500	31.817	32.137	32.460	32.786
3.5	33.115	33.448	33.784	34.124	34.467	34.813	35.163	35.517	35.874	36.234
3.6	36.598	36.966	37.338	37.713	38.092	38.475	38.861	39.252	39.646	40.045
3.7	40.447	40.854	41.264	41.679	42.098	42.521	42.948	43.380	43.816	44.256
3.8	44.701	45.150	45.604	46.063	46.525	46.993	47.465	47.942	48.424	48.911
3.9	49.402	49.899	50.400	50.907	51.419	51.935	52.457	52.985	53.517	54.055
4.0	54.598	55.147	55.701	56.261	56.826	57.397	57.974	58.557	59.146	59.740
4.1	60.340	60.947	61.559	62.178	62.803	63.434	64.072	64.715	65.366	66.023
4.2	66.686	67.357	68.034	68.717	69.408	70.105	70.810	71.522	72.240	72.966
4.3	73.700	74.441	75.189	75.944	76.708	77.479	78.257	79.044	79.838	80.640
4.4	81.451	82.270	83.096	83.931	84.775	85.627	86.488	87.357	88.235	89.121
4.5	90.017	90.922	91.836	92.759	93.691	94.632	95.584	96.544	97.514	98.495
4.6	99.48	100.49	101.49	102.51	103.54	104.59	105.64	106.70	107.77	108.85
4.7	109.95	111.05	112.17	113.30	114.43	115.58	116.75	117.92	119.10	120.30
4.8	121.51	122.73	123.97	125.21	126.47	127.74	129.02	130.32	131.63	132.95
4.9	134.29	135.64	137.00	138.38	139.77	141.17	142.59	144.03	145.47	146.94

	.0	.1	.2	.3	.4	.5	.6	.7	.8	.9
5.0	148.41	164.02	181.27	200.34	221.41	244.69	270.43	298.87	330.30	365.04
6.0	403.43	445.86	492.75	544.57	601.84	665.14	735.10	812.41	897.85	992.27
7.0	1096.6	1212.0	1339.4	1480.3	1636.0	1808.0	1998.2	2208.4	2440.6	2697.3
8.0	2981.0	3294.5	3641.0	4023.9	4447.1	4914.8	5431.7	6002.9	6634.2	7332.0
9.0	8103.1	8955.3	9897.1	10938	12088	13360	14765	16318	18034	19930
10.0	22026	24343	26903	29733	32860	36316	40135	44356	49021	54176
11.0	59874	66171	73131	80822	89322	98716	109098	120572	133252	147267
12.0	162755	179872	198790	219696	242802	268337	296559	327748	362217	400313
13.0	442413	488943	540365	597195	660004	729416	806131	890912	984609	1088163
14.0	1202605	1329086	1468865	1623346	1794078	1982760	2191292	2421750	2676445	2957934
15.0	3269020	3612832	3992792	4412713	4876810	5389704	5956553	6583004	7275337	8040483

INDEX

* ff. denotes that pages following the number also refer to the topic.